D0488120

DATE DUE

OC 25 04			

DEMCO 38-296

Traditional
Music
of the
Lao

Traditional Music of the Lao

Kaen Playing and Mawlum Singing in Northeast Thailand

TERRY E. MILLER

Contributions in Intercultural and Comparative Studies, Number 13

Greenwood Press
Westport, Connecticut • London, England

Library of Congress Cataloging in Publication Data

Miller, Terry E.
  Traditional music of the Lao.

  (Contributions in intercultural and comparative
studies, ISSN 0147-1031 ; no. 13)
    Bibliography: p.
    Discography: p.
    Includes index.
    1. Laos (Tai people)—Thailand—Music—History and
criticism.   2. Folk music—Thailand—History and
criticism.   3. Folk-songs, Lao—Thailand—History and
criticism.   4. Kaen.   I. Title.   II. Series.
ML345.T5M54   1985   781.7593   84-22538
ISBN 0-313-24765-X (lib. bdg.)

Library of Congress Catalog Card Number: 84-22538
ISBN: 0-313-24765-X
ISSN: 0147-1031

First published in 1985

Greenwood Press
A division of Congressional Information Service, Inc.
88 Post Road West, Westport, Connecticut 06881

Printed in the United States of America

10 9 8 7 6 5 4 3 2 1

Contents

Examples

Figures

Preface

Ironically, my first introduction to Asian music occurred involuntarily during a year's tour of duty (1969-70) in the Republic of Vietnam (South Vietnam) with the United States Army, and thus I owe a certain kind of thanks to the Government of the United States for prodding me into experiencing Asian culture. Research for this work was accomplished from late 1972 until early 1974 with the support of the Social Science Research Council's Foreign Area Fellowship Program, whose funds were provided by the Ford Foundation. Without this grant, the field work would have been impossible.

Since that initial field work, much has happened in my life, both to change my perspectives and to expand my research interests to areas as diverse as China, Scotland, and the Appalachian region of the United States. Through a teaching position in Ethnomusicology at Kent State University's Center for the Study of World Musics within the School of Music, I have had the opportunity to convey some of this material to my students. This experience has also helped me clarify a number of points that were doubtless muddled in earlier articles and lectures written as early as 1974.

As of this writing I have not had the opportunity to return to Northeast Thailand, but have kept in contact with friends there. It is likely that as time continues, more and more of what I have written about Northeast Thai culture will change from contemporary to historical description. Electricity has now come to most villages along with better roads. If the pattern seen in other regions holds true here, traditional culture will suffer, and some of the genres discussed in this work will become extinct if they have not already become extinct.

While it is likely that someone else attempting such a large scale work as this on Northeast Thai music might see things differently, it is just as likely that I also might if I had begun my research now. One's perspectives change. Moreover, some of the most important informants who both helped me and influenced my thinking have now either died or retired from active music making. In a sense, no one will ever be able to duplicate my experience; time has marched onward.

I am profoundly indebted to numerous individuals for their help to me in understanding Northeastern Thai music and culture. First and foremost is Prof. Jarǔnchai Chonpairot of the University of Sri Nakarin-wirot in Mahasarakam. Jarǔnchai led me on innumerable expeditions to remote villages where he successfully sought out one important informant after another. Through his interpreting, I was able to convey questions and concerns that will exceed my ability in Thai throughout my life. His advice was consistently sound and wise. Much technical understanding of the music then came in 1975 when we were able to work together while he was a student at the University of Michigan.

I am additionally indebted to numerous other Thai who aided my work. They include Prof. Kamtorn Snidvong of Bangkok, Prof. Sumret Kum-mong of the Mahasarakam Teacher Training College, Mr. Sompong Wunnachote of Kosum Pisai, and especially to kaen maker Tui Rǔang-siarun and kaen master, Tawng-koon See-aroon. Numerous other singers and instrumentalists willingly recorded and interviewed for me. Lastly I wish to thank the administrations of the University of Sri Nakarin-wirot in both Bangkok and Mahasarakam and that of the Mahasarakam Teacher Training College for their help in many practical matters.

Lastly, I wish to acknowledge my deep appreciation to Dr. Walter Kaufmann of Indiana University for his encouragement and sound advice during my student days when my study of Northeastern Thai music began.

While I have no pretensions of this work's perfection, it is as accurate and perceptive as I have been able to make it at this point in my life and intellectual development. Naturally, in the future as I learn more, further refinement will take place.

Terry E. Miller
Center for the Study of World Music
(School of Music)
Kent State University
March 11, 1984

The Transcription of Thai

The transcription of any non-Latin writing system into Latin letters is a compromise. In certain languages, such as Chinese, one may use a long accepted system such as Wade-Giles or the pinyin system adopted by the People's Republic of China. In the case of Thailand, there is no single accepted system of romanization. One has therefore to choose between two options, either a linguist's system that transcribes as minutely and as minutely as possible, or a layman's system that transcribes in less detail. The former approach usually entails the use of numerous symbols not found on ordinary typewriters or known to uninitiated readers. For those desiring a detailed system, there is the romanization devised by Mary Haas based on the international phonetic alphabet. For those desiring the second option, there is a plethora of solutions.

For better or worse I have chosen the latter option. Both Thai words in the title, kaen and mawlum, require symbols not found on the typewriter when transcribed according to Haas. Although not all may agree, I have concluded that the system I use reflects the actual sound of the word for most readers, especially those untrained in the international phonetic alphabet. It is also much easier to type and set into type. I take full responsibility for the shortcomings of the system. Its inspiration was the system proposed by A. B. Griswold in his Thoughts on the Romanization of Siamese (Bangkok, 1969).

Besides transcribing consonants and vowels which often have no equivalent in English or other Western languages, there is the problem of tonal inflection, for Thai (Siamese or Lao) is tonal. It is traditionally taught that Siamese (the language of Central Thailand, officially the Thai language) has five tonal inflections. In Northeast Thailand, however, the language is Lao and because it has not been systematized by officialdom, there is much variation from province to province both in Northeast Thailand and across the Maekong river in Laos. Not only does the number of tones vary but the inflections in each consonant group also vary from place to place. Therefore, which locale does one choose when showing tone, whether with numbers or diacritical markings? Both Siamese and Lao words are found in the text.

My solution is to provide in the musical transcriptions involving text both the original script and the romanization so that those who wish to know the details of pronunciation and tone may do so and those who are not interested in such matters do not have to deal with them. A tone chart for the language of Roi-et and Mahasarakam provinces is provided on page 10. Further, a glossary has been provided giving not only short definitions but the Thai script and romanization into the Haas system with diacriticals added.

One final problem remains difficult to solve, and that is personal and place names. Where individuals are well-known in an established spelling, such as Maha Sila Viravong, I have followed that spelling. Where they are not known in a romanized spelling, I have followed my own system. Place names are problematic in the same way, because some are well known on maps, such as province names, while others are not, such as obscure villages. In this case I have followed my own system throughout (except for the official name of the country--Thailand). In most cases I included the better known spelling in parentheses the first time it occurred. Some of them are close to the map spellings, such as Kawn-gaen replacing Khonkaen, while others are quite different, such as Oobon replacing Ubon or Ubol.

The following pages show in chart form the equivalents of the original Siamese or Lao letters and the romanized letters.

One last matter must be dealt with. When differentiating Siamese as written in Bangkok in Siamese letters from Lao written in Wiangjun (Vientiane) in Lao letters, differences in pronunciation are clear. For example, the Siamese word for poetry, glawn, is pronounced and spelled gawn in Lao. A difficulty is that in Northeast Thailand the Lao alphabet is not used. It is normal to spell words in the Siamese form, when there is an equivalent, and pronounce them in the Lao way. When there is no Siamese equivalent, a makeshift phonetic spelling may be used. For clarity's sake, I have chosen to romanize according to the Siamese spellings since Lao lacks the double consonants that differentiate words in Siamese. For example, lum pun is a nontheatrical genre involving one singer and kaen player while lum plun is a theatrical genre involving a troupe performing on stage. Pun is pronounced with a low-falling tone and plun with a high-falling tone, but in Lao both are pronounced pun. To avoid confusion, I have chosen to keep the Siamese spelling.

The Romanization of Thai

Consonants

Thai	Initial	Final	Thai	Initial	Final
ก	G	K	ผ ภ พ	P	P
ข ค ฆ	K,	K	ฝ ฟ	F	-
ง	NG	NG	ม	M	K
จ	J	T	ย	Y	-
ฉ ช ฌ	CH	T	ร	R	N
ญ	Y	N	ล ฬ	L	K
ฎ ฏ	D	T	ว	W	-
ฐ ฑ	D	T	ศ ษ ส ซ	S	T
ฑ ฒ ถ ท ธ	T	T	ทร	S	-
บ	B	P	ห ฮ	H	-
ป	B	P	น ณ	N	N

Vowels

Thai	Preferred	2nd	Thai	Preferred	2nd	Thai	Preferred	2nd
อะ	a	u	เออะ / เอ เออ	ย		อิว	iu	
อา	a	ah	เอีย	ia		เอว	eo	
อำ	um		เอือ	ua		เอว	eo	
อ	u	a	อัว อว	ua		แอว	aeo	eo
อี	i		อัย	ai		เอียว	io	
อี	ee		เออ	ย		ใ	rü	
อี อี	ü	eu	ไอ ไอย	ai		ใา	rü	
อุ	oo		ไอ อัย	ai		ฤ	lü	
อู	oo		อาย	ai		ฤา	lü	
เอะ เอ	e		เอา	ao		เอ	ü	
เอ	e	ay	อาว	ao		อรร	an	
แอะ แอ	ae		อุย	ui		ออ	ü	
แอ	ae		โอย	oi		อวง	uang	
โอะ	o	oh	ออย	oi		เอย	üi	
โอ	o	oh	เอย	üi		เอ	e	
เอาะ ออ	a		เออย	üe		เอ	ü	
ออ	aw	au	อวย	ue				

Traditional
Music
of the
Lao

I.

Northeastern Thai Music and
Its Cultural Context

A General Description

The cultural makeup of continental Southeast Asia is among the most complex and colorful on our planet. Within this relatively small subcontinent dwell at least 151 separate ethnic groups speaking a plethora of dialects grouped into four major linguistic families. On first appearance maps provide a misleadingly coherent picture of the region showing each major group--Thai, Lao, Burmese, Malay, Khmer, and Vietnamese--within its own national boundary. To assume that these borders define the limits of each culture would be erroneous. Wherever they live, both major and minor ethnic groups follow their own distinctive customs and, apropos to this study, express themselves musically in differing ways.

The modern nation of Thailand, a relatively small country, is comprised of four rather distinctive cultural regions, each with its own dialect, literature, musical styles, customs, and ethnic subgroups (see Figure 1). The Southern region (pak dai) is distinctive because part of its culture is Malay Islam and part Theravada Buddhist. The character of the North (pak nüa) has been affected by Lao and Burmese influences. Moreover, a large number of upland ethnic groups, unrelated linguistically to the Thai or Lao, inhabit this region. The Central Plain (pak glang), which dominates the country politically and has also attempted to impose its culture and language on the rest of the land in the interest of national unity, is Siamese, the result of earlier Mon and Khmer influence upon the Tai.[1] Lastly, the Northeast (pak isan) is Lao both historically and culturally; this region's musical culture will be the focus throughout this study.

The modern state of Thailand, meaning "Land of the Free" (Bra-tet-tai), with a population of more than forty-six million, covers some 514,000 square kilometers, somewhat smaller than the state of Texas.[2] Of these people, at least thirty-seven million live in rural areas and engage in agriculture, particularly rice growing, but also grow jute, harvest rubber, or mine tin in certain regions. The Northeast includes only 17 of 73 provinces of Thailand but covers 170,226 square kilometers or fully one-third of the total land area. Its total estimated population in 1970 was more than twelve million, but the rate of growth then exceeded three

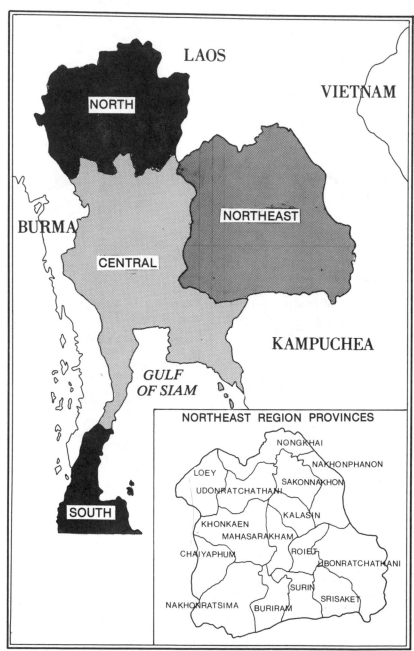

Figure 1.   Map of Thailand showing major cultural divisions with inset showing northeast region provinces.   (Sheri Foote, Cartographer)

percent a year, among the highest in the world. Today, the rate has fallen to 1.9 percent.

Research for this study was conducted primarily in Kawn-gaen (Khon Kaen), Mahasarakam, and Roi-et provinces with additional forays into Oobon (Ubon), Soo-rin (Surin), Nakawn-ratchasimah (Nakhonratsima), and Galasin (Kalasin) provinces. Figure 2 shows Roi-et province in greater detail since it was in this area that most of the fieldwork was done.

In contrast to Thailand, the modern state of Laos, whose land area is 236,000 square kilometers or nearly forty percent larger than Northeast Thailand, has a population of only three to four million.[3] All but about one half million of these live in rural areas, but as much as one-third of the population consists of non-Lao upland minority groups. Laos' sixteen provinces are relatively isolated from each other because the mountainous terrain and generally undeveloped state of the country preclude good roads or communications. Even though relatively small numbers of people are involved, the musical culture of the Lao living in the southern provinces bordering Thailand and Kampuchea (Cambodia) differs significantly from that of Lao living in the far north near China or the west near Burma.

While the modern state of Laos includes a tremendous variety of peoples within its borders, Northeast Thailand is much less diverse in its ethnological makeup. By far the dominant group is the Lao who, while close relatives of the Siamese in Central Thailand and the Shan of northern Burma, nevertheless differ from them in a few significant ways. Superficially, one of the most noticeable is diet. Whereas Siamese eat ordinary rice, Lao prefer sticky or glutinous rice which is steamed in a basket and eaten in lumps rolled in the hands. Neither sticky rice nor another Lao speciality called ba dek (fermented fish) are appreciated by the Siamese who generally dismiss the people of the Northeast as backward rustics.

In addition to the Lao, several provinces near the Kampuchean border, especially Soo-rin, Sisaget (Sisaket), and Boori-rum (Buriram), are inhabited by Khmer people as well as their ethnic relatives, the Kui, Soai, and Sui. Unlike the Lao, they eat ordinary rice and use the Siamese dialect when speaking to Thai people but cultivate a type of singing related to that of the Lao. Scattered throughout other areas of the Northeast, particularly the mountainous provinces, are people known as Pootai (Put-hai), Tai-yaw, Yuai, and Puan, most of whom migrated from the highlands of Laos during the last one hundred years; their singing illustrates a more conservative branch of the Lao culture. Finally there are Thai Korat living in the vicinity of Nakawn-ratchasimah (Korat) on the edge of the Korat Plateau, people who are culturally more akin to the Central Thai than the Lao.[4] Some mention should also be made of the many Chinese, Vietnamese, and Indians living throughout the Northeast who engage in business in the provincial and district towns. These groups have had little cultural influence on the indigenous peoples, however.

Village Life in Northeast Thailand

Though many Westerners consider Bangkok and Thailand as almost synonymous, it is the city which is least representative of Thai society. Cities are economically dominated by Chinese who immigrated to Thailand mostly during the nineteenth century, and while they have become more assimilated into Thai society than in most other Southeast Asian countries,

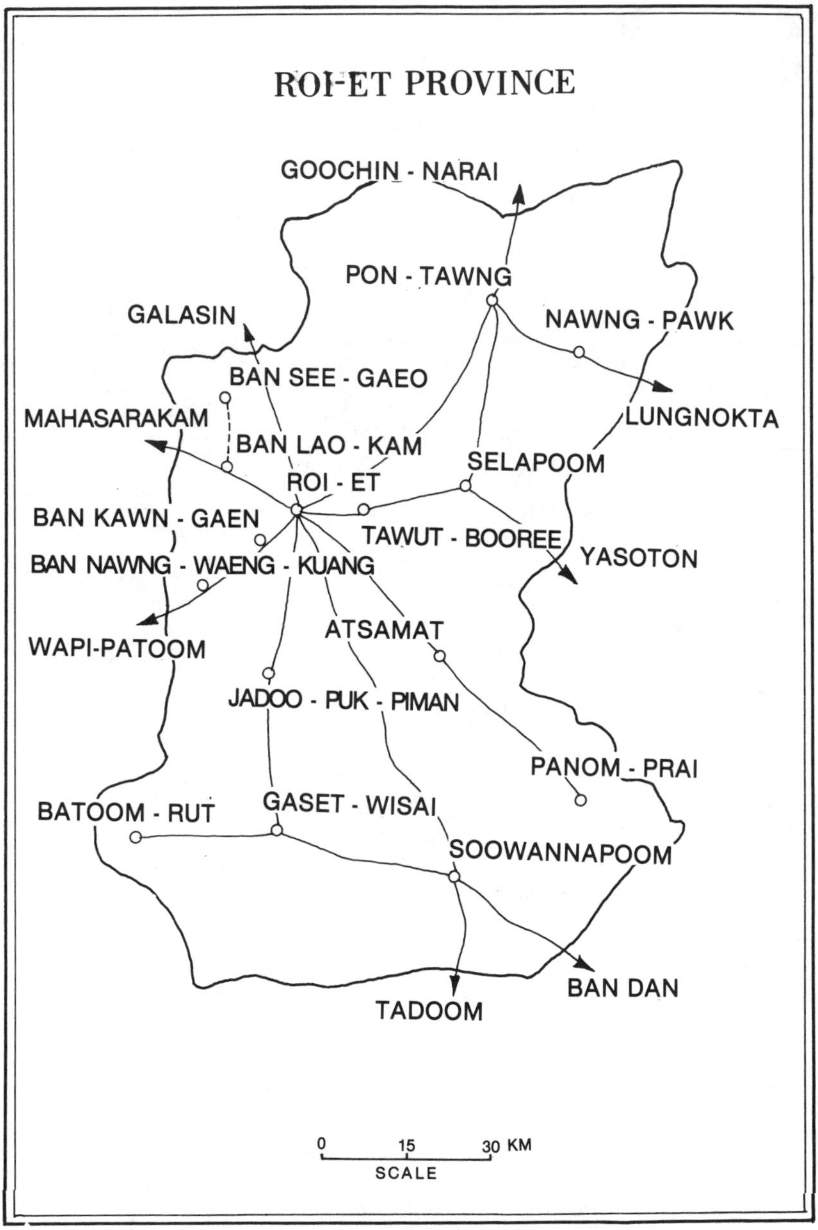

ROI-ET PROVINCE

GOOCHIN - NARAI

PON - TAWNG

GALASIN

NAWNG - PAWK

BAN SEE - GAEO

MAHASARAKAM

LUNGNOKTA

BAN LAO - KAM

SELAPOOM

ROI - ET

BAN KAWN - GAEN

TAWUT - BOOREE

BAN NAWNG - WAENG - KUANG

YASOTON

ATSAMAT

WAPI-PATOOM

JADOO - PUK - PIMAN

PANOM - PRAI

BATOOM - RUT   GASET - WISAI

SOOWANNAPOOM

BAN DAN

TADOOM

0   15   30 KM
SCALE

Figure 2. Map of Roi-et province in northeast Thailand showing important towns and roads. (Sheri Foote, cartographer)

they remain Chinese in spirit. The heart of Thailand beats in the villages. Here lives approximately eighty-four percent of the population, and, except for non-Tai minorities such as the Khmer, Sui, and upland groups, most of whom are farmers as well, nearly everyone engages in wet-rice agriculture. Unlike American farms which stretch quilt-like between cities, each family isolated from the next, Tai farmers live in tightly grouped villages surrounded by their fields. This system requires, however, that villagers walk many kilometers to their fields if they do not directly adjoin the village.

Northeastern villages are preferably located near a pond or swamp because water is such a precious commodity during the long dry season. Varying in size from about three hundred to two thousand people, villages dot the landscape throughout this relatively densely populated region where the population was until recently growing as rapidly as anywhere in the world. Within a village there is little economic variation from one family to another in evidence. Unlike in the cities where the contrast between rich and poor is astounding, village homes are uniformly modest.

Rice growing is the chief concern of villagers, although tobacco and jute have become important cash crops as well. Whereas the monsoon rains arrive with regularity in May in the Central Plain, the Northeast, because it is high on the Korat Plateau and cut off from the moist air by mountains, cannot depend on monsoon downpours to fill its rice fields whose soil holds water poorly. Consequently the Northeast is the poorest region of Thailand economically, though its rich culture provides another sort of wealth, however intangible.

It is in conjunction with festivals and celebrations associated with both Buddhist and non-Buddhist events that opportunities for performing and hearing traditional music occur. The cycle of festivals parallels the agricultural cycle both spiritually and practically since celebrations would obviously be out of place during periods of heavy work; rain also makes out-of-doors performances difficult. Just before plowing time in May, assuming the rains have arrived on schedule, Northeasterners observe Wisaka boochah, the day on which the Lord Buddha was born, received enlightenment, and died. Although this festival is rarely cause for musical performances, it may be considered the beginning of the cycle. In July when rice transplanting has been completed, the Buddhist Lent called Kao pansah begins during which musical performances are traditionally forbidden. At least once in their lives Thai males are expected to enter the temple (wut) as monks or novices to accumulate merit for themselves and their families, and they usually do this during Pansah when there is little work to be done. In October when the rains have stopped and the rice is maturing, Pansah ends, and most of the boys who had become novices shed their robes and return home.

The first important festival calling for musical performance is Boon gatin which occurs anytime between the full moons of October and November before the rice is cut. This is the time that villagers acquire merit for themselves by presenting the community of monks (sangha) with new robes and other gifts. As in most festivals of this sort, the monks go to the home of a donor on the first evening to chant blessings, return in the morning to chant again, then by accepting food transfer merit to the donors. On the preceding evening the donor is expected to sponsor some kind of entertainment for his guests and the village at large. The entertainment may be a performance of traditional singers, a traditional play, ligeh (likay) theatre from Central Thailand, or an outdoor movie. If a village acts as collective donor making more money available, perhaps a professional rumwong (dance) troupe may be added for the benefit of the unattached males. Rumwong consists of a rock band and a bevy of attractive girls who dance with any male willing to pay one baht ($.05) for the two-minute privilege.

In February Maka boochah occurs, the Buddhist All Saint's Day for which musical performances may be hired, but less often than for the next major festival, Boon prawetsundawn (commonly called Boon prawet) in late February or early March. Boon prawet (called Tumboon Mahachat in Central Thailand), is the day on which talented monks chant the story of Prince Wetsundawn, the jataka tale of the penultimate life of Buddha before enlightenment.[5] Lasting all day, the reading, whose style relates directly to traditional singing, will be followed by various entertainments or even a temple fair. Such fairs normally include traditional forms of music and theatre, movies, boxing, rumwong, food and drink stands, and an opportunity for informal meetings between boys and girls.

At the height of the dry season in mid-April comes Songkran, the traditional New Year, although according to the lunar calendar the festival should occur on December 9. The Thai celebrate not only Songkran but the Chinese and Western New Years as well, and in fact the latter is also occasion for traditional performances. Songkran begins early in the morning when the monks assemble to receive food from laymen. Later people come to pour water over a Buddha image set up for the occasion. Not only is the Buddha sprinkled, but everyone else eventually gets sprinkled, splashed, and drenched too. For three days both young and old engage in organized (and disorganized) water throwing throughout Thailand, a custom that can hardly be criticized coming as it does in the midst of the hottest weather of the year. Where water is difficult to find, villagers throw it nevertheless, though in smaller quantities. In the evenings traditional performances may take place.

Traditional entertainments often occur in conjunction with certain rites of passage also. Though most enter the monastery temporarily during Lent, ordination can occur almost anytime during the year. Because ordination is an important event in any household considering the merit bestowed, the family of the initiate must sponsor a performance or a movie if they can afford it. Similarly, after a person has been cremated and his remains disposed of, the family may sponsor a performance. While this may seem incongruous to a Westerner, the Lao attitudes toward death involve much less gloom; it is quite appropriate to celebrate the death of a loved one with a performance whose mood is both comic and earthy.

In May or June Northeastern Thai and Lao from Wiangjun south celebrate Boon bung-fai, the rocket festival whose origin is pre-Buddhist.[6] The long powder-propelled rockets (bung-fai) which various groups attempt to launch are sent to tell the sky god, Payah-taen, to send rain. While Lao normally behave in a modest manner, during Boon bung-fai lascivious and lewd behaviors are the order of the day. Men routinely parade about town wearing giant, artificial phalluses, imitate pregnant women, or go about operating copulating wooden puppets mounted on a bamboo stick meant to shock the girls. This festival's relationship to a fertility rite is obvious.

The most active time of year for traditional entertainments is from January until late May during which there are not only several important festivals, but Red Cross fairs and general temple fairs as well, these meant to raise funds for the charity involved. The January Red Cross fair in Mahasarakam, lasting seven nights, has not only food and drink stands, games, movies, boxing, and rides, but traditional singers and theatre, Central Thai theatre, and rumwong as well. Temple fairs have little to do with religion though they take place within the temple walls but contribute to the expense of maintaining the temple. They are similar to Red Cross fairs except usually smaller and last only two or three nights. In both cases a small fee is collected at the gate which allows guests to watch any entertainment except boxing without additional charge. Fairs of any sort, however, tend to be dusty, noisy, and commercial, hardly a "cultural" atmosphere.

Language, Scripts, and Literature

Sung and recited poetry must be understood in relation to the special requirements of the language. The Lao language is one regional manifestation of a larger family called Tai which includes Siamese (spoken in the Central Plain), Shan (northern Burma), Ahom (Assam), Nüa (Yunnan, China), Lü (Sipsong Panna in northern Laos), and various other Tai minorities. It remains uncertain whether Tai is a Sinitic language as Wuff contends or related to Kadai and certain Indonesian languages as Benedict claims.[7] Throughout the region the various Tai dialects are closely related though they are not always mutually intelligible on first encounter. All Tai dialects including Lao are tonal, that is, a given syllable in addition to being composed of consonants and vowels has a tonal inflection, either level or contoured. Regardless of where the word occurs in a sentence, its tone remains the same; indeed, it must remain so because without the tone or with an incorrect inflection the word cannot be understood except in context.

In both Siamese and Lao the letters of the alphabet--forty-four consonants in Siamese, twenty-seven in Lao--are divided into three classes, uksawn glang, uksawn dum, and uksawn soong. According to the length of the vowel, the final consonant if any, and tone marks, the tones will vary from uksawn to uksawn. Taking the dialect of Roi-et and Mahasarakam provinces, we find seven tones: mid, low, mid-high, mid-rising, rising, high-falling, and low-falling. Figure 3 illustrates this system.

While Tai languages are written in an alphabetical--as opposed to character--script based on Indian alphabets, there is considerable variation from one group to another. Though the Tai groups were not always as clearly defined as today, three distinctive variations in the script developed in the area of modern Thailand, one called tai wiang or tai noi in use among the Lao, one later called Siamese in use among the Tai of the Jaoprayah river valley, and another in use among the Shan and western Lao. The latter script has manifested itself into three separate but closely related variations. In Northern Laos especially around Muang Hou on the Chinese border the script used for all occasions is called lü while around Chiangmai in Northern Thailand the related script is called yuan, dua kum muang, or dua lanna. Thirdly, dua tam script is used throughout Laos and Northeast Thailand but only for sacred writings such as chant, doctrine, or certain non-Buddhist ritualists' manuscripts. The word tam comes from the Pali dhamma meaning the doctrine of the Buddha and his collected writings. These three northern scripts, tam, lü, and yuan, are closely related to the scripts of the western Shah which also show Burmese influence.

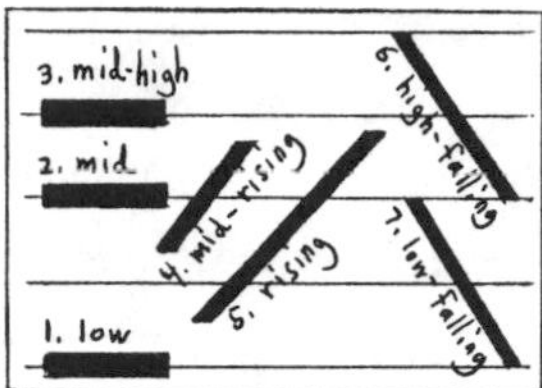

	1. short vowel nasal final / 2. long vowel / 3. long vowel nasal final	1. short vowel / 2. short vowel hard final	long vowel hard final	mai-ek	mai-toh
3. mid-high / 2. mid / 1. low (6. high-falling / 7. low-falling / 4. mid-rising / 5. rising)				|	∨
	(Tones from chart above.)				
UKSAWN GLANG	2	4	1	3	7
UKSAWN DUM	6	2	7	2	7
UKSAWN SOONG	5	4	1	3	1

Figure 3. The tonal inflections of the Lao language spoken in Mahasarakam and Roi-et provinces.

The old Lao script called tai noi or tai wiang emerged at the end of the sixteenth century after a gradual simplification from the thirteenth-century Sukhotai script. Tai noi gradually shed the "cerebral" letters which have been maintained in Siamese for many foreign words, and in practice sometimes eliminated tonal signs. This script was used for poetic and romantic literature, codes, administrative papers, correspondence, and other ordinary purposes. It has gradually evolved into modern Lao which, while much simpler and more cursive than Siamese, has restored tonal signs and certain consonants, mostly under Siamese influence.

Traditional manuscripts, called kumpee, nungsü pook (bundle book), or nungsü bai-lan (palm-leaf book), consist of narrow strips of dried palm leaf approximately fifty centimeters long and eight to ten centimeters wide. The writer uses a stylus to scratch the letters into the leaves, then fills them with ink or lamp black and rubs away the excess leaving the letters intaglioed in black. In the case of sacred writings, two holes are punched in each leaf dividing the strips into thirds. A cord strings the leaves together but through the left hole only. The manuscript must be wrapped in a protective cloth to prevent insects and the climate from destroying the fragile leaves. Extended jataka or local nitan ("tales") have cords through both holes with wooden end boards acting as a binding, These manuscripts may be very thick and heavy, even up to 875 leaves. Each leaf normally has four lines of writing on both sides with leaf numbers and titles at one end, though five or more lines are common to conserve palm leaf. Both religious material and traditional literature were written in manuscript form and are the point of origin for contemporary singers' poetry.

Today the use of such manuscripts and alphabets is gradually dying out in Northeast Thailand because of modernization emanating from Bangkok. As a result it is rare today to find men who are literate in the traditional sense. Few men, even monks, can read tai noi script, for hand-written kumpee have been replaced by palm-leaf books printed in modern Siamese. Laos, however, has preserved its traditional learning to a much greater extent simply because the difficult terrain, lack of money, and neverending warfare have prevented the spread of modernization beyond Wiangjun and a few lesser cities.

With the Northeast politically isolated from Laos and its traditional learning supplanted by Siamese, there was no longer a traditional way to write Northeastern Lao, though singers and poets continued to write poems. During the 1940s printers in Kawn-gaen began publishing small booklets containing poetry intended for singers, and though the language was Lao, the alphabet was Siamese. Where Lao and Siamese words were the same, there were no serious problems, but when they differed, the printers had to improvise a phonetic spelling. Among the difficulties were consonant clusters. While Siamese words commonly contained clusters such as in the word glawn (poetry), Lao drops the cluster leaving only the initial, glawn. When written in Lao letters this is clear, but in the printed Northeast Lao the cluster is retained but dropped in pronunciation. Certain vowels also change, such as kwai (Siamese for buffalo) to kui or kwun (Siamese for spirit essence) to kuan, though spellings are identical. Central Thai speakers, for example, cannot accurately pronounce these words because they may not know the Lao equivalent.

With tones, major problems arise. Central Thai traditionally is said to have five tones--mid, high, falling, low, and rising--and has a complicated system of signs and consonant groupings to indicate inflections. Northeastern Lao, however, has not been systematized to such an extent, and the tones vary both in number and interpretation from province to province. The same holds true in Laos where provinces are often separated by mountain ranges or forests. The printers in Kawn-gaen failed to evolve a consistent system for indicating tones and left correct intonation to the reader. Fortunately, in 1972 Somdet Pra Maha Wirawong published a 525-page Northeastern Thai-Central Thai Dictionary in Siamese alphabet which is both scholarly and systematic.[8] While his spelling system is consistent and can be pronounced in any of the provincial variants, this book is unknown to traditional poets and singers who continue to rely on their makeshift system.

Though there is little published material to explain Lao poetry, there is a great deal about Siamese poetry. In reading the latter studies two factors may confuse the uninitiated. While certain terms for poetic styles such as glawn and gap are common to both literary traditions, they are not actually equivalents, while parallel forms may have different names. The word glawn means not only poetry in general to the Lao, but one type of poem in particular, at least in everyday usage. Maha Sila Viravong describes six types of glawn,[9] but Northeastern singers generally speak of only one and refer separately to gap which is far less important than the former.

Glawn consists of stanzas each having four lines which according to Maha Sila Viravong are called in order: wak sa-dup, wak hup, wak hawng, and wak song. Each line is "an imparasyllabic line of seven feet, divided into two naturally unequal parts, the second having always four feet."[10] While most stanzas have four lines, many consist of only two, beginning either with the first or the third line of a regular stanza. In constructing his lines, however, the poet may affix a variety of adverbial or conjunctive expressions of an exclamatory, interrogative, or supplicatory nature before (kum boopabot--prefix) or after (kum soi--suffix) the main part of the line to complete the thought. Rhythmically, a line has four beats or accents which in a simple line of seven syllables would fall on syllables 1, 3, 5, and 7. Including the prefix and/or suffix, lines may commonly have up to twelve or rarely even sixteen syllables.

Furthermore, each phrase of a glawn stanza must obey a pattern of tonal signs. The rules, as summarized by Thai Nhouy, are (1) the third syllable (end of the first hemistich) of the first, third, and fourth lines, and also the last syllable of the second line, must be given the accent to (√); (2) the third syllable of the second line, and also the last syllable of the fourth line, must not have any accent; (3) the last syllable of the third line must always be either given the accent ek (') or formed with a consonant of the lower series and a vowel composed with the finals k, d, or p.[11] In addition the fifth word of the last line must also have a to accent.

1. wak sa-dup	___	___	√	___	___	___	___
2. wak hup	___	___	none	___	___	___	√
3. wak hawng	___	___	√	___	___	___	'
4. wak song	___	___	√	___	√	___	none

ทุก ที่ หน้า บ่ง เบตต์ เบิ่ง ไหล
เป็น ป่าง ทุกข์ ฉลาด ปะมาบ มี มั่อ
กำ รัก ทับ โก้ ทอง ทิว ละ ท่าว
แม่ หฺอด แห้ง ทิว น้อย มฺอด ตาม[12]

2 2 1	6 7 6 5
took tee nah	nawng net nüang lai
2 2 2	7 6 6 7
ben bang took	sawat baman mee mua
6 2 7	5 6 6 2 2
kum huk ton	tü tuang tua la tao
2 1 1	5 7 7 2
mae hawt haeng	hui maw-i mawt dam

Meaning:

Everyone's tears are flowing,

> For it is a time of great sorrow.
> Love floods the mother's heart;
> She feels so sad that she is nearly dying.

Alliteration and interior rhyme are integral to glawn, but external rhyme is not. While two and three repetitions of a consonant or vowel are cultivated, four exceed the limits of good taste though such cacophony may be used for special effect.

yüan yak tao	tung haeng hoi haeng
dün daw-i luang	gua gai lü gai
löi kio kün	kao ngawn müa ngawn
küt mae bah	boon hai hum hai[13]

Meaning:

> His great fatigue makes it difficult to continue travelling;
> He crosses through a large forest,
> Then reaches the top of a hill.
> Thinking of his mother, he begins to cry.

It should be noted that the pairs haeng, gai, and hai are different words by virtue of differing tones. A good poet strives to achieve a great variety of rhythms by adding uncounted syllables which alter the flow of words, or he may divide words over the caesura or from the end of one line to the next, a technique called yutdipung (enjambment) according to Thao Nhouy.[14]

The second and lesser style is called gap or glawn gap, the word being derived from the Sanskrit gawaya.[15] Although the number of syllables per line may vary, seven is usual. The last word of each line must rhyme with a word in the following line, the third being most common. These pairs, whose vowels ordinarily rhyme, have matching tone marks as well, but pairs with tone marks alternate with pairs lacking such marks. While Siamese glawn dalat also uses this rhyme pattern, though less strictly and combined with other patterns into stanzas, Lao gap runs continuously without separate stanzas. Gap is sometimes used for introductions in singer's poetry as a contrast to glawn, but a few works have been written entirely in gap. Gap poetry is also used in a genre of singing called süng performed by roving bands of revelers, usually inebriated, as they parade around town during certain festivals seeking whiskey money. The best known is süng bung-fai, songs for the rocket festival in June.

> om poot to namo ben kao
>
> koi si wao dung dae düm mah
>
> namo na mah wun ta wun tawng
>
> nawm get gawng wai gaeo tung sam[16]

Meaning:

> Om Buddha namo must come first.
> I will tell the old story

with the words <u>namo na mah wun ta wun tawng</u>.
I bow my head to the Three Gems.

Musical Instruments

An enumeration of past and present musical instruments in Northeast
Thailand and Laos includes some twenty-five varieties of which ten are
aerophones, four are chordophones, four are membranophones, and seven
are idiophones.

Without doubt the most important of the seven aerophones known
today is the <u>kaen</u>, a bamboo mouth organ whose sound is generated by
tiny metal free-reeds (see Figure 4). A more complete description of this
instrument will follow since it is basic to this book. Similar to the <u>kaen</u>
in principle is the <u>look bee kaen</u>, a single-tube reed-pipe known among
the hill-dwelling Pootai both in Northeast Thailand and southern Laos.
This instrument's pitches are similarly generated from a metal free-reed,
but the single tube is fitted with six or seven finger holes allowing the
player to blow seven or eight pitches. The <u>bee sanai</u> is a water buffalo
horn with both ends open and a metal free-reed larger than but similar to
that of the <u>kaen</u> fitted over a hole cut in the concave side. Also found
in Cambodia where it is called <u>sneng</u>, the <u>bee sanai</u> is capable of only two
or three pitches and is a favorite noise-maker at the <u>bung-fai</u> festival
(see Figure 5). The <u>klui</u>, a vertical bamboo flute, while well-known, is
actually of more significance in Central Thailand where it functions in
certain classical ensembles. Of less musical importance is the <u>wot</u>, a
children's toy constructed of eight bamboo tubes varying from about
eight to twenty-one centimeters long (see Figure 6). The tubes are
formed into a circular bundle around a longer handle and sealed into place
with <u>kisoot</u>, a type of black, sticky beeswax. At the bottom end the tubes
remain sealed by their unpierced nodes but are open at the other. A
rounded mound of ordinary beeswax or <u>kisoot</u> is formed over the open end
but not closing the pipes completely so that air blown over the ends
causes whistle-like pitches to be sounded. Although an old man from
Galasin province named Pao in the 1970s became locally known for playing the <u>wot</u>, in fact it is normally thrown like a dart by children in the
fields as a musical toy. In being used this way, the wind produces the
sound. The two remaining wind instruments barely deserve mention. The
<u>bee goo füang</u> is a child's toy flute made from a green rice stalk, and the
<u>bee bai dawng glue</u> is a cone-shaped kazoo made from a banana leaf. Of
these wind instruments only the <u>kaen</u> and <u>klui</u> are specifically mentioned
in old Lao literature.

Two instruments whose names are mentioned in traditional literature
are unknown today, the <u>kai</u> and <u>suan-lai</u>. Several older singers whose
texts were drawn from such literature thought that <u>kai</u> was an old word
for <u>kaen</u>, although the latter term is also encountered in the literature.
The <u>suan-lai</u> is almost certainly a kind of oboe (double-reed aerophone)
similar to the Cambodian <u>sralai</u> and Central Thai <u>bee</u>. Among other
aerophones no longer used are the <u>sung</u> (Chinese <u>xiang-lo</u>), a large conch-
shell trumpet, and the <u>bee tae</u>, a trumpet-type instrument used to signal
the time during certain periods of the night, and especially around noon,
a period known as <u>yamtae</u>.

The most important of the chordophones is a plucket lute called <u>pin</u>
or less commonly <u>süng</u> (see Figure 7). There is no standard form for <u>pin</u>
other than its having a wooden corpus and wooden neck with five to eight

Figure 4. A traditional <u>kaen</u> player in Roi-et province, Mr. Pun Chonpairot.

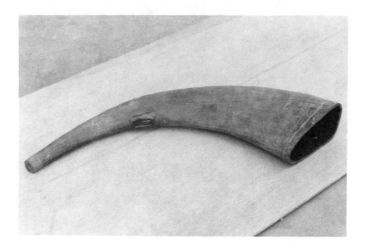

Figure 5. Water buffalo horn with free-reed.

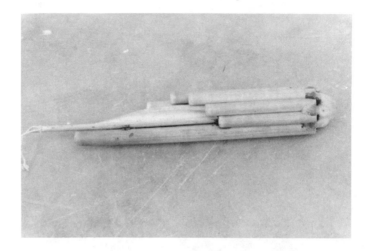

Figure 6.   The <u>wot</u>, a bundle of flute pipes thrown by children.

Figure 7.   A <u>sŭng</u> or <u>pin</u> (<u>gajupbee</u> in Laos), a plucked lute.

frets. There may be from two to four metal strings, one of which is a melodic or "singer" string, the others tuned a fifth lower being drone strings; they are plucked with a piece of buffalo horn. While the pin repertory is severely limited to three or four pieces, players have nevertheless created a very distinctive style in which one drone string may parallel the melody in fifths while the remaining strings produce unstopped drones. Pin combined with kaen have become the standard accompaniment for mawlum plün theatre, and in fact the best-known pin solo today is called "lum plün." Still, the antiquity of the instrument cannot be doubted, however contemporary the Northeastern pin repertory may appear. The word pin in Tai is derived from a Pali-Sanskrit word vina.[17] The Northeastern pin is more closely related in form in the Siamese grajupbee, a four-stringed long-neck lute, and to the Northern süng, a small plucked lute, than to the Northern chest-resonated chordophones which are called pin (pin-pia and pin-num-dao).

Of secondary importance are two types of bowed instruments, the first called saw mai pai ("bamboo fiddle"), the second saw bip ("metal can fiddle") (see Figure 8). The former, which is rarely seen, consists of a section of stout bamboo about one meter in length over which one or two strings are strung over a bridge to upper tuning pegs. Played with a curved bow, this instrument is technically a bowed tube zither. The more commonly seen is the saw bip whose corpus is a metal can such as for kerosene or Hall's Mentho-Lyptus Lozenges fitted with a wooden neck and two wire strings. Unlike the bow of the Siamese saw-oo and saw-duang fiddles whose hairs pass between the two strings (as in the Chinese erhu as well), the bow of the saw bip is separate from the instrument. Last is the sanoo, a musical bow which is attached to large kites. As the wind changes the tension on the bow, random melodies are produced by a strip of dried palm leaf or rattan (see Figure 9). The sanoo will be discussed in another context in Chapter VI.

The most widely encountered membranophone is the glawng yao ("long drum") or glawng hang ("tail drum"), a single-headed drum whose hardwood body is shaped somewhat like an hourglass (see Figure 10). The glawng yao, which is played with the hands, is usually played in combination with a large bronze gong called mong, a pair of cymbals called chap yai, and a smaller pair of cymbals called ching (sing in Lao) usually to accompany dancing. All of the above instruments are also known in Central Thailand, as in the ramana lum dut, a large flat frame drum called glawng düng in the Northeast. Smaller drums such as the ton, also known in Central Thailand, are sometimes found in the Northeast as well. Lastly, pairs of long, barrel drums called glawng seng or glawng jing are beaten in competition to attain the highest pitch, a din that defies description (see Figure 11).

Two Northeastern idiophones are not found elsewhere among the Tai in Thailand, the kaw law and hoon or hün. The latter is a bamboo jaw harp approximately twenty-five centimeters long (see Figure 12), the former is a vertical wooden xylophone peculiar to Galasin province (see Figure 13).[18] Another traditional idiophone is the gup gaep consisting of pieces of hardwood about thirteen centimeters long, five centimeters wide, and from one to two centimeters thick. These are played in pairs, one pair in each hand, clicked in varying patterns to mark the time. A similar instrument in Central Thailand is called grup sepah and accompaneis sepah recitation.[19] The Vietnamese have a similar instrument called cái cap kè, this word being similar to the Lao words gup gaep and

Figure 9. The sanoo or musical bow mounted on large kites.

Figure 8. A two-stringed saw bip made from a Hall's lozenge can played by Tawng-koon See-aroon in Roi-et province.

Figure 10. A small glawng yao troupe with two "long drums," a cylindrical drum, and a pair of cymbals (chap yai) at a festival in Mahasarakam city.

Figure 11. Two pairs of contest drums (glawng seng) during competition in Kawn-gaen's TV 5 television station.

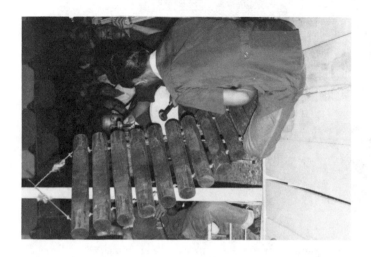

Figure 13. The vertical xylophone of Galasin province, called kaw law or bong-lang.

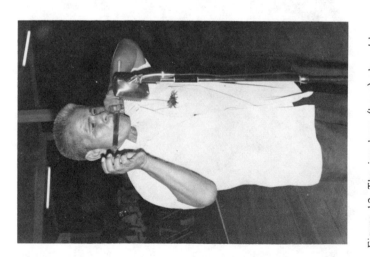

Figure 12. The jaw-harp (hoon) played by Sootee Chai-dilut

said by Trần văn Khê to be an onomatopoetic term.[20]

Lastly, the Pootai, especially in southern Laos, use an instrument called ngawp ngaep (see Figure 14). The instrument consists of two sticks of wood about thirty centimeters long, the lower side of one being scalloped or cut into saw teeth. The upper piece and sometimes the lower as well have at one end some coins or bottle caps held in place by a nail which pierces them. As the player clicks the two pieces of wood together in his left hand, he rubs the saw-toothed portion over a stone or piece of wood producing a combination of clicking, jingling, and scraping. The instrument is often heard in the ensembles which accompany the southern Lao singing styles.

Trần văn Khê again describes a closely related instrument called cái phach or cái sinh tiến in Vietnamese or sapèque clappers in French which consist of two pieces of wood about twenty-seven and twenty centimeters long respectively. The shorter of these, which is placed above the other, has two brass nails each with three coins and the longer has one nail with three coins. The longer, moreover, has saw teeth cut into the lower side. Instead of a stone, however, the player rubs the teeth over another piece

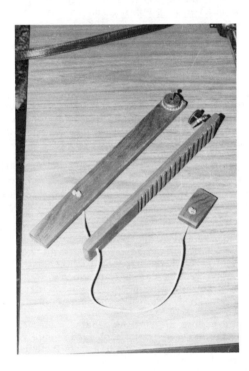

Figure 14. Used primarily in southern Laos, the ngawp ngaep is shaken, struck, and scraped.

of wood about eighteen centimeters long. This instrument is still used in central Vietnam, and records of it go back to the eighteenth century.[21]

Whereas the musical cultures of the Siamese, Khmer, Burmese, and Indonesians (Javanese and Balinese especially) emphasize ensemble playing involving a variety of non-soloistic instruments, Northeastern musical culture is primarily represented by but one instrument, the kaen, and that played alone or with a singer. Traditional Lao literature additionally mentions it among the pinpat or pat ensembles which might include some of the same instruments found in the Siamese ensembles. But because this literature describes the Lao court, a court which increasingly sought to imitate the more brilliant courts of Angkor and later Bangkok, the kaen's inclusion in the ensemble is not thought to be significant. Most discussions of Lao music mention the kaen's place in the contemporary Lao ensemble called sep noi, but because of tuning differences as well as because the traditional manner of kaen playing differs radically from ensemble playing, it seems more likely that the kaen, a truly Lao instrument, was merely added to the imported ensembles for court use. In contemporary practice, at least as far as Northeast Thailand is concerned, the kaen has three purposes: (1) to accompany singing, (2) to perform solos, (3) for use in kaen wong ensemble in schools, a non-traditional use.

Theoretical Concepts

Vocal music, because of its close relationship to literature, Buddhism, and tradition, is thought more important than instrumental music. "Intended as it is to be read aloud or sung, Laotian poetry, or verse, is essentially musical and rhythmic."[22] The definition of song as heightened speech best prepares the reader for understanding the various Siamese and Lao words which are usually translated "to sing." Four words must be discussed in this regard--rawng, wah, kup, lum--though only two are customarily used among Northeasterners--kup and lum. The Siamese term rawng, though it also means "to cry out," is the standard word for "to sing." While youthful speakers of Lao now use the Lao equivalent--hawng-- for "to sing," in fact hawng means only "to cry out" in Lao. Rawng, which is usually combined with pleng meaning "to sing a song," implies a fixed melody to which the words must adjust themselves regardless of their tones. Singers rawng Siamese classical songs, popular songs, and Western songs, but when rendering Siamese folksongs one uses the verb wah. Wah has various meanings including "to say," "to insult," "to scold," or "to speak out." The Siamese also use the verb kup for certain types of recitation, particularly kup sepah, the reading of poetry to a fixed melody accompanied by two pairs of wood castanets called grup.[23] According to Mosel kup literally means "to eject" or recite words with voice modulation or melody.[24] While birds and animals may rawng, only humans can kup.

The Lao, however, use the verb lum that in a musical sense is encountered in Siamese only in reference to lum dut (a genre of Central Thai repartee folksong) and lum num (a melody from Buddhist chant). Lum (in its musical meaning) neither appears in the Haas Thai-English Student's Dictionary nor under "sing" in the major English-Thai dictionaries known to me. Lum has often been confused with and misprinted in Siamese publications as rum meaning "to dance" because both Lao and Siamese speakers, finding the consonant r difficult to pronounce, often alter it to l (e.g., lawng pleng rather than rawng pleng). Mosel, however, correctly

states that lum is a kind of song "in which the words are primary, the
melody being adjusted to fit the sound and grouping of the words (as in
setting a poem to music). The rhythmic intervals are necessarily irregular
in that they must accommodate to the word groupings and their meanings."[25] Mosel, though, then implies incorrectly that lum is to kup (kup
lum) as pleng is to rawng (rawng pleng), for pleng is a noun and lum is a
verb.

A number of other meanings further complicate the term lum. It may
mean "a story according to the rule of verse," such as lum pra wet, the
story of Prince Wetsundawn, the penultimate life of Buddha before enlightenment. It may also refer to the body of a human, animal, or anything,
living or inanimate minus appendages. Similarly it is a classifier for tubu-
lar objects such as boats, airplanes, and bamboo, e.g., hua sam lum ("boat--
three tubes"). This latter definition together with its meaning as a trunk
or stalk (e.g., lum pai--"bamboo stalk") is known to the Siamese. Lastly it
refers to Lao singing generated by word-tones.

While the term lum is usually throughout the Northeast as well as
Southern Lao, the word kup describes Central and Northern Lao styles,
such as kup sum nua, kup ngum, and kup siang kuang, referring to place
names. While kup also means "to drive a car or animal" or combined with
dam means "to follow," in its musical meaning it too implies that the tones
of the words generate the melody. Both the Northeast Lao-Siamese dictionary and Allen Kerr's Lao-English dictionary, however, skirt the issue
defining the term kup as simply "to sing."

While lum implies a direct relationship between tone and pitch, there
is in fact no simple system for realizing melody. There are many different kinds of lum, each with different modes, rhythms, and moods, and yet
all are lum in principle. The word therefore has very general application
as in lum isan, meaning Northeastern singing. As a fundamental concept
in creating melody, lum may be as old as the Lao people, although the
resulting melodies will have changed over the years and from region to
region.

A Lao singer is called a mawlum. Maw alone means "doctor" and
while some translate mawlum as "singing doctor," this is more innocent
than helpful. Maw means a "skilled person" as in mawyah (yah--"medicine,"
folk-medicine doctor), mawdoo (doo--"to see," fortune teller), or maw-kuam
(kuam--"law," lawyer). Northeast singing has also been called lum kaen in
reference to the bamboo reed organ which accompanies the singing. In
Central Thailand, especially during the nineteenth and early twentieth
century, lum isan was known as aeo lao. While some Siamese dictionaries
translate aeo as "love song," in fact it has no meaning except that erron-
eously applied to Lao singing. Aeo in Lao means "to implore" or "to cajole," as a child nags its mother for milk. In Northern Thai, however, it
means "to court a girl" (aeo sao), and this may have influenced the Siamese, knowing that mawlum often sang love poems.

Lao musical theory is neither written nor articulated systematically.
Players and singers imply the distinction of scales and rhythms in non-
technical language which grows out of their classification of vocal genres.
In the minds of performers, however, there are no abstract concepts of
scale or meter and thus no exact terms for them.

While the Northeast Thai tuning system (considered to be all the pitches
available on the kaen) is seven tones in an octave consisting of both half
and whole steps and approximating the pitches of a Western diatonic major
scale, traditional music is rarely if ever built on seven-tone scales.

Through analysis, two scales, both pentatonic, are seen to be used in Northeast Thailand. The first comprises five pitches with a prominent major third (C to E) while the second has a prominent minor third (A to C). In Example 1 the lowest pitch indicated is the "tonic" or finalis since both singers and instrumentalists cadence on it, but in the case of the first scale, the C (fourth above the finalis) functions as a secondary tonic between full cadences. Only the lower G and A respectively are tonics, however, for the equivalent pitches an octave above lack the release of the lower notes.

Example 1. The two scales found in Lao music.

Two terms, lum tang sun and lum tang yao, began to be used about 1945 when Mr. Soonton, the leader of the Soontara-pirom troupe in Bangkok, coined them for the benefit of audiences to describe different singing styles. Lum denoted Lao singing technique based on word tones while tang denotes regional style of playing or singing and less commonly scale or mode. In Lao usage tang does not have the Central Thai meaning of a version of a melody for a particular instrument or as taught by a particular teacher. The Lao term wat, meaning style of singing, dancing, or playing, is interchangeable in meaning with the Siamese term tang, but it is rarely encountered. Sun means "short" and implies syllabic text setting while yao means "long" and implies melismatic text setting.

Both terms referred to the major divisions of mawlum glawn, the non-theatrical vocal genre in which male and female singers alternate accompanied by the kaen. The first portion followed the first scale, was sung syllabically, and in tempo giusto, specifically duple meter. The second portion followed the second scale, was set more melismatically, and sung in parlando-rubato or speech rhythm. Extending the terminology to cover other styles, e.g., lum döi, which follows the second scale but in meter, is not done; singers simply refer to this type as lum döi, which implies its own combination of scale and meter.

In seeking Northeastern Thai terminology to denote theoretical phenomena, we have been forced to compromise by using terms in ways that go somewhere beyond their normal meaning. While Northeastern Thai singers would not distinguish scales by calling them the "sun scale" and "yao scale," such terminology is consistent with local thinking and solves a labeling problem in English. To distinguish metrical from speech rhythm, however, we shall have to use the Italian terms tempo giusto and parlando-rubato.

Recited Genres Relating to Northeast Thai Singing

There are a number of literary genres in the Northeast and Laos which are performed in a sing-song style of recitation that is neither singing nor speaking but somewhere between these two. They include tet (sermons in Lao read by Buddhist monks), soo-kwun (a Brahministic ceremony in which a ritualist reciting texts in Lao calls back the kwun or "spirit essence" of

the participant, the term having been originally <u>soot-kwun</u> from the Sans-
skrit <u>sutra</u>), <u>sung</u> (a responsorial chant sung especially at the <u>boon bung-fai</u>
[<u>rocket</u>] festival), <u>pa-nyah</u> (ritualized courting in which boys and girls test
wits by reciting memorized proverbs and excerpts from Lao literature),
and <u>an nungsu</u> (reading of epic-length localized <u>jataka</u> and Lao stories from
traditional <u>nungsu pook</u> manuscripts at funeral wakes). In general throughout Thailand and Laos it is rare to encounter anyone who reads poetry
aloud in anything but a sing-song style since poetry through its manipulation of rhythmic and tonal patterns is essentially musical. Pali chant
recited in the temple, too, is never spoken but given dignity and added
importance through sing-song recitation in spite of the non-tonal nature of
Pali.[26] Non-Buddhist ritualists, to increase the authority and efficacy of
their words, may have originally imitated these chant styles in heightened
speech, and because the tonal nature of Lao tends to generate scale patterns almost involuntarily, the step to melody was a small one indeed.

An nungsu

Of the literary forms which are recited, the one having the closest
relationship with <u>mawlum</u> singing is <u>an nungsu</u> or literally "reading a
book."[27] The book, however, is not a modern printed volume but a traditional palm-leaf manuscript called <u>nungsu pook</u> ("book in a pile") or <u>nung-</u>
<u>su bai lan</u> ("palm-leaf book") (see Figure 15). The art of copying such
books is now nearly lost, for printed "manuscripts" have replaced the
traditional ones. Although such manuscripts tend to deteriorate rapidly
because of climate and insects, many temple libraries contain <u>nungsu pook</u>
dating as far back as one hundred years. While monks <u>tet</u> from similar
books, those used in <u>an nungsu</u> were written in <u>glawn</u> poetry using <u>tai noi</u>
(old Lao) alphabet (see Figure 16). Temple libraries tend to have multiple
copies of certain stories because laymen may make merit for themselves
by hiring former monks to make such copies which are then donated to
the temple.

Immediately after a person dies relatives and close friends come to
the home each evening for three successive nights to participate in the
<u>ngun huan dee</u>, literally "good house party." Traditionally young and old
alike spend the nights listening to older men read aloud from <u>nungsu pook</u>
the epic Lao stories drawn from both <u>jataka</u> and local sources in a kind of
sing-song called <u>an nungsu</u>. Today the practice has become extremely rare
in the Northeast since interest in traditional literature is diminishing and
very few men can still read in this style. Today's youth prefers to play
cards, talk, or listen to the radio.

Mr. Jun Pijan, age fifty-six (1973), of Ban Nawng-doo near Barabu
reported that he learned to read when he was a monk more than twenty
years earlier. Besides copying manuscripts, Mr. Jun reported having read
the stories of <u>Jumba-seedon</u>, <u>Pa Daeng Nang Ai</u>, <u>Galaget</u>, <u>Sung Sin-sai</u>,
<u>Koon Tung</u>, and <u>Nang Pom-hawm</u>. Another informant, Mr. Moon Sotipun,
also called Paw-yai-jan Moon ("old writer monk"), age seventy-two (1973),
found his recitation suffered when unable to imbibe some alcohol first.
Mr. Moon's expertise, however, was offset by his age and poor vision, a
condition aggravated by the fact that reading takes place at night with
only a small oil light or at best a kerosene latern. Stumbling and other
mistakes are therefore inherent to <u>an nungsu</u>. The following excerpt from
the story <u>Sio-sawat</u> read by Mr. Soot-tee Chai-dilut, then aged sixty-six,
of Ban Kawn-gaen near Roi-et illustrates <u>an nungsu</u>. In all recorded

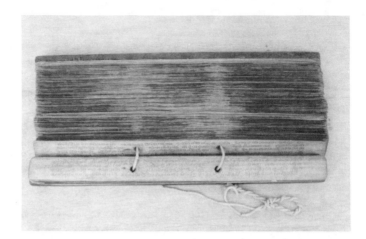

Figure 15. A relatively large palm-leaf book (nungsü pook) in old Lao script containing an epic-length story.

Figure 16. Close-up view of Figure 15 showing the script called dua tai noi.

excerpts the scale pattern was consistently d f g a with d as the "tonic"
pitch and a few rises to c. It is significant that mawlum, although they
are singers rather than readers, sometimes refer to the lum tang yao
scale pattern as an nungsü. Indeed, increasingly the tempo of an nungsü
reading and adding kaen accompaniment would nearly constitute lum tang
yao singing (see Example 2).

Another informant, Loon Saen-kot, age forty-two of Barabü district,
read from an eighty-year-old manuscript fully 34 centimeters thick repeating the well-known story of Jumba-seedon (Four Jumba Trees). Mr. Loon's
eyes were better than those of his teacher, Jun Pijan, but he had to practice for nearly an hour before he would record the excerpt (see Example
3).

The importance of an nungsü in relation to mawlum cannot be over-
emphasized. Not only do mawlum sometimes refer to one of their two
scale patterns as an nungsü, but kaen soloists improvise two basic pieces
called an nungsü yai and an nungsü noi which imitate mawlum in the two
kaen modes described by the words yai ("big") and noi ("small"). The
rhythm of an nungsü, like lum tang yao, is parlando-rubato and flows
according to the words. It is the word-tones which determine the direction
of the melody, although good readers add embellishments of their own
which may result in melodies like those sung by mawlum. The connection
with the temple is important, for while monks do not perform an nungsü
for the faithful, the practitioners of the art learn to read, write, and
recite the manuscripts in the temple. Formerly all learned monks could
perform an nungsü.

Pa-nyah

Although spoken, rather than recited or sung, pa-nyah in Lao is derived
from the Pali word brut-ya or brut-chaya meaning "philosophy." In converting Pali and Siamese words into Lao the br sound changes to p and the
y sound to ny. Although the Lao spelling of the word is unsettled--pa-
nyah, pun yah, bun-yah, pan-yah--the meaning remains the same.

Pa-nyah, translated "courts of love and poetry" by Thao Nhouy Abhay
in the Kingdom of Laos,[28] was one of the ritualized courtship customs
which took place during the evenings especially from November to February when the weather was at its most pleasant. The young men walked
from their homes to those of their girlfriends playing the kaen. Upon
arriving, the suitor and his friends might be invited onto the open verandah
of the girl's home where she and her friends might be spinning silk or
performing some similar task. Pa-nyah was a contest of wit, a literary
match, in which the males competed with the females for superiority in
parrying each other's verbal thrusts. The opposition's indirect, poetic, but
nonetheless outrageous questions and suggestions had to be answered with
statements which firmly put down the opposition. The mood might be
melancholy or light-hearted, with laughter often filling the air.

Although there is a form called pa-nyah pasit which derives its material from proverbs, ordinary pa-nyah consists of fragments and quotations
from Lao poetic literature. These excerpts are rarely complete stanzas
and are usually preceded by a phrase meaning "O my sister" (oh naw nawg
oi) or "O my brother" (oh naw ai oi). A line of pa-nyah consists of an
introductory phrase, a main phrase consisting of from seven to twelve
syllables broken down into four main beats, and an optional suffix which
adds politeness and requires one additional beat. The poetry must be

Example 2 continued on next page.

11. PEE WAH KÜN KUT KAW BOK BAO BANG YOO

12. KAW GAE TAN POO HOO PAI KAH YAH SA DIAN - - - - - - - - - - - -

Example 2. An nungsü from the story Sio Sawat read by Soot-tee Chai-dailüt, Mahasarakam, September 18, 1973.

♪ = CA. 200; D SOUNDS C

1. DAE NUN POO MAN AWN MOI   SOM NGAM TUNG SEE

2. PEE LAE NAWNG WAWN WAI NAH MAE DON

3. GAW JUNG BAK GLAO WAO KAI   HET UN MEE

4. MAE MAN DAH NANG UK KEE KAT WEN BAWNG KAH

5. (BANG FOONG) PÜNG FOONG GUM (? ?) PAH NEE JAK MAN DAH

6. UN WAH MAH (?) WAH GÜT MAH YAM DAI HAO SAI HAI YAM NUN

7. AO BAI TIM NON TEE LAI LAWNG

8. BOON BOON SOI BAWNG NUM MAH KAH SOO WUN

Example 3 continued on the following page.

9. UN WAH AI YA GAH TAO PUA MIA TUNG KOO

10. AO YOO LIANG BEN GAEO LOOK DON

11. UK KEE POO BAH BUNG TUM MA HET

12. KAO KAO WAH SOM SAI NGUAN SIA NGIANG LUAT DAI

Example 3. An nungsü from the story Jumba-seedon read by Loon Saen-kot in Ban Nawng-waeng, Bua-mat sub-district, Barabü district, Maharasa-kam province on November 28, 1973.

beautiful and indirect, replete with simile, metaphor, and pun, conveying the sentiments of love however sharply barbed.

The search for informants skilled in pa-nyah produced a fair number of women, all in their sixties, but only two men. The two recording sessions observed were similar in that the male and females took turns sparring while competing for sympathetic laughter from the audience. In one case three old women competed with a man whose memory was rather hazy but nevertheless held his own until he ran out of material. Pa-nyah is merely spoken although the poetry together with the word-tones give it a melodic smoothness distinctly different from, for example, a market conversation. It is competitive alternation between male and female, however, which leads directly to mawlum glawn where the best known subject is glawn gio, courting poems in which the two singers engage in similar competition. The following example, freely translated by Jarunchai Chonpairot, was taken from a pa-nyah excerpt published in the Program of the Northeast Thai Music Festival.[29]

(male) O my dear, I wish to ask you about the big tree in the center of the woods if I may. I want to know whether many people live there. A black crow wishes to eat the fruit of that tree and smell its fragrance. But I am not handsome; I am black as the crow. [Are you married or single? I love you but I fear I will not succeed because I am ugly.]

(female) O my dear, I am like a small tree on the heights waiting for the rain to pour down. If the fifth month [April] comes but brings no rain, the small tree will soon die. [I am single and want a boyfriend.]

(male) Can this really be true? A big tree without a ghost or a pretty girl without a lover would burst the breast of Nang

Tawranee [the goddess who protects the earth]. If the ghost who protects the fields [pee da-haek] has no coconut shell [water bowl], the earth will dry up in dust. If you are pretty, you must already have a lover. [I cannot believe that you have no lover.]

(female) My dear, since the time when I was a seedling there were no vines to entwine themselves around me. Now that I am a sapling, still no vine embraces me. [I have no boyfriend.)

(male) You say that the tree has no vines, but why then is it overgrown? If the place under the house is too small, how can you keep a buffalo there? I want to die and become a water bowl which will be warmed when you hold it. O, luck, why do you not come to help me live with her? [The implication is that she is lying.]

(female) I was a virgin pure like a daeng jing melon. Since I became a girl [sao] no boyfriend has slept with me. Since I became a girl no boyfriend has talked with me. You are the first one I've met. Please protect me and keep me as your lover. I will never forget you.

NOTES

1.   The term Tai indicates the greater linguistic family in contradistinction to Thai which indicates citizens of the modern nation of Thailand. The Siamese are the inhabitants of Central Thailand.

2.   United Nations, Secretariat, United Nations Statistical Yearbook, 24th ed. (New York, 1973), p. 8.

3.   Kingdom of Laos, Ministere du Plan de la Cooperation Service National de la Statistique, Annuaire statistique (Vientiane, 1970), pp. 10-11.

4.   Korat is a shortened form of Nakawn-ratchasimah. Nakawn was shortened to kawn, then simply ko. Ratchasimah was similarly shortened to rat.

5.   Phya Anuman Rajadhon, "Thet--Māhā Chat" in Essays on Thai Folklore (Bangkok: The Social Science Association Press of Thailand, 1968), pp. 164-77.

6.   Marie-Daniel Faure, "The 'Boun' Bang-Fay," in Kingdom of Laos, ed. René de Berval, trans. Teissier du Cros et al. (Saigon: France-Asie, 1959), pp. 272-82.

7.   Kurt Wulff, Chinesisch und Tai: Sprachvergleichende Untersuchungen (Copenhagen, 1934).

   Paul K. Benedict, "Thai, Kadai, and Indonesian: A New Alignment in Southeastern Asia," American Anthropologist 44 (1942): 576-601.

8.   Somdet Pra Maha Wirawong, Potjanah-noogarom pak isan--pak glang [Northeastern Thai--Central Thai Dictionary] (Bangkok, 1972).

9.   Maha Sila Viravong, Sunta-luksana [Versification] (Vientiane, 1961), pp. 16-22.

10. Thao Nhouy Abhay, "Versification," in Kingdom of Laos, pp. 351-2.

11. Ibid., p. 353.

12. Bang-kum, Sung Sin-sai, ed. Sila Viravong (Vientiane: 1972), p. 61.

13. Ibid., p. 148.

14. Thao Nhouy Abhay, "Versification," p. 357.

15. Maha Sila Viravong, Sunta-luksana, p. 14.

16. Tawng-poon Ponsawut, Gap sung bawng-fai (Kawn-gaen: Klungnah-nawitayah, 1962), p. 1.

17. Dhanit Yupho, Thai Musical Instruments, 2nd ed., trans. David Morton (Bangkok: Department of Fine Arts, 1950), p. 87.

18. See Terry E. Miller and Jarernchai Chonpairot, "The Ranat and Bong-lang: The Question of Origin of the Thai Xylophones," Journal of the Siam Society 69 (1981): 145-63.

19. Dhanit Yupho, Thai Musical Instruments, p. 11.

20. Trần văn Khê, La musique vietnamienne traditionnelle (Paris: Presses Universitaires de France, 1962), p. 172.

21. Ibid., pp. 172-3.

22. Thao Nhouy Abhay, "Versification," p. 348.

23. H. H. Prince Bidya, "Sebhā Recitation and the Story of Khun Chāng Khun Phan," Journal of the Thailand Research Society 33 (March 1941): 1-22.

24. James N. Mosel, Trends and Structure in Contemporary Thai Poetry, Data Paper no. 43 (Ithaca, New York: Cornell University Press, 1961), p. 51.

25. Ibid., p. 50.

26. Although Pali is non-tonal, it is written in Siamese letters, many of which automatically cause tonal inflections. Consequently it is common for monks to chant Pali according to Siamese or Lao tonal inflections.

27. The term also means "to read a message" or "to read a love letter."

28. Thao Nhouy Abhay, "Courts of Love and Poetry," in Kingdom of Laos, pp. 206-9.

29. Pawn-see Chaisan, "Pa-nyah," in Program of the Northeastern Music Festival (Galasin, 1972), p. 21. (In Thai)

II.

Nontheatrical Vocal Genres

Introduction

The term mawlum properly refers to a Northeastern Thai or Lao singer whose style is traditional and who derives the melody from word-tones, a technique indicated by the word lum. Although the term is used loosely, referring to both professional and amateur singers, it is commonly used among Westerners in reference to the singing itself, a grammatical impropriety. Still, for English speakers it is common to refer to Lao singing as mawlum, e.g., mawlum singing. The Central Thai sometimes refer to traditional Lao singing as lum kaen, lao kaen, aeo lao. The first of these was coined in 1959 by a monk, Tanjaokoon-tamtirarat-maha [His Holiness] Moo-nee in his essay Rüang lum-kaen [The Story of Lum-kaen][1] to avoid the misnomer aeo lao widely used among the Siamese for more than one hundred years. Aeo has no meaning in Siamese but means "to court" or "visit" in Northern Thai and "to cajole" or "nag" in Lao. Aeo lao, though referring to mawlum in common usage, has no proper literal meaning.

A mawlum singer must be literate in order to learn written poetry, must receive extensive training, performs for an audience, and establishes a reputation on the basis of excellent vocal technique, pronunciation, ability to dance, as well as his rapport with the audience. The ingredients for professional singing as opposed to folk singing are therefore present. The mawlum pee fah genre sung by female mediums to cure victims of malevolent spirits, however, clearly falls within most definitions of folk music since one becomes a mawlum pee fah by virtue of having been cured by one, there being no requirements of training, literacy, or singing ability.

This chapter and the following one describe the nontheatrical and theatrical vocal genres but without musical examples, a detailed discussion of singing technique being reserved for Chapter IV.

My research in Northeast Thailand has uncovered fifteen varieties of nontheatrical mawlum which may be categorized into five groups. They

are: (1) a genre in which a solo singer accompanied by kaen sings epic-
length tales, called lum pün or lum rüang; (2) six genres in which two or
more singers accompanied by kaen sing alternately and in competition.
The most common is known as lum glawn, but lum jot and lum gup gaep
are closely related. Lum ching choo, lum sam sing ching nang, and lum
sam glü all involve three or more singers, the first two of mixed sexes,
the last all male; (3) an extension of Buddhist sermons (tet) called tet lae
in which monks sing poems in a vocal style similar to lum glawn; (4) six
theatrical genres involving troupes or companies. The most common
today are lum moo and lum plün although lum wiang and nung bra-mo-tai
are still played. Ligeh lao and lum moo maeng dup dao, although no
longer performed, were important predecessors to today's genres; (5) a
ceremony to cure persons afflicted by spirits performed by old women who
sing and dance throughout. It is known variously by four terms, lum pee
fah, lum pee taen, lum tai tüng, and lum song.

Although most of these genres may be found in all sixteen provinces
of Northeast Thailand, musical activity centers in five provinces along
the Chi River from Oobon in the southeast to Kawn-gaen in the northwest
with Yasoton, Roi-et, and Mahasarakam provinces between them. The
province of Löi, Chaiyapoom, Galasin, and northern Nakawn-ratcha-simah
also have much musical activity but have not been the traditional areas
of innovation or concentration of performers. The culture in Nakawn-
ratcha-simah province, which borders Central Thailand, has a distinctive-
ness of its own that is both Siamese and Lao. Boori-rum, Soo-rin, and
Sisaget provinces bordering Kambuchea (Cambodia) have large numbers of
ethnic Cambodians and Kui while Sagon-nakawn, Nakawn-panom, and
Nawng-kai provinces to the northeast along the Maekong are somewhat
mountanous and partly inhabited by Pootai and other highland Lao groups.

Performs have travelled widely throughout the Northeast for many
years, but such travel was slow and uncomfortable, either by ox-drawn
wagon or horseback. The musical influence of one province on another
was therefore rather slight since most performers restricted themselves
to a small area. Since about 1965 the Thai Government has been attempting to blunt a low-keyed but nevertheless teancious insurgency in the
Northeast, especially in Nawng-kai, Sagon-nakawn, and Nakawn-panom
provinces, by providing long-overdue development. As a consequence there
are now excellent highways throughout the region, though secondary roads
connecting villages often remain rugged. Today's performaners may play
in Oobon one night, in Galasin 245 kilometers to the northwest the next,
and in Oodawn province 180 kilometers further northwest the next. The
isolation that formerly allowed regional variations to develop has given
way to a more cosmopolitan atmosphere where singers and players freely
borrow from any styles which they encounter.

Beginning in November with the gatin festival, performances resume
with the end of the Buddhist lent (pansah) and the planting season but
become most plentiful during December, January, February, and March;
during March and April performances diminish as the weather becomes
increasingly hot and during May and June when the rains return the number further diminishes. Each provincial town in the Northeast has a Red
Cross Fair at least once a year lasting up to seven days during which mawlum is a required entertainment. The Red Cross Fair in Mahasarakam
held January, 1974, included outdoor movies, games, restaurants, rumwong

dancing, boxing, rides, popular music groups, mawlum moo, mawlum plün, and mawlum glawn. In such festivals each troupe, ride, restaurant, or entertainment attempts to overpower the competition with badly worn recordings of popular music played through powerful amplifiers and giant speakers. Needless to say the combination of din, dust, and confusion from milling crowds tends to create a crude and commercial atmosphere.

The audiences which attend mawlum performances must sit on the ground before the stage since seats are rarely provided. At mawlum glawn performances one is more likely to encounter old women with their grandchildren plus a few old men since this genre has lost much of its popularity with young people. Mawlum moo and especially mawlum plün audiences, however, are much more youthful since these genres have adopted such devices as rock bands and young mini-skirted girls to attract audiences. In most villages, however, it is rare to find anyone who would not make the effort to attend a free performance. In the cities and towns, although the overall percentage of the population which attends is far less, the numbers are nevertheless greater. Though performances may last all night, children remain throughout often asleep on the ground since child-rearing practices in Thailand do not ordinarily require children to go to sleep at any particular time.

With regard to origin, education, and occupation, mawlum singers are amazingly homogenous. Except for some of the old women who sing mawlum pee fah, every singer encountered was literate and reported having at least four years of primary education, the maximum then provided free by the Thai Government. With few exceptions all singers came from rural villages in the Northeast and all engaged or had earlier engaged in rice farming. The few who no longer farmed during the planting season included only the best professional singers like Ken Dalao or young beautiful females who could afford to preserve their beauty through idleness during the planting season. The singer's social status, life styles, income, and the attitudes and stereotypes held by fellow villagers regarding mawlum, as well as sexual license, and eligibility in marriage will be discussed in relation to specific types of mawlum.

History

Among the assumptions of many Thai and Westerners is the belief that mawlum singing is as ancient as the Tai people. His Holiness Pra Moo-nee writes that because there are still Tai people who use a kind of kaen in Yunnan and Guangxi provinces in southern China that mawlum is at least as old as the alleged original Tai kingdoms there, approximately one thousand years.[2] Many Western scholars believe that Asian music preserves itself through strict tradition allowing little change if any. Consequently writers of music history texts tend to group Asian music with Classical Greek and Roman music though they may discuss contemporary forms such as Chinese drama and Indonesian gamelan orchestras. As will be demonstrated, Northeastern Thai music has changed dramatically even within living memory, although the rate of change has accelerated during the present century.

Ironically the most interesting historical documents regarding Northeast Thai singing come from Central Thailand. It has been mentioned previously that as a result of Siamese invasions of Wiangjun in the late eighteenth century, and especially in 1827, a significant portion of the population was forcibly deported to Central Thailand especially around Sara-booree, Lopbooree, Ratbooree, and Brajinbooree provinces north and west of Bangkok. As the Lao spread throughout Central Thailand things Lao became a fad among the Siamese. Not even the royal family could resist the fashion.

King Mongkut (1804-1868), known as Rama IV and officially as Pra Chomklao-chao-yuhua, who reigned from 1851 to 1868 restored the custom of appointing a Second King, a practice which had not been followed for some 250 years. Mongkut appointed his brother, Prince Chutamani (1808-1865) to this post in 1851 giving him nearly equal status and a coronation of great splendor. His residence, called the Palace of the Front and now the National Museum, faces the Sanam-luang ("royal grounds") near the main palace in Bangkok. The Second King's official name was Pra Pin-klao.[3] Sir John Bowring, an envoy from Great Britain, described a meeting with the Second King in 1855 in which his host performed on the Lao kaen; at a meeting two days later he entertained Bowring with Lao dancers and kaen music.[4] The Chronicles of the Fourth Reign includes a description of the Second King's musical activities.

> During his lifetime, the Second King had constructed, at baan sii thaa (Ban See-tah) district, a small place for pleasure and open air enjoyment where he had a Laos-style pavillion erected for his personal convenience. He enjoyed playing the Laotian reed mouth-organ known as khaan, and he often jour-neyed to the town of phanad-nikhom [Müang Panut-nikom], to the Laos district of sam prathuan [Sumbratuan], within the city limits of nakhɔɔnchajsii [Nakawn-chaisee], and to baan-siithaa district, within the limits of saraburii [Sara-booree], where he would pass the time playing the Laotian musical instrument. He could perform the Laotian type of dance [fawn] and could skillfully perform the Laotian comedy-singing known as ɛɛw [aeo]. It is said that if one did not actually see his royal person, one would have thought the singer were a real Lao.[5]

After the Second King's death in 1865 King Mongkut immediately made known his fear that Lao musical culture would completely supplant Siamese genres and therefore banned Lao musical performances in a proclamation issued "on Friday the fourteenth day of the Waning Moon in the twelfth Lunar Month, in the Year of the Ox," that is, the seventh year of the decade, M.E. 1227 (1865).[6]

> His Majesty the King directs this royal decree to all government officials and all citizens in and out of the capital: Thailand has long been an assembly point for for-eigners from near and far. Alien singing and dancing have occasionally been performed alongside ours, and this adds to the honor of our country. Since they are alien entertain-ments, however, the propriety of imitating them is question-able. It is of course good that Thai are able to imitate others such as monks who can chant Mahachat [the story of Prince Wetsundawn] in other styles such as that of the Lao, the Mawn, the Burmese, and the Khmer. Still, alien singing and dancing should not have priority over ours. Ours should maintain their priority and others should be a little less important.

The situation has now changed. Thai have abandoned
their own entertainments including beepat ensemble, mahori
ensemble, sepa-krüng-tawn [a kind of story telling in sing-
song accompanied by pairs of wood blocks called grup],
brop-gai, sukrawah, pleng-gai-ba-gio-kao [three types of
folksong], and lakawn rawng [a play with singing]. Both men
and women now play laokaen [mawlum] throughout the kingdom. Those who play in the beepat or mahori ensembles
must sell their instruments because they are no longer hired.
Laokaen is always played for the topknot cutting ceremony
and for ordinations. The price is as high as ten to twelve
dum-lüng [forty to forty-eight baht]. His Majesty the King
finds this kind of situation unfavorable. We cannot give the
priority to Lao entertainments. Laokaen must serve the
Thai; the Thai have never been the Lao's servants. Thai
have been performing laokaen for more than ten years now
and it has become very common. It is apparent that wherever there is an increase in the playing of laokaen there is
also less rain. This year the rice survived only because of
water originating in the forests. In towns where there was
much laokaen it rained only a little and there was little
rice growing. Even though the farmers were able to plant
rice near the end of the season, too much water from the
forests destroyed the rice in floods. Consequently the King
has been worrying about this, and through his authority he
now requests all Thai who remain loyal and grateful to him
to stop performing laokaen. Please do not hire laokaen or
perform it yourselves. Try this for a year or two. Thai
entertainments including lakawn, fawn, rum, beepat, mahori,
sepa-krüng-tawn, brop-gai, sukrawah, and pleng-gai-ba-gio-
kao ought to be revived. They should not be forgotten and
finally lost. You are requested to stop performing laokaen.
Try this for a year or two and see whether the amount of
rain becomes sufficient again or not.

Anyone who disobeys this proclamation will be taxed.
Both the player and the owner of the house will be assessed
a stiff tax. Those who play secretly will be fined by two
or threefold.[7]

There is no known documentation describing the results of this proclamation, but its effectiveness is attested to by the nearly complete lack
of mawlum performances originating in Central Thailand today. Kaen are
known to be made in a number of Central Thai provinces although it has
not been determined whether these makers came during the forced migration of the nineteenth century or later. Stern and Stern, who described
mawlum singing in Kanchana-booree province near the Burmese border,
fail to state when the Lao living there arrived.[8] Were they from among
those coming in the early nineteenth century and able to preserve their
style with no influence from later developments via radio, they might
reveal something of earlier practice, but this remains to be investigated.

In more recent years when transportation became available, a pattern
of migration from the Northeast to Bangkok of villagers seeking work
developed. Because of poor economic conditions and a rapidly growing

population at home, Northeasterners now inhabit Bangkok in great numbers holding such menial jobs as bus boys, servants, gardeners, taxi drivers, and so forth. According to Mr. Soonton Awpisoon-tarang-goon, an official in the Ministry of Culture and leader of the elite Soontara-pirom mawlum troupe in Bangkok, it was not until the administration of Field Marshall Piboon Songkram after World War II that mawlum performances returned to Bangkok. In 1946 a mawlum performance took place at the Ratdumnun (Rajdamnoen) Boxing Stadium which was first advertised by sound trucks. Migrant Northeasterners, upon hearing their music, followed the trucks to the stadium where nearly three thousand people heard the performance.

Mawlum pün

It is generally agreed among informants that the oldest genre of lum surviving in Northeast Thailand is lum pün. The word pün, which is found both in Lao and Siamese, means floor, foundation, tradition, and first, as in nitan pün müang (literally, old stories of the city; more loosely, traditional stories). Following these meanings, pün alone has come to mean a story or folktale about a person or nation passed down from generation to generation. In practice these include in addition to stories of local origin, Lao versions of the jataka tales. Lum pün requires only one singer as opposed to lum glawn in which a male and female alternate. Lum pün is also sometimes called lum rüang ("story"). Mawlum pün are traditionally male, but a few women have been known to perform this genre. The traditional accompaniment is kaen, formerly the long kaen gao with eighteen tubes, now the ordinary kaen baet with sixteen tubes.

Without written documents, there is no way to trace the history of lum pün, but this genre's relationships with an nungsü pook (reciting a story) tet nitan (Buddhist chanting of stories), and tet boon prawet (Buddhist chanting of the story of Prince Wetsundawn) are indeed close and significant. While both an nungsü and lum pün draw from the same repertory of tales, only the former is read directly from nungsü pook manuscripts. Even though the poetic forms used are basically identical, the literary glawn of the manuscripts is not quite as suitable for singing since it often includes prefixes and suffixes; sung glawn furthermore utilizes end rhyme more than nungsü pook style which restricts itself to more subtle interior rhyme and alliteration. Singers therefore must prepare their own poetic versions of the epic stories though both details and even phrases of the original may be retained.

A number of writers, most notably Brengues and Brandon, emphasize that the singers of earlier generations were wandering minstrels, comparable to Troubadours and Minnesingers, and that they wove bits of gossip, news of the court, and other timely material into their singing.[9] They are compared to Homer, implying that the poems were extemporized in the manner of the epics that Albert Lord has described from Yugoslavia in his book The Singer of Tales.[10] There is, however, no evidence known to me that this is the technique involved. All singers interviewed had memorized poetry from written sources, and none claimed to improvise their material except in shortening the story to fit the occasion. Singers in Laos, however, where the tempo is slower, can improvise longer passages. It remains uncertain whether or not lum pün singers formerly wandered from village to village spreading the news since these claims were made by Western writers and have not been substantiated by living singers.

Lum pün was formerly very common and highly appreciated in the Northeast, but during the past forty years its popularity has plummeted sharply. One informant said this trend became noticeable about 1940, another, 1955. The Lao as well as the Siamese apparently lack sentimentality for the old, an attitude which continues to shape the evolution of musicial forms in the Northeast. When audiences no longer preferred lum pün, singers stopped performing it. Lum pün has now become so rare that only seven persons were known in 1974 who could demonstrate it, and only four of them performed actively, but two were of advanced age. Because there are no students learning this genre, it will probably become extinct in Northeast Thailand within twenty years.

Mr. Pao Boot-prom (born 1915) of Roi-et province is the most active lum pün singer in Northeast Thailand and claims to perform an average of twenty nights a month during the months November to March and from May to July (see Figure 17). Pao also has the largest lum pün repertory, seven stories, whose total duration would require nine nights each running from 9 p.m. to about 6 a.m. They are: (1) Tao Galaget; (2) Tao Sooriwong; (3) Tao Lin-tawng; (4) Napak glai-gradon; (5) Tao Bae; (6) Tao Ma-yui; and (7) Wiangjun (Vientiane). All but the last are likely localized jataka tales; Wiangjun is a traditional history of the fall of the Lao capital to Siamese forces in the early nineteenth century, a story which requires two full nights.

Figure 17. Lum pün singer, Pao Boot-prom, and his kaen player at a festival in Mahasarakam city.

While Pao served as a monk during his youth, it was not until he was twenty-eight in 1943 that he began his musical training. His teacher, Ajan ("teacher") Gun of Ban Laeng-tak-lom, Selapoom district, Roi-et province, who was seventy when Pao studied with him and who died in 1963, required Pao to learn the texts orally through imitation. Ajan Gun divided each story into parts, and Pao practiced and mastered each part before going to the next. When Pao trained his students, however, he wrote out the entire texts and required them to memorize each story as a whole. Of Pao's five students only one is still living, and he can perform only Tao Bae and Tao Sooriwong. That the memory required for such performances is extraordinary is obvious although memorization is facilitated by the construction of the stanzas, their sing-song form, and a certain dependence on stereotyped phrases.

Before the advent of electricity, amplification, and raised wooden stages, all of which began penetrating the Northeast only in the 1950s and 1960s, mawlum of all types were performed on straw mats on the ground. The only light was provided by gabawng lamps whose oil came from a type of tree found locally. Consequently the audience sat very close to the singer, and he had to rotate periodically to see everyone. Today both mawlum pün and mawlum glawn perform on small wooden stages about three to four meters on a side, covered with a tin roof. Both lights and amplification systems are powered by a gasoline generator nearby.

Seventy-two-year-old (1974) Tawng-si Hawirot of remote Ban Jaeng in Roi-et province along the Chi River no longer performs publicly, but his voice remains clear and strong. While he was primarily a lum glawn singer, he also demonstrated lum pün in two excerpts, both from the Wetsundawn jataka. Although Tawng-si began as an ordinary mawlum using kaen accompaniment, he later became a mawlum gup gaep accompanying himself with two pairs of wooden blocks called gup gaep. (I shall deal with this subject further under mawlum glawn.) Soot-tee Chai-dilüt, while able to demonstrate lum pün, had been a kaen accompanist, and his excerpts performed without kaen were only meant to demonstrate the style.

Two other informants, while considering mawlum pün, perform a variation called mawlum rüang or hüang as pronounced in Lao. Brandon refers throughout his book to mohlam luong when he means mawlum moo because in popular usage the terms have become confused. Old lum rüang, however, is a king of mawlum pün in which the singer, by changing headgear, clothes, and positions acts out the story as several characters. While women rarely sang lum pün, they did sing lum rüang. Tawin Boot-tah of Kawn-gaen province was the only mawlum rüang interviewed because Ms. Jumbee of Roi-et province, the other known mawlum rüang, lived in an extremely remote village, Mr. Tawin speculated that the style came from Wiangjun, Laos, about 1932, but such estimates are rarely reliable since he had no way of knowing musical practice in other provinces before the advent of good roads. Mr. Pao, nevertheless, claimed that a Ms. Tao of Gra-nuan district, Kawn-gaen province was the first mawlum rüang and that when he met her in 1936 she was already well-established. Her stories included Tao Sooriwong and Nang Daeng-awn. While the late Ms. Tao wore fancy clothing and changed scarves to indicate characters, Ms. Jumbee is said to dress in a plainer fashion.

Lum glawn

In contrast to lum pün performed by one singer, lum glawn is performed by two singers: two males, a female and a male, or rarely two females
(see Figures 18-20). A discussion of certain related genres involving more
than two singers such as lum ching choo or lum gup gaep accompanied by
the singer himself will be dealt with after all aspects of lum glawn have
been covered. While the word glawn means "poetry" in general, it also
refers to a specific poetic form. And while it is true that all mawlum
genres involve sung poetry, the term lum glawn in the minds of Northeasterners refers to but one variety.

Unlike kaen players, who are normally self-taught, mawlum glawn
singers all report having studied with teachers. With few exceptions the
teachers were practicing mawlum who taught privately in their homes.
Singing is not known to have been taught in either temple or government
schools nor are there conservatories or college level music programs in
Thailand for Northeastern music. The Fine Arts Department in Bangkok,
which specializes in music, dance, theatre, and architecture, restricts itself to Siamese culture, particularly that of the court nor does the College
of Dance in Roi-et teach lum. Aspiring mawlum choose their profession
freely with or without parental guidance; there are no customs regarding
the inheriting of musical talent or the exclusiveness of the profession for
a divinely approved elite, customs known in some non-Tai musical cultures.
Asked why they became mawlum, most singers replied that they enjoyed
singing, were attracted by the income possibilities, or because other members of the family were singers. It would be reasonable to compare mawlum study with piano instruction in the United States where many aspire
to become musicians under both competent and incompetent teachers, but
only a small percentage actually became professional.

Figure 18. Typical modern performance of lum glawn.

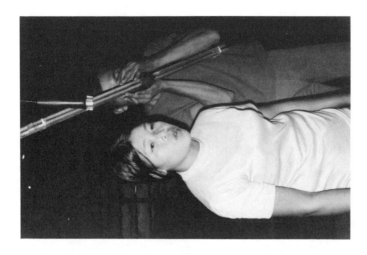

Figure 20. Mawlum glawn singer Bunlung Tomoolah with her kaen accompanist, Mr. Somboon.

Figure 19. Mawlum Tawng-yoon accompanied on kaen by Tawng-koon.

Because children grow up hearing mawlum and becomes acculturated
to its scales, rhythms, poetic forms, and practices, beginning students are
already able to sing to some extent, and may go to teachers only after
acquiring the basic techniques from amateurs within the village or family.
The average age for beginning is about fifteen though many begin as
young as twelve and some as late as twenty-five. Mr. Sui Seetawng
(born 1905), whose training predates that of other informants, reported
that he began musical study in 1918 at age thirteen with Ajan Suang of
his home village. Otherwise his only formal education was in a temple
school where he learned to read the traditional alphabets. Sui studied
singing in the evening after the farm work was completed. Because
there is no musical notation, students learn the technique of singing by
imitation combined with the acculturated lum technique. Sui reported
that neither he nor his teacher wrote out the poems he learned but rather
he had to remember them by rote. While Sui studied in this fashion for
five or six years, he noted that there is no specific period for study since
it depends on the skill and motivation of the student. When he had mastered a lesson, the teacher gave him a new one. Study ends when the
student feels ready to begin a singing career. Although the teacher may
have dictated the texts to his students, the poetry was not improvised
and had ultimately come from a written source.

When Sui began his study the most popular genre of lum glawn was
lum jot ("problems" or "questions") also called lum jot-gae ("to solve problems") in which two singers of the same or differing sex compete by
asking questions and posing riddles concerning religion, literature, geography, history, and other aspects of Lao culture. Students had to master
a vast repertory of answers to the most often asked questions as well as
the questions themselves before beginning competition. A mawlum without an answer might be so embarrassed and disgraced as to have to leave
the stage. Mr. Tawng-si reported that he began to compete in lum jot-
gae without formal training using his own poems but could not compete
successfully and only then went to a teacher.

Sui stated that when he went to study with his teacher he had to
greet him by bowing his head to the floor three times and as he rose
place his hands in the prayer or wai position. When he began his study he
paid his teacher six baht, another twelve baht when he learned how to
fawn (dance), and finally twenty-four baht when he learned potent words
called kum aw (magic chant) which will be described in more detail later.
The expense was considerable since then an ox cost six baht.

Mawlum Soot-tee-sompong (born 1914), who began study at age fifteen
in 1929, reported that his teacher, Ajan Gasem Sanawng-kwun of Ban
Dawn-ngua, Oom-mao subdistrict, Tawut-booree district, Roi-et province,
required him to live at his home and work in the fields. He therefore did
not have to pay for his training. Ajan Gasem dictated the poems to be
learned to Soot-tee-sompong who copied them into notebooks for later
memorization. Upon memorization the student performed for his teacher
at full speed receiving suggestions for improvement. Virtually no informant reported vocal coaching as known in the West, and most of the effort
went into learning the poems and expressing them properly in lum.

Other singers reported similar experiences. Kumboon Sing-senee (born
1935) stated that she learned her texts by rote from her teacher, Mawlum
Moo-saw, of Piboon-mungsahan district, Oobon province. Mawlum Tawng-
yoon (born 1919), who began study at the age of twenty in 1939, first
learned to repeat her texts without music but soon added the melody. She

said she memorized by first learning the general outlines, then the
details, and must still practice periodically when the material becomes
unfamiliar. She, like most younger singers, still keeps a collection of notebooks filled with her poems. Mawlum Blian similarly still keeps his notebooks though he has been singing for thirty years. Mawlum Bunlung
Tomoolah (born 1952), who at twenty-two is an established singer, began
study about the age of seventeen in Oobon with a female singer named
Somwung Tawngsee who gave her texts to copy into notebooks. Bunlung
lived at the teacher's home for three months paying three hundred baht
a month. After she had memorized the texts she would sing them for the
teacher. She reported that she still returns to her teacher occasionally to
learn new poems, but when copying poems from other teachers or singers
she must pay ten to fifteen baht each.

Mawlum Chawiwan Dumnun (born 1945) stated specifically that singers
do not do vocal exercises nor do they regularly practice though they may
do so before a recording session. Her teacher listened only after the texts
had been memorized, and if difficulties remain the teacher would demonstrate. She said the first poems had to be spoken to the teacher, then
sung. First she learned the wai kroo or ceremony to honor her teacher,
then an introduction to the audience giving her name, home village, and
so forth, and finally repertory.

The wai kroo ceremony, whose origin is Buddhist, is a part of most
musical genres in Thailand and Laos. Kaen makers perform wai kroo once
a year, Siamese ligeh troupes do likewise before each performance, and
mawlum glawn and mawlum moo troupes must also wai kroo. To perform
the ceremony the student must assemble certain ritual items on a tray.
These may vary to some extent but Chawiwan's description is typical.
Known collectively as kruang boochah (sacrificial offering), kai (articles
for worship), or kai aw (articles for worship specifically for mawlum), they
consist of five pairs of candles and flowers, five sui (flowers placed in
banana leaf containers), a pair of large candles (tien lem baht), a bottle
of rice wine (lao), an egg, and an amount of money varying from one and
one-half baht to twelve baht. Sometimes a woman's skirt (sin) and an
ordinary piece of cloth may be required. After lighting the two large
candles the student prays the wai pra or incantation to the Buddha spoken
in Pali. In another incantation called kata aw the student invokes the
Buddha, the dhamma (doctrine), and the sang-ga (the community of monks
and novices) for protection from evil. When finished the tray is placed on
a high shelf until after the performance when the wai pra is repeated.

Mawlum Bunlung's description varied only a little but added several
details. In the home of the performance's sponsor she assembles the kai
consisting of pairs of candles and flowers in two groups, one five, the
other eight (kun hah kun baet), a piece of white cloth, two large candles,
and twelve and one-quarter baht supplied by the householder and kept by
the singer. If the singer is male, a bottle of rice wine is added. She
stated that the incantations and prayers are spoken silently. She invokes
the aw lum or kata aw to help her sing well and prevent loss of memory
and the voice, saying them seven times after which she drinks water.
She may also invoke aw sai aw gun words which besides protecting her
may be used against her competition causing him to lose his voice, forget
his texts, or sing badly. Kata are also known generally as potent words to
frighten away ghosts, help students perform brilliantly on exams, or protect soldiers in battle. They are usually in Pali but the meaning is rarely
known to the reciter.

At least three informants, Kumboon, Wichian (born 1934), and Blian Winon-sook (born 1923) are active teachers of mawlum. Kumboon claims to have taught about forty students and at the time of the interview (1973) had three or four. Depending upontheir interest students may study for a month or a year. Except during the planting season when she suspends teaching, students come two or three times a month for coaching after first memorizing their poems. The lum principle notwithstanding, she claims her students must sing exactly as she does.

Repertory

The writers of the poems are almost without exception male, this being a rule of tradition quite possibly stemming from the lack of schooling afforded females in the past when only temple schools were available. All male mawlum glawn who were interviewed had written poems, some extensively. Professional singers pride themselves on either writing their own poems or obtaining them from reputable teachers. A number of writers, some apparently amateurs, have published both lum glawn and lum moo poems in small paperbound books printed in Kawn-gaen. Although books of this type date back as far as 1902 when some were published in Bangkok, the vast majority appeared in the 1940s, 1950s, and early 1960s. To my knowledge these booklets are no longer printed. Brandon is mistaken in assuming that these booklets are singing aids published by the Mawlum Association of Kawn-gaen.[11] I did not find a single singer among the forty-two recorded or interviewed who had used such books, for they are intended for amateurs.

Though without the advantage of an extensive and systematic study of Lao literature and mawlum poetry, I offer a tentative classification of poetry types encountered among informants. Other classifications are possible and new categories may become known, but the following is based on how the singers themselves group their poems.

1. Glawn wai kroo used to pay respect to the teacher.
2. Poems in which the singer introduces himself and requests a similar exposition from his partner.
3. Glawn jot or dowatee used in debate-style mawlum to discuss aspects of Lao literature, history, geography, religion, and science.
4. Glawn sat to brag and show off the voice.
5. Glawn sasanah about the Buddha's life, doctrine, and the story of Prince Wetsundawn.
6. Glawn gio, courting poems which may vary from earthy humor, explicit reference to parts of the body and sexual acts to indirect, poetic sentiments characteristic of pa-nyah.
7. Glawn dün dong, poems describing a walk in the forest and extolling the beauty of nature.
8. Glawn nitan, poems taken from epic stories of both jataka and local origin as well as from well-known Central Thai masterpieces.
9. Glawn pitigam appropriate for ceremonies such as ordinations, soo-kwun, funerals, weddings, and so forth.
10. Glawn betdalet, miscellaneous poems which discuss virtually

any topic from current events and propaganda to comments
on life in general. Among titles encountered are "Concerning Progress," "Rumwong Dancing," "How People Dressed
in the Past," "This Changing World," and "Lum Plūn."

While some of the above categories may be sung in lum tang yao, all
those listed could be sung in lum tang sun. The poems used for lum tang
yao are usually sad in mood since the singer must bid farewell to the
partner, the audience, and the sponsor. Among the varieties encountered
are the following:

1. Glawn lum lah, poems to bid farewell
2. Glawn gio, courting poems
3. Glawn nitan, excerpts from stories
4. Glawn sasanah, concerning religion and the life of the
   Buddha
5. Glawn lawng kong, a type of poem dealing with an
   imagined boat trip on the Maekong. Mawlum Kum-
   pawng's famous "Lawng kong" was composed from
   information found in old books since the author had not
   made such a trip. For convenience he had the Maekong
   flow through Saigon (Vietnam) before reaching the
   South China Sea, since Saigon is a well-known place.
6. Glawn betdalet, miscellaneous poems with such titles as
   "Thinking of Wiangjun," "Wishing Well to a Soldier
   Departing to Vietnam," and "Flying to America"

Mawlum singers are typically vague about the extent of their repertor-
ies since few have ever attempted to count their poems. Many are able to
learn poems very quickly from hearing them on the radio or from friends
and thus have not written them down. Since older poems become obsolete
if the subjects are topical and new poems must be added to keep abreast
of current events, it is difficult to tabulate repertoires satisfactorily.

Mawlum Bunlung provided the most extensive discussion of repertory.
Her library consisted of twenty-one paperbound notebooks of varying sizes
full of handwritten texts in both her hand and that of her father. Asked
to estimate the number of individual poems, she responded that she knew
about one thousand in lum tang sun each lasting approximately three
minutes and seventeen in lum tang yao, each about five minutes. The
tang sun figure must be accepted with some skepticism since if literally
true she can sing fifty hours without repeating a single text, and this at
age twenty-two.

S.J. Tambiah's informant, Mawlum Tawng-see, who had been performing for more than forty-five years, estimated his repertory at 350 poems,
each lasting about five minutes.[12] Mawlum Blian in Oobon city merely
estimated his repertory at three nights. That mawlum need exceptional
memories is indisputable, especially recalling Mawlum Pao's repertory of
seven lum pun stories requiring nine nights for complete performances.
The nature of the poetry with stereotyped phrases plus other devices
such as alliteration make the poetry easier to memorize than if it were
entirely original. Few mawlum admit to having memory lapses during
performances, but I have observed singers encounter this problem during
recording sessions when the usual devices for covering lapses such as
changing poems or taking a sudden break were felt to be unacceptable.

In several instances singers, even famous ones, perform with their notebooks open before them to prevent any lapses. In short, singers need not
only exceptional memories but techniques to cover failures since an exact
rendition without blemishes is the ideal.

Performance Practice

Most older informants report that when they were young, singers
travelled from village to village on foot, ox cart, or horseback and performed in an intimate setting at a home or temple. The singer stood on
a straw mat surrounded by the audience necessitating that he rotate
periodically. A light called gabawng powered by a kind of tree sap was
hung on a pole with a long spike sometimes driven into the pole so that
the audience could place sadung coins on it. If the kaen player were not
being paid, he could try to get these; otherwise the performers divided
the coins equally. During the past ten to fifteen years two significant
changes have occurred. First, mawlum glawn began performing on small
wooden stages erected for the occasion probably in response to mawlum
moo's practice. Though these platforms raised the singers above the
audience making them easier to see, they also eliminated the close rapport between audience and singer. The inability to hear from a distance
was corrected by the second change, the advent of electrical generators
to run both amplifiers and lights. Lacking training in vocal techniques,
few mawlum know how to project their voices properly, and many cannot
be heard at all in the open air. Since competing forms of entertainment
at fairs and tumboon also have amplifiers, such equipment has become
necessary for survival. Singers typically stand within a few inches of the
microphone or even hold it near their mouths causing distortion and feedback.

Contemporary performances take place before audiences seated on the
ground on three sides of the stage.   Because the kaen player cannot get
close to the microphone, he sometimes cannot be heard in proper balance
with the singer, and there are no stage walls to project the sound. The
only furnishings on stage might be a couple of chairs; in one corner is the
amplifier, in another a pitcher of water and a glass. Sometimes the top
of the stage frame is decorated with a cloth banner announcing the occasion or the names of the singers. The audience may come and go as it
pelases; some stand near the table, others sit in the darkness far away
but near the loudspeakers in trees.

Singers formerly wore traditional clothing styles. Women wore a
white sin (long, wrap-around skirt) with a long-sleeved blouse of any color,
and the men wore a shirt and a silk sarong called padalong. The wearing
of traditional clothing is now thought to be a sign of ignorance, conservatism, and poverty. Officially, government civil servants, teachers, and
students may not wear traditional dress while on duty but must dress in
Western-style skirts and blouses or trousers and shirts. Thai want to
avoid appearing conservative and thus adopt Western dress if at all
possible. Mawlum today, to display their propensity and progressiveness,
rarely wear traditional clothing although some females wear long Central
Thai dresses. Men wear trousers, white shirts, and neckties; women wear
fashionable skirts--even mini-shirts--and blouses. The men wear their hair
short and women have beauty-shop permanents.

Complete mawlum glawn performances such as were common a generation ago are now increasingly rare because competition from mawlum

moo and mawlum plūn has all but eliminated lum glawn from fairs and
tumboon. A traditional performance begins about 9 p.m. with one of the
singers introducing himself and inquiring about his partner. In lum jot, a
competitive form of lum glawn, both singers were often male, and the
format then consisted of questions and answers regarding knowledge. The
more characteristic type of lum glawn heard today consists partly of questions and answers but dwells more on love, usually an imagined love affair
proceeding between the two singers. Whether the two sing together regularly or have met for the first time, they begin by inquiring about the
marital status of the other, engage in pa-nyah style dialogue doubting the
truth of each other's words, and bait each other with suggestions that may
become sexually explicit.

About 5 a.m. when the performance and imaginary love affair are
nearly completed, the scale changes to yao and the rhythm to parlando-
rubato, the portion called lum tang yao. The subjects are uniformly sad,
bidding farewell to the audience, the host, and especially to the singing
partner since unrequited love must predominate. This portion, although
lasting a mere fifteen minutes, is the emotional climax of the night and
regains the attention of the audience. By now many of the younger
members of the audience who came to hear the love banter have returned

Although the bawdy aspects of mawlum have been over-emphasized by
some writers, they nevertheless exist. Male singers are more inclined to
introduce this type of material into a performance than females, but
whether it continues then or not depends on the audience's reaction.
Some people might be insulted or the other singer might react negatively.
Mawlum Ken Dalao, famous for his lusty poetry, often had difficulty finding singing partners because few females could compete with this sort of
banter or enjoyed the embarrassment from it. When Mawlum Ken found
a woman who could repel his insults with equally bawdy material, he
married her.

Singing partners are normally not married to each other although many
informants reported that if circumstances were favorable they might sleep
together. They were also quick to point out that mawlum were no less
moral than ordinary people but merely had more changes to engage in
illicit love affairs. While audiences tolerate married male singers since
Thai men commonly have affairs outside marriage, they do not tolerate
married females unelss they are already famous when they get married.
There is little doubt that male members of the audience engage in sexual
fantasies with female mawlum, but when the singer is married their interest fades.

The portion of the performance which begins at 9 p.m. is sung throughout to the sun scale (see p. 24) in tempo giusto, although short passages
may be sung to the yao scale while maintaining the giusto meter. This
latter phenomenon is called see pun dawn or see tun dawn, a characteristic which will be further explained in Chapter IV. Ordinarily each singer
performs from fifteen to thirty minutes, then yields to the other. Poems
average about fifty lines each but are strung together at the discretion of
the singer. Although such a performance becomes very monotonous to
Western ears since the words cannot be understood, it is the text, not the
melody, which holds the audience's attention. While one singer performs,
the other often dances in the traditional style called fawn, but the singer
too may take short breaks to dance with the partner. Although the night
air may grow cold and damp and members of the audience fall asleep,
the singing continues without interruption until near daybreak.

home allowing the grandparents to return to hear lum tang yao. The audience, though it enjoys lum tang sun, savors the beautiful language, plaintive melody, and melancholy mood of tang yao in a different way.

It is lum lah [singing goodbye] that melts the hearts of the listeners and makes them very sad. Some people may even cry. Older people long for the happiness of their youth; younger people long for departed lovers.[13]

Although lum tang yao traditionally ended an evening of mawlum glawn, since the late 1940s a third portion has been added called lum dŏi which allows the performance to end on a cheerful note. The dŏi are sung in the yao scale but in tempo giusto in any of three varieties, dŏi tumadah ("ordinary"), dŏi kong (referring to the Maekong river), and dŏi pamah ("Burmese dŏi"). These may be sung singly or as a medley. The subject is nearly always courting, even of a bawdy nature, but unlike in earlier portions singers alternate more frequently. Like lum tang yao, lum dŏi lasts only fifteen or twenty minutes after which the audience departs for home.

That the origin of dŏi singing should remain unknown although it occurred during the singing careers of many informants is one of the anomalies of musical research in Northeast Thailand. Estimates of the date of introduction varied from 1934 (Tawng-si) to 1954 (Ken). It is widely felt that dŏi tumadah is Northeastern in origin because it is lum in principle, but dŏi kong and pamah are thought to have come from the North. Pamah, meaning Burma, does not necessarily indicate a Burmese origin, though. Jarŭnchai Chonpairot has shown that it is related to the Siamese classical tune "Pamah rum kwun" ("Burmese ax dance") and a Northern Thai melody called "Pamah." Both kong and pamah, however, use popular song texts in Siamese, not Lao, indicating a non-traditional, possibly even commercial origin. Both mawlum and soldiers have travelled around Thailand, the latter especially during World War II, and have heard songs in other regions. The term dŏi derives from dai (south) meaning southern Laos and indicates an origin outside Northeast Thailand.

Today such lengthy performances of lum glawn are increasingly rare because audiences are younger and demand more action, a desire more readily gratified by mawlum moo, mawlum plŭn, movies, or popular music groups. Many performances now last only until 1 a.m., and I have observed the use of lum tang yao alternating with lum tang sun. Lum glawn is increasingly common on the radio where shows last just thirty minutes and include all three portions. Some predict that someday lum glawn will exist only on radio, although there is evidence that mawlum moo's popularity has not affected lum glawn in some areas such as Oobon.

Members of the audience normally remain passive during a performance. In Siamese ligeh if the troupe is skilled and the lead players handsome, the show is constantly interrupted by people presenting actors and actresses with necklaces of flowers with money pinned to them, but I have never seen this in the Northeast. The old Northeastern custom of erecting a light pole with a spike on which the audience placed coins is no longer known. Except for occasional laughter and yells from appreciative men during bawdy passages, there is little interaction between performers and hearers. This is especially so today because mawlum glawn audiences have become older, and the young people are more likely watching movies and other modern entertainments. When singers performed on a mat within reach of the audience, there was more interaction, but the raised stage, bright lights, and amplification have all but eliminated such rapport.

Because so many Western writers mentioned the element of improvisation in mawlum, I queried nearly every informant on this subject. If we understand improvisation only in reference to the text as opposed to the melody, which is obviously extemporized, then there is rarely any improvisation. A few veteran performers who also write poetry admit that they can improvise short passages of poetry but always qualify this with the criticism that these passages are inferior to memorized ones. When singers appear to be improvising, it is more often prose spoken in rhythm. Some listeners think that certain texts are spontaneous because singers speak of a particular occasion, but this comes about by blanks in the poem or a slight juggling of the words. Improvisation was more common in lum jot style where singers discussed material in Pali terms which fit into glawn poetry with great difficulty and where answers to difficult questions might not be in the singer's repertory. Usually the kaen player will stop during these prose passages. The slower singing in Laos, with its many kaen interludes, admits more text improvisation, but even this may be derived from panyah.

Before 1949, when a sponsor wished to engage a mawlum glawn or mawlum moo troupe, he had to hire the performers and negotiate the fee himself. It was in 1949 that Field Marshall Sarit Tanarat sponsored the founding in Kawngaen of the first mawlum association called Samakom-song-sum Mawlum Isan under the direction of Kumdee Sarapon. The present director, Boon-paeng Wong-kok-soon, also founded the Sahapun Mawlum Bratet Tai (Union Mawlum Association of Thailand) in 1972 to sponsor radio programs. During the past twenty-four years at least seventy-two more associations have been founded which act as booking agents. Although the following figures are known to be incomplete, especially from Oobon province, the locations and numbers of associations in 1973 will give some indication in which provinces mawlum performances predominate: Kawn-gaen, seventeen; Mahasarakam, eight; Udawn-tani, eight; Chaiyapoom, six; Roi-et, five; Galasin, five; Oobon, four; Löi, four; Sagon-nakawn, three; Nawng-kai, three; Nakawn-panom, three; Boori-rum, two; Nakawn-ratchasimah, two; Yasoton, one; Petchaboon, one; Sisaget, one.

The list from which the above figures were taken was compiled by an association in Kawn-gaen and is thus more complete for that portion of the Northeast. Not surprisingly there is but one association in Khmer-dominated Sisaget and none listed in Soo-rin, also a Khmer area. The seven provinces along the Chi River from Oobon to Kawn-gaen and into neighboring Oodawn province number forty-eight while the remaining nine provinces together have only twenty-four. Except for a few possible associations founded recently in southern Laos, and mostly to serve Northeastern Thai, mawlum there remains largely untouched by this phenomenon.

An association is usually headed by a president, vice-president, and secretary although some are headed by one man, and others, such as the oldest and largest in Kawn-gaen, by a total of fifteen men. Singers or troupes wishing to be listed with the association pay a ten-baht fee and a ten percent commission on each engagement. Although association presidents rarely have reliable statistics at hand, several claim to have as many as one thousand mawlum glawn registered. With so many singers registered, however, and fees generous, it is no wonder that the mawlum associations display more evidence of wealth than performers. They are often housed in new buildings with relatively comfortable facilities, the walls covered with photos of singers and troupes. Many associations have small recording studios in which they tape radio programs. Contact with performers is maintained by telegram, letter, or courier to avoid multiple engagements on the same day.

The associations have benefited Northeastern singers in many ways. They provide opportunities for young unknown singers to perform since these would not normally be asked directly by a sponsor. They make it possible for troupes and soloists to arrange full schedules in advance and thus plan their travel. They have also removed any doubt that mawlum singing is both a business as well as an art. The romantic notion of mawlum mixing gossip and news into their stories as they travelled like minstrels and troubadours from village to village is quite untrue today if it ever was true. In spite of the fact that many amateurs can only attempt to earn a living by singing, the associations legitimatize the professional nature of mawlum.

There is apparently no way to know how many mawlum glawn are active in Northeast Thailand since most singers join more than one association. Estimates vary widely from a few hundred to a few thousand. Brandon's estimate of 5700 performers in 1963--400 male mawlum glawn, 400 female mawlum glawn, 400 kaen players, and 300 amateur and professional mawlum moo troupes averaging 15 members totaling 4500 performers--must be doubted since his figures are simply too neat.[14] There is no doubt that the number changes constantly as new singers launch careers, old singers retire, and poor singers withdraw.

Singers establish reputations according to their talents. They are not members of a musical elite that demands respect regardless of talent nor are they in the same class with ordinary people since only trained and talented people sing mawlum. In this sense neither poverty nor location of birth can prevent a determined young person from pursuing a singing career since training may be obtained from some teachers in exchange for work. In this sense mawlum singers are not much different from Western musicians. Although there are no music critics judging their work in newspapers, mawlum know that the audience is the ultimate judge. If audiences reject the singer because he performs badly, he will not be hired very often, and fee levels are determined by the laws of supply and demand. Exceptional singers are much less common than ordinary ones and therefore command higher fees.

The following factors, gleaned from conversations with Jarunchai Chonpairot and the singers themselves, are significant in judging a singer:

1. He must possess a strong, clear, and "sweet" voice.
2. He must be well-read and able to memorize numerous poems.
3. His pronunciation must be clear for otherwise the audience cannot understand his texts.
4. His health must be good or he will become tired and his singing deteriorate.
5. He must be able to maintain good rhythm and coordination with his accompanist, an ability that comes with experience and practice.
6. The emotional quality of his singing must be sincere and deeply felt.
7. He must be intelligent, able to choose apt texts, and able

to make quick and appropriate replies to questions,
riddles, and challenges.

Besides live performances, mawlum glawn often appear in other media,
particularly radio, television, and on disc and cassette recordings. There
are government-operated radio stations throughout the Northeast which
program at least thirty minutes of mawlum glawn each day as well as
allow some private individuals who make their own programs to broadcast
them during rented time. Mr. Sumran Wongsajun of Mahasarakam, until
his death, operated such a studio in which he recorded local singers, the
advertisements which paid for his programs, and announced performance
engagements for nearby mawlum glawn and mawlum moo troupes. Singers
must listen to their radios each day at certain hours to learn of their
coming engagements although they may also be notified by telegram or
courier. The government-operated TV 5 station at Kawn-gaen sponsored a
mawlum glawn contest in 1972 followed by a mawlum moo contest in 1973.
Each week throughout the year contestants appeared on television and
were judged. The winners received only trophies, but their enhanced reputations allowed them to increase their fees steeply.
Commercial interests in Bangkok have not overlooked the potentially
rich market for recordings of popular and movie music which appeal to the
rural people of each region. Thus beginning about 1963 a new genre of
popular song began to appear in contrast to current pop songs. Urban
popular songs, called pleng look groong ("children of the city"), are sophis-
ticated and highly Westernized. The lyrics, in Central Thai, are relatively
polished and subtle. Accompaniment is provided by Western instruments
though the style is extremely conservative by contemporary American and
European standards. The new genre, called pleng look toong ("children of
the fields"), however, is marked by simple poetry, direct sentiments, and
a general lack of sophistication. The subjects are the lives of ordinary
people, especially villagers. For singing styles the composers, most of
whom live in Bangkok, plunder any and all regional folk and art forms including mawlum glawn and mawlum moo. The accompaniments are provided by regional instruments or Western instruments imitating them.
Among the most popular are arrangements of doi kong. A number of
successful mawlum glawn and mawlum plün singers have gone to Bangkok
and made ever greater fortunes singing pleng look toong. One such person,
Samai An-wong, is best known for his popularized kaen playing in the
movies. Composers and arrangers take the most prominent characteristics
of these regional styles and work them into otherwise popular-style compositions.

Mawlum and Politics

Because new mawlum texts can be quickly written and learned, several
genres have great propaganda potential. While the Thai government has
not attempted to censor mawlum, although a few singers were arrested in
the past for expressing strong criticism of the government, they have
nevertheless offered employment to singers and writers who wished to
promote the government and fight Communism. Because singers attract
substantial audiences wherever they go, they have the power to sway
men's minds. The earliest known incident involving a mawlum and politics
is described in Francis Cripps' book The Far Province, an Englishman's
account of his life in the Mahasarakam area in the 1960s. Cripps' story of

Mawlum Noi has been confirmed by my informants who further noted that he is now dead but was considered a god-man when alive. His efforts to foment a revolution were furthered through his ability to sing ideas as well as speak them.

Democracy came to Mahasarakam in 1932 after the ending to absolute monarchy in Bangkok. This change was marked by catastrophic floods which destroyed the crops and covered the fields with sand. Mo Lam Noi, the little minstrel, travelled around the province commenting on these inauspicious developments to the accompaniment of his panpipes. His sweet music charmed the people. He warned them not to respect monks who wore yellow robes but had lost their holiness; they should not send children to school when they ought to be working to help their parents; and they should not pay their taxes now that the government of the King had been betrayed by democracy.

Mo Lam Noi, the little minstrel, had a friend called Mom Rachawong Sanit (Prince Charming). Mom Rachawong Sanit was a powerful noble who would seize Korat and rule that city. As for Mo Lam Noi, he would return to Vientiane and re-establish the kingdom of Laos. Together the two rulers would lead the people in a glorious campaign. They would smite Bangkok and the decadent central plain. Moreover, the taxes paid to Mo Lam Noi were to be reduced: they need only pay two baht a head.

But on June 20, 1933, Mo Lam Noi was brought before the court at Mahasarakam and sentenced to four years in gaol.

Very soon magicians appeared at Ban Chiang Hian, a village by the road to Roi Et. For themselves, they said, they knew how to fly in the sky. If anyone wanted to learn to fly they should find a pair of white shoes and come to be taught. The villagers came to Mahasarakam to buy their shoes; Chinese traders hurried about finding white shoes to sell. In the evenings at Ban Chaing Hian the people gathered to cheer the magicians. Soon, it was said, they would fly into the prison to rescue Mo Lam Noi, the little minstrel, who was still confined there.

But officials brought the magicians to court for investigation. On November 10th, 1933, they were each sentenced to six months imprisonment. It transpired, to the distress of their followers, that they were quite unable to fly out of the gaol.[15]

Periods of democracy appeared sporadically after the 1932 coup d'etat in which the absolute monarchy was overthrown, though military men ruled in the intervening periods. During elections candidates for public office in the Northeast made a practice of hiring mawlum glawn to aid their campaigns. The singing might perform to attract audiences to hear the candidate or insert material glorifying the candidate. Needless to say with a constituency inexperienced in democracy, wealthy candidates found it easy to buy votes by providing the people with favorite singers. The elections held in early 1975 were preceded by campaigns featuring mawlum singers. At least one former representative from Sagon-nakawn province carried a kaen with him to Bangkok to symbolize his Lao cultural background and regional-nationalistic feelings.

The most extensive efforts ever made to harness mawlum for propaganda purposes were made by the United States Information Service (USIS) during the late 1950s and 1960s. The efforts in Thailand were less extensive than those in Laos, but the Thai government continued the program into the 1970s. Operating from Bangkok, USIS first began hiring mawlum glawn about 1965 or earlier, gave them instructions as to what themes to emphasize, and sent them into the Northeast to sing. Before launching the effort, however, USIS did not make a technical study of mawlum nor did it have any musical specialists who understood the dialect. The effort mostly failed since singers tended to deliver their "messages" without subtlety, and audiences became bored or even left. In 1966 USIS in Bangkok ceased hiring singers for live performances and began making films. Of the four types--a documentary about the Northeast with mawlum sound track, Central Thai documentary with mawlum sound track, a documentary created by a mawlum moo troupe, and films of mawlum glawn singing propaganda texts--the most successful were the documentaries with mawlum sound track.

An experiment with a mawlum moo troupe, filmed in 1966, failed because USIS merely hired a troupe, showed them an earlier film about Communist terrorists, and asked them to stage a sixty-minute performance before the cameras apparently believing they could improvise the story. The troupe leader did not understand his material nor did he have the imagination to perform it in an interesting way, and the film was poorly received. In total USIS made ten films of "straight mohlam" and two or three sound track films but had discontinued their use by 1969.

Their efforts in Laos originated in the Wiangjun office and were more extensive and long-lived. Brandon, who discusses this subject in great detail,[16] notes that USIS first tried mawlum propaganda in 1957 at a fair at That Luang, a famous sixteenth-century Wiangjun temple. The message was subtle and did not refer directly to Communism. Throughout the rest of the 1950s and the following decade USIS continued to hire mawlum glawn troupes consisting of two singers, one male and one female, and a kaen player. All performers, however, came from Northeast Thailand since the Lao singers were too difficult to locate, train, and hire. Brandon notes that from July, 1962, to July, 1963, when three teams were under contract, more than six hundred USIS-sponsored performances were given. Statistics indicate that mawlum glawn attracted audiences averaging 1550 whereas USIS films attract an average of only 430. The U.S. Government estimates that nearly one million people viewed their programs in Laos or a third of the population.

A typical USIS mohlam performance is made up of half a dozen thirty-minute routines and lasts about three hours. Twenty minutes of each routine is standard mohlam fare, joyfully graphic accounts of lovemaking and courtship. Ten minutes is propaganda "freight." Propaganda items are fashioned to suit the need, but at any time around ten are in the repertory: five are basic items included in every performance and five are supplementary items used less often.

The basic items in late 1963 were: Lao self-help for well-
digging, school-building, and similar projects; support the
Royal Lao government; pro-Buddhism; American economic aid;
and Lao history. These boil down to three basic themes; en-
courage consciousness of a Lao national identity capable of
withstanding Communist blandishments; tell the story of
American economic help; and support practical, worthwhile
community development projects. Anti-Communist slogan-
eering has never been part of the program. Abstract appeals
have no meaning for the Lao farmer.[17]

Both the Thai and Lao governments continued to use mawlum as a
means of swaying citizens' minds at least into the mid-1970s. In early
1974 when the neutralist government of Laos was still in power, a military
radio station in Wiangjun permitted me to copy cassette tapes of propaganda mawlum from their "library." Mawlum Soot-tee-sompong said that
talented musicians from among the soldiers are given the rank of sergeant
and ordered to entertain the troops with inspiring texts. In Thailand the
Ministry of Information contracts with mawlum writers in the Northeast
to produce poetry informing the people of recent government-sponsored
development projects such as new schools, dams, and roads, recent events
such as floods and droughts, or anti-Communist material. One such writer,
Mr. Pim of Kawn-gaen, showed me a typed list which he had received
outlining the topics to be dealt with. The government, according to informants from Northern Thailand, has employed a mawlum moo troupe to
play a pro-birth control story both there and in the Northeast. A well-
known doctor in Müang Pon south of Kawn-gaen employs a male assistant
who functions as an amateur mawlum singing about birth-control.

On the subject of mawlum and politics, Tambiah writes:

The 'nationalizing' role of mau lum singers may be compared
to the role of radio and television as communication media.
The village mau lum singer informed us that in Udorn she had
recently bought mau lum texts for about 100 baht, put out by
the government in cooperation with certain American agencies.
These new texts have as their themes rural development,
animal husbandry, government slogans for various development
drives, anti-communist propaganda, nuclear rockets (jarnad
[jaruat] nuclear!), psychological warefare (songkram chitta-
vitya), and provincial reorganization of the north-east.[18]

Genres Related to lum glawn

Whereas mawlum glawn does not require regular partners, there are
three related genres which do. These are called lum ching choo, lum sam
glü, and lum sam sing ching nang. The word ching means "contest" and
choo a "lover" or "minor wife." Although a few lum ching choo troupes
are said to consist of two female singers and one male, most consist of
two males and one female. According to Jarünchai Chonpairot, the two
males, both being boyfriends, compete with each other in the manner of
lum jot in a display of knowledge to impress the female to live with the
winner. Today ching choo singers dwell almost entirely on love though
they may use dün dong poems ("walking in the forest") and nitan (story

poems) as well.

Two informants, Mr. Som-mai Chai-hanit and Ms. Nootin Seeyot, both of Ban Dawn-yom, Ta-kawn-yang subdistrict, Müang district, Mahasarakam province, were the only ching choo singers we could locate because the genre has now lost its popularity and become rare. Som-mai, who learned lum glawn before lum ching choo, began to study the latter genre at age fourteen in his home village from Ajan Chalee who also wrote the texts. Beginning at 9 p.m. a performance would last until dawn or for a shorter period if the sponsor could not afford a full night. Using poems in both glawn and glawn gap form lasting approximately ten minutes each, the singers rotated their turns first using lum tang sun and then near midnight changing to lum tang yao and lum dŏi. If the performance was to continue, they began once again in lum tang sun and continued until dawn when tang yao and dŏi were again sung.

Because the topics never change, texts may be handed down from teacher to student. Nootin said she still had her notebooks of ching choo poetry. The troupe performed widely during the 1950s although Nootin evidently did not join until 1967 and then sang for only three years. Besides performing in Northeastern provinces, Som-mai mentioned travel to Petchaboon, Gumpaengpet (Kamphaengphet), Nakawn-sawan, and Chainat provinces in Central Thailand. He knew of but one troupe still performing, that led by Mawlum of Ban Nawng-idŭ, Kok-pra subdistrict, Guntara-wichai district, Mahasarakam province. Because lum ching choo's format is more contrived than that of ordinary lum glawn, Mawlum Sui Seetawng's estimate that the genre is about seventy years old may be reliable. Now sixty-nine (1974), Sui (of Ban Tawng-lang in Kawn-gaen province) said that lum ching choo first came to Kawn-gaen province from Chaiyapoom province when he was a child.

Mawlum Sui himself was the originator of a genre called lum sam sing ching nang ("three man contest for a girl" or literally "three lions contest for a girl") which is an extension of lum sam glŭ ("three friends"). In the latter genre three men, one singing as a farmer, one a trader, and the other a government official, perform a kind of musical seminar in which the topics may range from good-humored banter to open criticism of government policy (Figure 21). Sui said that sometimes the police would come and arrest the men, and thus he avoided this problem by adding a female to create lum sam sing ching nang and by eliminating criticism of government policy. Although Sui had performed lum glawn and especially lum jot since his training began in 1918, it was only in 1963 that he began performing lum sam sing ching nang. The troupe is no longer active because Mawlum Tawng-pet, the trader, is now dead, but Sui's student Soi Mee-tawng-lang, age forty-five, who played the farmer can still perform his poems along with Sui who wrote the poetry and played the official. Two females, See-tawng and Noo-liab, both of Ban Gawk near Kawn-gaen, alternated performances.

Each of the three men had to impress the woman with the benefits of his particular trade. The official claimed he was rich but nevertheless honest; the farmer said he could provide food; and the trader claimed great wealth and material goods. After a kaen introduction the farmer began, followed by the trader, the official, and finally the girl. Each round took one hour and most performances consisted of ten rounds or ten hours. Based on his experience, Sui stated that in lum sam glŭ, lum tang sun was followed by lum tang yao, but lum sam sing ching nang had no lum tang yao. In fact Mawlum Soi could not perform it at all. The poetry

Figure 21. Mr. Sui Seetawng of Kawn-gaen province, the creator of the genre called <u>lum sam glü</u> in which he sang the role of government official.

tended to be entertaining and humorous, some of it quite bawdy. Even at age sixty-nine Mawlum Sui was quite able to give a convincing and lively performance indicating that the genre, although limited apparently to one troupe, was an entertaining one.

Although little known and rare today, <u>mawlum gup gaep</u> is significant because it is the only genre in which the singer provides his own accompaniment. <u>Gup gaep</u> consist of four pieces of hardwood each measuring approximately thirteen centimeters long, five centimeters wide, and one centimeter thick which are held in pairs in each hand. They are closely related to the Central Thai <u>grup sepah</u> whose measurements are slightly larger.[19] <u>Grup sepah</u> are used to make a rhythmic accompaniment for <u>sepah</u> recitation and were played by the reciter himself. The only <u>maw-lum gup gaep</u> who could be located, Mr. Tawng-si Hawirot of Ban Wung-pai, Mahasarakam province, age seventy-one (1974), stated that he thought <u>gup gaep</u> had come to the Lao from the Khmer living in Soo-rin province. He mentioned that he had known of Lao <u>mawlum gup gaep</u> who learned from Khmer singers using a similar accompaniment, but he also thought the instrument might have come from Chinese opera. The Chinese have a similar instrument called <u>shuang-mu</u>[20] which like the Khmer model is larger than the <u>gup gaep</u> seen in Roi-et province. It may also be significant that a Khmer-speaking <u>jariang</u> singer from near Soo-rin who recorded for me and was accompanied by <u>kaen</u> nevertheless snapped his fingers in rhythm when dancing during interludes as if playing gup gaep.

Tawng-si (Figure 22) first launched his career in mawlum jot without the aid of a teacher but soon discovered that his poems and skills were no match for his competition. In 1927 at the age of twenty-four he began study with Ajan Juntah of Ban Blui-dan in Roi-et province, and according to the informant became so skilled that he could not find a partner who could compete with him. He therefore decided to become a one-man show and began gup gaep training with Mawlum Kumpai from Goompa-wapee district in Oodawn province in 1935 at age thirty-two. He claims to have a repertory of 350 poems each lasting about five minutes and says he has performed in Central Thailand, Laos, and throughout the Northeast.

Figure 22. Mr. Tawng-si Hawirot, the last surviving mawlum gup gaep, in his home in Roi-et province.

The Role of mawlum in Northeastern Culture

Mawlum singers and their position within Northeastern society may be viewed from two vantage points, that of the urban dweller and that of the villager. It can be said with some certainty that the larger the Thai city, the less it reflects traditional culture. This is especially true of Bangkok whose population is more modern and Westernized than any other in Thailand. In the Northeast, Bangkok's culture first penetrates the cities through the larger schools, movie theaters, and modern shops. Cities of differing regions are more uniform than villages since they tend to replace their regional identities with a generalized urban-Thai culture. The attitudes of city dwellers towards mawlum singers are therefore irrelevant to villagers but at the same time decisive since future trends are first set in the cities. When mawlum glawn or mawlum moo troupes play in the cities and towns, however, they may demand higher fees since city dwellers tend to have more money to spend than villagers.

Because most urban Thai in the Northeast are better educated than their village brethren, they tend to become more like Central Thai than Lao. The better educated, the more developed their preferences for Central Thai culture or, beyond a certain degree of sophistication, for Western culture. It is therefore not surprising that urban dwellers hold mawlum singers in low esteem, calling them country bumpkins, reactionaries, and relegating them to among the lower classes since they make their money merely by singing and dancing. The Chinese, Vietnamese, and Indian merchants in towns have virtually no interest in this type of entertainment and simply dismiss it as a form of local folk music. The mawlum stereotype holds that singers are lazy though not drunkards or debtors, that they are stupid, old-fashioned, and symbolize the village's resistance to modernization. If someone dresses badly he might be told, "oh, you look like a mawlum moo." Performers are not considered artists since it is thought anyone can play the kaen or sing mawlum.

Villagers' attitudes are quite different, however. Because they know the mawlum personally and that they are also farmers, villagers accept singers as worthy citizens. Whereas an urban dweller would discourage his children from pursuing a singing career, preferring those of either a teacher or government official, a villager would normally not object to his children learning to sing since there is prestige and money in this profession. While mawlum do not rank much above ordinary villagers in the rural hierarchy which puts monks in the highest position, old men and women next, then teachers, headmen, parents, and farmers, they do not suffer from the stigma attached to theatrical people that is prevalent in some cultures. While male mawlum are thought to have more active sex lives than ordinary farmers, the mawlum counter that they are no less moral than ordinary men but merely have more opportunities. Female singers are not looked upon as theatrical prostitutes nor are their chances for making a good marriage diminished by a singing career.

Mawlum singers may be viewed in at least four roles in rural society, those of teacher, entertainer, moral force, and preserver of tradition. Their role as teacher was especially significant when lum jot was common, for singers then engaged in a verbal battle of wits and knowledge, and through hearing the audience also learned a great deal about history, literature, geography, religion, and customs. Today the trend to glawn gio (courting poems) and the emphasis on love rather than knowledge has reduced this role to some extent.

Because mawlum must possess obvious musical talent and study singing with a teacher, they are both artists as well as entertainers. Singers are appreciated for their vocal and expressive skills. While a beautiful girl with musical talent has some advantage over a homely girl with similar talent, a beautiful girl without talent cannot succeed in mawlum glawn and may be forced to turn to other media such as the movies. It could be said that mawlum glawn tend to be more artist than entertainer while the

opposite is often true of mawlum glawn tend to be more artist than entertainer while the opposite is often true of mawlum moo and especially mawlum plun. Any successful mawlum glawn can easily learn to be a mawlum
moo, but few mawlum moo or mawlum plun, because their standards are
somewhat lower, could hold their own as mawlum glawn. Without the
bright lights, flashy clothes, and popular rhythms, mawlum plun especially
would pale in comparison to lum glawn.

Because mawlum singers are not burdened with the anti-theatrical
stigma, they may use the high regard with which they are held as a forum
for exerting a positive attitude towards traditional institutions and morality. Most male singers, especially those of earlier generations, had served
as monks for extended periods of time. In the temple they became deeply
imbued with Buddhist morality and learning. They emerged from the
temple as learned men and although few became village leaders or ritualists, they were nevertheless respected by their peers. As artist and entertainer they were as much a part of Buddhist ceremonies as the monks who
chanted. Their stories were often the same as those read by the monks,
and their poetry was derived from the palm-leaf manuscripts of the temple
library.

Their most significant role is that of preserver of tradition. Though
they are under great pressure from urban-oriented audiences to abandon
their traditions in favor of more progressive trends, they yield no more
than is necessary to maintain their competitive edge. In this regard mawlum glawn singers are far more conservative than mawlum moo or plun
since the latter genres have become popular and comeptition is fiercer.
Even a talented troupe that fails to follow the trends can lose its audiences
if it resists "progress." Singers' texts, drawn from traditional literature,
reflect life, customs, and the morality of the past. They provide examples
of good behavior to follow, however old-fashioned, and in this sense resist
the social changes already affecting the cities. Mawlum formerly sang
often of Wiangjun and the old Lao kingdom, and a few old people still
long for a return to their relatively glorious past, but today most look to
Bangkok. The language of the texts tends to be more conservative than
heard among ordinary speakers, and mawlum poems are full of words and
phrases which young people no longer understand; indeed, some younger
singers do not understand the meaning of their own words.

> The mau lum singers not only preserve and propagate
> regional traditions; they are also the channels through whom
> certain stories and epics, popularly known and appreciated
> in central and northern Thailand, are passed on to north-
> eastern villagers. They sing stories about the life of the
> Buddha which are nationally known and are heard in a differ-
> ent form in the temple. Today they appear to be agents
> for disseminating ideas and slogans of national importance.[21]

What of the future? How will traditional music respond to the pressures that continue to build on it? If past experience is any guide, the law
is survival of the fittest. Audiences in Northeast Thailand and Thailand
generally are more and more dominated by young people whose tastes are
not as conservative as those of their parents. It can be said that audiences
are fickle and trendy; they respond to quantity rather than quality. In any
contest the loudest and most brightly lit troupe wins. Audiences expect
successful troupes to impress them with the trappings of success--flashy

clothes, good lighting, more than adequate amplification, brilliant scenery, pretty girls, and a good rock band. Whatever the role past or present of mawlum in society, audiences still expect entertainment. They expect progress, not conservation. Consequently few mawlum glawn wear old-fashioned clothing, the young girls in mawlum moo and plun wear mini-skirts, the men wear modish clothes and large Japanese wrist watches for all to see.

The mawlum pee fah Ritual

Mawlum pee fah (singing pertaining to the pee fah or "sky spirit") is one of the least understood and accessible musical genres in Northeast Thailand. Few Westerners have witnessed the ceremony, and no writer to my knowledge has either described it or explained its significance in any language. S. J. Tambiah's excellent monograph Buddhism and the Spirit Cults in Northeast Thailand discusses in great detail all other aspects of the spirit world, the ritualists, ceremonies, and meaning, but because he witnessed the mawlum pee fah ceremony only once and very late in his field work, he was unable to discuss it in context with other phenomena.

Mawlum pee fah differs from ordinary mawlum genres in many signifi-cant ways. Chief among these is that the singing is but a vehicle of ver-bal expression within the ceremony and does not constitute a "performance" as in lum glawn. Lum pee fah cannot be approached in any other way than as a cultural phenomenon; the singing is merely one aspect of it. The ritualists are not trained singers, and they become mawlum pee fah by virtue of a non-musical experience. The ceremony's purpose is to mollify malevolent spirits (pee) which have caused someone to become ill, either physically or mentally. A mawlum pee fah ritualist is not unique in this respect, however, for she is merely one of many who perform such palli-ative functions. But lum pee fah is unique because the ceremony is sung rather than spoken.

In the Northeastern villager's world, spirits are legion. There is no contradiction in simultaneously being a Buddhist and believing in spirits. It is mostly agreed upon by historians that the Tai were animists before becoming Buddhists and that the belief in spirits has persisted from time immemorial.

An attempt to list all the various types of pee might well constitute an entire chapter. The following list, however, enumerates the chief spirits encountered in lum pee fah as well as provides a sampling of some of the most important lesser pee.

1. Pee fah, pee taen, or payah taen. It is agreed by informants that the term pee fah is a general one and pee taen a specific name for the highest ranking spirit (some say tewadah or angel) who lives in the fifteenth level of heaven,[22] or accord-ing to Wirawong[23] at the jadoo-maharat level of heaven. Wirawong, who states cryptically that the word taen comes from the tian language, advises that the pee taen is not a pure god but a high-ranking ghost. The pee taen fixes the lives of people, their birth, marriage, deaths; it also pro-tects villages, provides fortunes, and supervises somewhat loosely the activities of lesser spirits. It is generally agreed that the pee taen or pee fah does not make people ill but can intercede with other ghosts to affect a cure. Tewadah

may act in a similar capacity.

2. Pee dum or pee chüa, meaning "low class spirit" or "evil
   spirit," also called pee küa. They are prone to cause
   illness because of quarreling in the family.
3. Pee da-haek or pee nah, ghosts of the fields.
4. Pee bao, a kind of spirit which eats raw food and possesses
   people, sometimes causing them also to eat raw food.
5. Pee bawp, the most serious and violent form of spirit
   possession in which the ghost eats the liver, stomach, and
   intestines and eventually kills the victim; pee bawp chüa
   may result from learning magic words while pee bawp wicha
   stem from the failure of ritualists to observe rules and
   procedures in dealing with amulets, an affliction to which
   people learned in the Brahmanistic science called saiyasat
   are prone.
6. Pee pet, a type of ghost which assumes very tall forms such
   as that of a palm tree at night and frightens unlucky individuals.
7. Pee prai, meaning "wind spirit," is a ghost which assumes
   animal forms and haunts people when they are severely ill.
8. Pee prong, similar to pee bao, is a ghost that possesses
   its victims at night and causes a bright light to shine from
   their nostrils.
9. Pee hoong, ghosts of people who died accidental and premature deaths. While pee hoong are dangerous generally,
   the most vicious are those of unborn children who died in
   the womb.
10. Pee um, a phenomenon in which a spirit makes its victim
    sleepy and places weight on the chest making breathing
    difficult.
11. Pee het, a light-hearted ghost that enjoys frightening
    people who are especially frightened by ghosts.
12. Da-boo-ban (ancestors or grandparent of the village), a
    permanent, guardian spirit who watches over a village.
    They are also called pee ban, pee boo dah, and pee poo dah.
13. Jao-paw-pa-kao (white clothed father), a guardian spirit
    similar to the da-boo-ban who protects the temple.

Of these, all villagers know and believe in the pee fah, pee ban (da-boo-
ban), pee nah, and pee chüa (pee küa).

The village ritualists are also numerous, some being specialists, some
able to work with many types of spirits. Informants often contradicted
each other in defining the nature and function of many of these ritualists,
however. The following list includes all known ritualists although few
villages will possess all of them:

1. Pra and nen, the monks and novices who live at the Buddhist
   wut (temple).
2. Maw kwun or pram, a Brahmanist who calls the kwun with
   recited texts appropriate to the situation.
3. Jum or gajum, a male chosen initially by possession who acts
   as an intermediary with the guardian spirits of the village and
   temple. His function is to intercede with these spirits when

they have been offended as well as make ritual offerings
to them semi-annually. In performing his functions the jum
uses ordinary speech, not recitation, as the ghost speaks,
through him.

4. Tiam, a medium for hire who may be male or female and
   is chosen by possession; the tiam is required when the jum
   is unable to solve a problem. The tiam in order to function
   must be possessed during the ceremony but like the jum
   does not sing or recite. The term, however, is used
   loosely especially with regard to women who perform
   ceremonies dealing with all types of spirits. It is believed
   that women are more prone to possession than men. Tiam
   literally means "side by side" or "two spirits in one body"--
   the ghost and that of the tiam. A tiam's life is fraught
   with restrictions and the home is a holy and dangerous
   place.

5. Maw doo (doo, "to look"), a fortune teller or astrologer
   who works with charts and other paraphenalia. They are
   commonly seen in towns along the streets telling fortunes.

6. Maw lek (lek, "numerals"), also a fortune teller and
   astrologer but said to work with numbers and deal with
   spirits of the fields.

7. Maw maw (maw, "crest" or "hill"), a fortune teller (maw
   doo) who may use many different techniques, especially
   that using a large cloth with animal pictures. The term
   maw derives from reading the "hills" of the palm.

8. Maw song (song, "to enter," "to seek," or "to be possessed"),
   a diviner and diagnostician. The exact nature of a maw
   song varies among informants, and the term is sometimes
   used interchangeably with maw doo. Tambiah's informants
   defined maw song as a diagnostician who is not possessed
   but learns his art. He is the first ritualist to be seen by
   an afflicted person seeking the cause of the illness.
   Jarünchai said that a maw song has the inner power to
   force possession in the ceremony during which he may ask
   the spirit questions regarding such diverse subjects as love,
   the prediction to winning lottery numbers, and the cause of
   sickness. A maw song may test the efficacy of protective
   Buddha images and in extreme cases use weapons on the
   owner in a dangerous ceremony called blook pra ("awaken
   the monks"). The maw song is not said to sing or recite.

9. Maw yah (yah, "medicine"), a folk doctor who uses herbal
   medicine and ritual texts.

10. Maw tam (tam, from dhamma, Buddhist doctrine), an
    exorcist of spirits. The seriousness of spirit possession
    usually by the dangerous pee bawp often results in emotional
    and even violent ceremonies which have become extremely
    rare during the past generation.

11. Maw wichah (wichah, "knowledge"), a general term for
    experts in such areas as love magic (maw saneh), protection,
    the control of epidemics, and other matters. Because they
    deal in magical texts and amulets, the risk of mishandling
    these is great and consequently maw wichah are prone to
    possession by pee bawp.

12. Maw sawng (sawng, "to look" or "call for possession"), a
    little understood ritualist who is said to be a maw doo
    who uses no charts but depends entirely on mediation.
    Some informants said he performed the ceremony by sing-
    ing.
13. Mawlum pee fah, old women who perform a ceremony
    accompanied by singing and kaen music in which a person
    afflicted by a spirit is cured.

Various informants in various places discuss or describe four types of
mawlum pee fah ceremonies, and while most were able to describe the
differences among them, there was little consistency from one informant
to another. Whether the differences claimed have any validity or not, the
four ceremonies are all basically the same. They may vary in the details
from village to village, but there is no consistent pattern throughout the
Northeast that justifies discussing them separately. The terms are mawlum pee fah, mawlum pee taen (in reference to the pee fah by its proper
name), mawlum tai tüng (pertaining to a "group" of spirits or immortals
"in the sky" or a high place), and mawlum song (song, "to enter").
    According to virtually all informants, if a person has become ill and
cannot be cured by the maw yah (folk doctor) or modern doctor, the
affliction is suspected to have been caused by a spirit. Pee cause illness
for many reasons. Pee hai-pee nah (field spirits) may do so because their
path is blocked by a paddy dike; other spirits may desire that a spirit
house be built for them, feel neglected, offended, or merely capricious.
The spirits of ancestors may cause troubles because there is tension within the family or village over unequal distribution of property or marital
difficulties. Eventually the root causes must be eliminated as well as the
spirits themselves appeased.
    If a ghost is suspected the person must go the maw song, maw doo, or
maw maw who identifies the ghost and the appropriate ritualist who can
effect a cure. If the village or temple guardians have caused the problem,
the person will be referred to the jum; in difficult cases a tiam will be
called too. Tambiah, because he was unable to learn much about mawlum
pee fah, fails to delimit their areas of responsibility. According to my
informants they deal with problems caused by almost any ghost including
the village and temple guardians, and their ritual role appears to overlap
that of other practitioners. The mawlum pee fah will be consulted when
the victim has no pain or obvious symptoms, but seems weak without
cause. Neither folk nor modern medicines have any effect on the disorder.
Mawlum pee fah will also be called as a last resort when other ritualists
have failed and the victim is near death.
    In some cases the mawlum pee fah fulfill the function of the maw song
in determining whether a ghost caused the illness and which ghosts in
particular. If no ghost seems to be involved they may recommend returning to the maw yah or a modern doctor. Mawlum Sui stated that only the
leader performs the first portion in which this determination is made, but
in other cases witnessed the entire group was involved. It is the responsibility of the mawlum pee fah to attract the pee fah or pee taen into their
bodies and then pursuade him to reveal which ghost is involved. When the
offending spirit has been identified, it may be summoned with the aid of
the pee fah although other ghosts may also come to possess the mawlum
during the ceremony.
    The pee fah is lured to the ceremony by various means including an

altar, dancing, and singing. The altar, called <u>kai</u> or <u>krüang boochah</u>, may
be a metal household tray or a woven basket called <u>padok</u> of the type upon
which traditional meals were eaten. The objects vary somewhat from ceremony to ceremony but are always items of beauty, fragrance, or comfort
offered to the <u>pee fah</u> and which also bribe the offending spirits from the
victim. These may include betel nut, cigarettes, flowers, cloth, money, a
mirror, a comb, an egg, rice, perfume, water, a pillow, candles, and thread.

Typically there was some discrepancy between what the <u>mawlum pee
fah</u> wear in practice and what they are said to wear by informants who
may have based their descriptions on both exceptional and ordinary ceremonies. Tambiah, in describing the costume of <u>tiam</u> (mediums) states:

> The costume consists of a black waist cloth or skirt, and a
> blouse, head cloth, and handkerchief all red in colour. If these
> are worn by a male, he resembles a female; if worn by a female,
> she resembles a man. That is to say, the mediator assumes
> somewhat of a transvestite appearance.[24]

A lady in Ban Nawng-waeng-kuang who had seen many <u>pee fah</u> ceremonies
said that the women must wear trousers called <u>pah salong</u> or <u>pah kuap</u>
similar to those worn at ordination ceremonies, a cloth around the head,
one around the waist, and another over the shoulder. The proper color is
blue-black and the material is silk. The <u>mawlum</u> also wear a chain of
papaya or <u>jumbah</u> flowers over their ears. A fifty-seven year old informant in the same village basically agreed but added that the preferred color
today is white and that the clothes must be beautiful so to attract the
<u>pee fah</u>.

In practice the group at Ban Nawng-koo-bawn in Roi-et province dressed in better-than-ordinary wrap-around skirts (<u>sin</u>), blouses of white or
other colors, but wore a white cloth over the shoulders as a Protestant
minister wears his stole. Some wore a short chain of papaya flowers over
one ear. The women at Ban Lao-kam in Roi-et province dressed similarly
except their blouses were all white. Because the ceremonies take place
inside homes on straw mats, shoes are never worn.

One becomes a <u>mawlum pee fah</u> by virtue of having been cured by one.
They sing to express the spirit which has possessed them. Thus there is no
training, no vocal or literary requirements nor the necessity of displaying
extraordinary powers. While men are obviously among those cured and
may then become <u>mawlum pee fah</u>, in fact I did not encounter any men
who had ever participated except as <u>kaen</u> players. Although young women
too may function as <u>mawlum pee fah</u>, the women are likely to be forty-
five or older. While the word troupe has been used in reference to the
<u>mawlum pee fah</u> of one village or locality, in fact they are not so well
organized. When it has been determined that a <u>pee fah</u> ceremony is in
order, the available <u>mawlum pee fah</u> assemble and may number from two
or three to ten. Several informants stated that there is no official leader
but the woman who has sung the longest is looked to for leadership; she
does not train the others nor do they perform a <u>wai kroo</u> ceremony for her.
Mawlum Sui claimed, however, that the leader of the group has special
curing powers, that the other members were cured by her, and that they
must honor her in a <u>wai kroo</u> ceremony. While Mawlum Sui may indeed
have observed these things in his home village, his remarks must be qualified for he had gotten somewhat drunk by the time he made them.[25]

The first ceremony which I recorded, observed, and photographed was

in a private home in Ban Nawng-koo-bawn south of Roi-et city on the
night of September 2, 1973 (Figures 23-25). The victim had undergone the
ceremony a few days earlier, but the mawlum pee fah agreed to perform
it a second time for our benefit. During the afternoon old women came
to prepare the kai, but the ceremony did not begin until nearly 8 p.m. after
the evening meal. Besides the seven participating mawlum pee fah there
was a kaen player, Mr. Tawng-koon See-aroon of a nearby village, and the
victim. Kaen players are always male and during the pee fah ceremony
they are called maw-mah or "skilled horseman" because the pee taen is
said to go from place to place on a horse. When the kaen player begins,
it is said "the horse is running." An informant in nearby Ban Nawng-
waeng-kuang noted that a pair of flowers ought to be placed on the kaen
for otherwise it will be hard to blow. Tawn-koon did not observe this
custom, however. About thirty other villagers filled the house to watch
the ceremony.

The singing during the ceremony was similar to lum tang yao, slow,
non-metrical, but sung in short phrases and with little ornamentation. The
mawlum sing as they feel directed by the spirits, entering at random without regard to other singers or the kaen's part. This singing will be described in greater detail with a transcription in Chapter IV.

Figure 23. A lum tai tŭng ritual led by Mae Noo in a remote Roi-et province village.

During the ceremony the mawlum assume new identities and names as
ghosts come and go. Among the ghosts that visited them were the daboo-
ban (village guardian) of Ban Nawng-waeng-kuang, a spirit called Tao Hong-
Kum of Ban Hong (formerly a müang or principality), Jao awn from Wiangjun who had learned of that city's fall to Siamese forces from another visiting ghost, and Nya-paw-koon-lek, a god who oversees the rains. Two other
ghosts who live together at Muang Ja-doon, formerly of Oong-moong of
Ban Kah, also visited, Jao mut and Nya-paw-mun-du.

Figure 24. Participants in <u>lum tai tüng</u> bow to the altar.

Figure 25. The <u>kai</u> or altar in <u>lum tai tüng</u>.

The exact mechanics of how ghosts enter and affect the participants and how the victim is cured remain vague.[26]   The mawlum offer the kai as enticements for spirits but also try to charm them with singing and dancing.   It is felt that the victim will be cured if he or she can be made to dance thus showing not only possession but allegiance to the offended spirit.   In some cases the spirit demands further actions such as building a spirit house or propitiatory offerings to be made, usually on wun pra (holy days).   The kaen player is necessary to provide accompaniment to the singing and dancing but seems to have a spiritual role as well though it is not well understood by informants.   Gagneaux in an article about the kaen in Laos mentions this aspect in reference to mediums in general. "Accompanied by a tambourine, the kaen playing helps the medium, usually a woman, cause the spirits to enter her and allow her to make predictions. The kaen thus serves as a connecting link between the world of spirits and that of men."[27]

The ceremony witnessed at Ban Lao-kam differed little from that in Ban Nawng-koo-bawn except that it was much simpler and less dramatic (Figure 26).   There was no victim present and thus no ghosts came, and furthermore the ceremony took place on a hot afternoon.   During this ceremony, however, the mawlum began drinking small glasses of rice wine. Soon afterwards they began acting drunk, their singing deteriorated, and their actions became more and more reckless.   At the end, however, they no longer appeared inebriated and insisted that they had not been drunk but merely pretending.   This ceremony differed somewhat from the other in that the mawlum danced in place and sang to a greater extent.

Figure 26.   A lum pee fah ritual in Lao-kam village in Roi-et province.

NOTES

1.   Tanjaokoon-tamtirarat-maha Moo-nee, "Rüang lum-kaen" [The Story of lum-kaen], in Maradok chao isan [The Heritage of the Northeast], ed. Boon-rüang (Bangkok, 1962), p. 393.

2.   Ibid., p. 402.

3.   H.R.H. Prince Chula Chakrabongse, Lords of Life (London: Alvin Redman Ltd., 1960), p. 184.

4.   Sir John Bowring, The Kingdom and People of Siam, 2 vols. (London, 1857; reprint ed., London: Oxford University Press, 1969), 2:324, 328-9.

5.   Jao-pra-yah Ti-pah-gor-ra-wong, The Dynastic Chronicles, Bangkok Era, the Fourth Reigh (B.E. 2394-2411) (A.D. 1851-1868), 2 vols., trans. Chadin Flood (Tokyo: The Centre for East Asian Cultural Studies, 1966), 2:354-5.

6.   M.E. is an era properly called Tiunlasakaraj in Pali which began on March 21, 638 A.D. in which years are grouped into decades.

7.   Quoted in Tanjaokoon-tamtirarat-maha Moo-nee, "Ruang lum-kaen," pp. 417-19; translated by Prof. Sagon Sonsenah of the Mahasarakam Teacher Training College, Mahasarakam, Thailand.

8.   Theodore Stern and Theodore A. Stern, "'I Pluck my Harp': Musical Acculturation Among the Karen of Western Thailand," Ethnomusicology 15 (1971):186-219.

9.   James R. Brandon, Theatre in Southeast Asia (Cambridge: Harvard University Press, 1967), p. 68.

10.   Albert Lord, The Singer of Tales (Cambridge: Harvard University Press, 1960).

11. Brandon, Theatre in Southeast Asia, p. 213.

12. S.J. Tambiah, "Literacy in a Buddhist Village in North-East Thailand," in Literacy in Traditional Societies, ed. J. Goody (Cambridge: Cambridge University Press, 1968), pp. 114-15.

13. Jarünchai Chonpairot, "Mawlum," in Program of the Northeastern Music Festival (Galasin, 1972), p. 8. (in Thai)

14. Brandon, Theatre in Southeast Asia, p. 213.

15. Francis Cripps, The Far Province (London: Hutchinson and Company, 1965), p. 191.

16. Brandon, Theatre in Southeast Asia, pp. 298-300.

17. Ibid., pp. 299-300.

18. Tambiah, "Literacy in a Buddhist Village," p. 115.

19. See p. 17.

20. Liang Tsai-ping, Chinese Musical Instruments and Pictures (Taipei: Chinese Classical Music Association, 1970), p. 11.

21. Tambiah, "Literacy in a Buddhist Village," p. 115.

22. The Northeastern Thai conceive of heaven as having twenty-six levels divided into three loka.

23. Somdet Pra Maha Wirawong, Northeast Thai--Central Thai Dictionary, p. 193. (In Thai)

24. S.J. Tambiah, Buddhism and the Spirit Cults in North-East Thailand (Cambridge: Cambridge University Press, 1970), p. 284.

25. Mawlum Sui, who was interviewed about lum glawn, lum sam sing ching nang, and lum pee fah, requested a bottle of rice whiskey before we started. During the interview he consumed the alcohol and by the time we had gotten to mawlum pee fah he had become drunk; finally the interview had to be suspended when he became boisterous.

26. See Terry E. Miller, "The Mawlum Pee Fah Ceremony of Northeastern Thailand" in Proceedings of the Saint Thyagaraja Music Festivals, Cleveland, Ohio, 1978-81, ed. by T. Temple Tuttle, pp. 82-97 (Cleveland: Greater Cleveland Ethnographic Museum, 1981).

27. Anne Marie Gagneaux, "Le khene et la musique Lao," Bulletin des Amis du Royaume Lao 6 (1971), p. 180.

III.

Theatrical Vocal Genres

Predecessors to Contemporary Genres

Unlike the non-theatrical genres of mawlum which can be traced back
more than one hundred years in written documents, the theatrical genres
in the Northeast are of recent origin. Moreover, their advent came as a
direct result of stimulation from Siamese dramatic genres, principally
ligeh, though certain Northeastern genres were also factors. The contemporary genres in the Northeast, mawlum moo ("group" mawlum) and mawlum plün ("spontaneous" mawlum) are nevertheless only temporary stages
in an ongoing development that began with relatively crude imitation of
ligeh slightly more than a generation ago. In comparison it may be said
that mawlum glawn has reached a certain peak of artistic development,
and since its performance requires considerable skill and sophistication, its
developmental dynamics are now relatively slow. In contrast, the theatrical genres, because they are more for entertainment and must compete
with other twentieth-century genres including movies and popular music
groups, are forced to respond both continuously and rapidly to changes in
public taste or face oblivion.

Informants queried concerning the history of these genres, even singers
during whose careers they developed, were surprisingly vague as to when
and how mawlum moo and mawlum plün began. Two explanations may be
offered. First, the earliest developments occurred in relative isolation,
since before about 1960 travel in the Northeast was extremely difficult.
Secondly, it may be said that informants generally seemed unaccustomed
to thinking about the past in anything but generalities and thus were unable
to pinpoint events without great difficulty. Moreover, the various reports
given by informants on the development of dramatic styles are often inconsistent and contradictory, giving the impression that the earliest manifes-
tations were ephemeral in nature.

There is general agreement among informants that the first dramatic
genre in the Northeast was ligeh-lao, i.e., Siamese ligeh theatre in Lao
style. Exactly when and how ligeh-lao began are difficult to determine.
Of the eight informants who volunteered information on ligeh-lao, only
three had had direct contact--Mawlum Soot-tee-sompong of Roi-et who as
a young man performed ligeh-lao, Mawlum Tawin of Kawn-gaen province

who although not a ligeh-lao player was able to demonstrate the singing
style, and members of a long defunct ligeh-lao troupe located in a remote
village in southeastern Mahasarakam province. Soot-tee-sompong thought
that Northeasterners who had migrated to Bangkok for work saw ligeh
there and upon returning to their native region attempted to imitate it.
Mr. Pim, a lum moo script writer from Kawn-gaen, stated that Central
Thai speakers from Korat who moved to Kawn-gaen imported ligeh for
their festivals. Jarünchai Chonpairot further asserted that when the central government began modern administration in the Northeast, they often
sent governors from other regions who might import entertainments more
to their tastes. Yet none of these reasons would seem to account for the
appearance of ligeh, though, for those who migrated to Bangkok for work
were not usually performers, Mr. Pim's story accounts for only one small
area, and it seems unlikely that a governor would import a genre identified
with the lowest classes of his home region to entertain Northeasterners
using both alien dialect and musical style.

It is the last point, ligeh's foreignness, which makes it difficult to
understand its introduction into the Lao-speaking Northeast. Its language
is not only Siamese but the musical instruments were also Siamese, principally the ranat (xylophone), kawng wong (tuned bronze gongs on a circular
frame), bee (oboe), ching (small cymbals), and various drums (dapon, ton,
ramana, and glawng dut).[1] Similarly, the singing style was Siamese,
principally renditions of classical tunes and various recitation styles.
While the stories were drawn from both classical and modern Siamese
literature, the performance and exact wording of the poetry were improvised to a scenario.

What probably arrested the interest of the Northeasterners were ligeh's
visual aspects, the brilliantly painted backdrops, colorful costumes vaguely
related to those of Siamese lakon and kon (dance dramas), and glittering
jewelry. While the Northeastern people eventually realized they could not
copy ligeh's Siamese musical characteristics, they slavishly imitated the
visual aspects with the result that casual observers could not tell the
difference. James Brandon, who mistakenly thought mawlum moo (mohlam
luong) was principally played in Laos and originated about 1925, did not
detect the fundamental differences between the two.

> Likay was introduced into Laos early in the twentieth
> century . . . Likay troupes, speaking standard Thai, played in
> northeast Thailand for the Lao-speaking Thai people of that
> region. From there it was but a short trip across the Mekong
> River to play for audiences in Laos. Around 1925, the khen
> was substituted for Thai musical instruments and mohlam
> singing replaced most of the Thai dialogue and dance while
> the stories, costumes, and staging practices of Thai likay were
> retained.[2]

Ligeh is currently popular throughout Central Thailand and especially
in the Korat (Nakawn-ratchasimah) area where several hundred troupes
are said to flourish.

According to a Thai-Khmer singer from Soo-rin province in the Khmer
area of the Northeast, ligeh has been known in that area for many years,
and as early as 1932 there are said to have been ligeh-khmer (ligeh in the
Khmer language) troupes playing too. This latter genre nearly died out
but has lately been revived, for two troupes in Jom-pra district, Soo-rin

province were again playing ligeh-khmer in 1974. The troupes are said to consist of three to four musicians and six actors. As in ligeh-tai, they use no script but their costumes differ. The instruments include a fiddle with cylindrical body (so i in Khmer, saw duang in Thai), Indonesian oboe (bee jawah in Thai), ching (small cymbals), and dapon (drum).

But there are also Lao people living in these provinces, and they no doubt saw either ligeh-tai or ligeh-khmer. The leader of the Oobon Putana mawlum moo troupe, when asked about the origin of lum moo, thought that it came from Boori-rum and Korat province. Mawlum Wichian of Oobon estimated that mawlum moo (probably ligeh-lao) began about 1935 in Ban Dang-dek in Guntara-rom district thirty kilometers east of Sisaget city. In fact the earliest known troupe of ligeh-lao actors began in 1929 in Ban Goot-numsai in Jadoopuk piman district in Roi-et province haltway between Roi-et city and Sisaget city. Another informant who "invented" a related genre called mawlum moo maeng dup dao (maeng dup dao is the name of a convivial song), also called ligeh samai boran ("old-period ligeh"), said that he had seen ligeh-tai performed in southern Mahasarakam and Roi-et provinces as early as the mid-1930s. There is every reason to believe, then, that one route of entry for ligeh was by way of Korat, Boori-rum, Soo-rin, and Sisaget provinces into bordering areas of Roi-et and Mahasarakam provinces during the late 1920s and early 1930s.

A second route was through Kawn-gaen province further west. Mawlum Tawin Boot-ta, whose brother founded the first troupe identified as mawlum moo, said that ligeh-lao preceded ligeh-tai in his home province. About 1937 there were already troupes performing in Ban Don, Ban Nawng-koo, and Ban Non-goo in Muang district, Kawn-gaen province. He said it was not until 1944 that a ligeh-tai troupe came from Soong-nun district of Korat province. The members, however, came to perform for food and rice indicating that their economic situation was not good. The appearance of ligeh-lao before ligeh-tai suggests an earlier influence, but the informant being only forty-two years old (1973) was not able to elaborate.

Ligeh's infusion into the Northeast was necessarily gradual since transportation was extremely difficult. Because the Northeast is situated on a broad plateau having few rivers and uncertain rainfall, transportation links via river or canal are obviously out of the question. Roads were poor until the 1960s. Troupes could move only slowly by oxcart or horseback from village to village, and the spread of ligeh would have depended on new groups learning the genre and venturing further north. The railroad no doubt enhanced movement. The mainline from Bangkok to Korat had been completed in 1900, but it was not until 1941 that the two branches--to Nawng-kai in the north and to Oobon in the east--were finished. It is easy to see how ligeh might have moved east from Korat into Boori-rum and Soo-rin and north into Kawn-gaen via rail during the 1930s or slightly earlier. Beyond the rail lines movement became more difficult, and the youngest troupes manned by Northeasterners began to convert the genre into something more to their liking.

With difficulty we located several surviving members of a long defunct ligeh-lao troupe living in remote Ban Nawng-waeng, Kam-bawn subdistrict, Wapi-patoom district, Mahasarakam province near the Roi-et border. The principal informant, Mr. Pimpah, age sixty, said his troupe studied in 1931 with the troupe mentioned earlier from Jadoopuk-piman district dating from 1929, when the latter group visited his home village. All members of that original troupe are now deceased, however. The younger troupe from

Ban Nawng-waeng performed until 1943 when they quite because several members had become too old, but Mr. Pimpah mentioned having trained another troupe in that village whose fate is unknown.

The troupe, which numbered sixteen or seventeen men and women, walked from village to village, performing in at least three provinces--Mahasarakam, Roi-et, and Nakawn-ratchasimah. They played but one story, Nang Daeng-awn, a Northeastern jataka tale, but unlike ligeh-tai, performed from a fully written script. A teacher, now long deceased, wrote the script in glawn poetry based on old nungsü bai-lan sources (palm-leaf books). As in ligeh-tai they opened with an awk kaek, a short melodic section in Indian or Malay style which attracts the attention of the audience. Their singing was otherwise ordinary Northeastern lum tang yao or an nungsü style, but sung unaccompanied. Their instruments were only the kaen which played lai sootsanaen during parades, two drums (ramana and glawng yao), and cymbals (ching) which accompanied dancing. Their performance, therefore, was mostly Lao in style since there were no Central Thai melodies or instruments, but also unlike ligeh-tai because it was performed with a script.

Since stages were unavailable, the troupe played on the ground before a plain white cloth or sometimes a colored cloth. The women wore Lao sin skirts and the men long-sleeved white shirts with jong-graben trousers modeled after those of ligeh; both wore glittering necklaces. This troupe's ligeh-lao was therefore far removed from ligeh-tai both in music and appearance, a fact not surprising considering their isolation and their never having seen ligeh-tai. It seems then that the remote villages and towns of the Northeast filtered out most of what was obviously Siamese as the genre moved from Korat deeper into the Lao cultural areas.

Three other informants in Roi-et province basically confirmed these conclusions. Mr. Pao, a mawlum pün, remembered that ligeh-lao played before a white cloth, used ligeh costumes and some Siamese lakon crowns or hats, but otherwise differed little from the troupe described above. He noted that those who played ligeh-lao began with a faithful imitation but gradually localized it through a change to Lao singing, instruments, and dancing. Mr. Tawng-si, a mawlum gup gaep, estimated that ligeh came about 1924 playing only one story, the jataka of Prince Wetsundawn. He recalled their using Siamese instruments, however, principally ranat, kawng wong, ching and a fiddle plus the Northeastern pin, and that they played in ordinary clothes without a backdrop; their singing was said to be Northeastern style lum pün.

Only a few kilometers from the village where Mr. Pimpah's ligeh-lao troupe lived was another in which a second early genre of theatre flourished known as mawlum moo maeng dup dao or ligeh samai boran ("old period ligeh"). The former designation refers to an insect and title of a widely known convivial song noteworthy for its bawdy lyrics which was inserted into the play; most call the genre simply maeng dup dao, and the term mawlum moo was probably added later. Mr. Lee Müang-gaeo, age fifty-six (1974), of Ban Süa-gok in Wapi-patoom district, Mahasarakam province, provided information about the early history of this genre, but there remain a number of insoluable difficulties. He said that he and several friends "invented" this theatrical genre about 1928 adding that it preceded the appearance of ligeh-lao by three years though he admitted having seen ligeh-tai previously. Indeed, the nearby ligeh-lao troupe had begun performing in 1931 confirming his story. The major difficulty is that the informant was only twelve at the time, a bit young to be composing poetry and forming a commercial troupe. Perhaps he was only twelve and now claims a greater role than he actually had.

While Mr. Lee said that previously a ligeh-tai actor had been in the area teaching new troupes, he did not comment on that genre's influence on his own troupe. He said that he and several friends from the same village chose the story of Tao Kooloo and Nang Ua because they were familiar with it and it was popular among the villagers. Mr. Lee and his friends together wrote the poetry for the singing and speaking parts, as well as the text for the maeng dup dao melody. Exactly when they stopped performing is problematic for Mr. Lee said the advent of mawlum moo in the early 1950s pushed aside the troupe, but other informants said they had quit performing during the 1940s.

The troupe consisted of thirteen performers, eight male and five female singers plus four male musicians who played the kaen, pin, saw bip (a two-stringed fiddle whose body was a discarded metal can), and ching. The singers performed on a straw mat on the ground before a white cloth with the musicians between them and the audience. Lighting was provided by several gabawng lights. Their costumes were not like those of ligeh but basically local dress plus a necklace (sungwan) and a chadah hat borrowed from ligeh for certain characters. Mr. Lee claims to have performed in "every village in Roi-et province" and throughout Mahasarakam, Soorin, and Boori-rum provinces as well. Before they ceased performing they trained eight other troupes in nearby villages, few of which performed for more than two or three years. The training consisted of teaching the text and a month's coaching.

One of these troupes, from Ban Nawng-waeng-kuang on the road between Wapi-patoom and Roi-et in Roi-et province, was able to perform excerpts during the Northeastern Music Festival in Mahasarakam in 1972 and 1973 although they had been inactive for many years. One of the singers, Mr. Mai Aigwa-dee, age forty-three, said that Mr. Lee trained his troupe about 1951 and that they performed for several years, quitting before the advent of electricity. The troupe had sixteen members, seven male and five female singers plus four musicians, exactly as in the original troupe. Each member had a notebook with his text but these are now lost. The characters were as follows: Tao (Prince) Kooloo, male; Nang (Princess) Ua, female; Tao Kooloo's lover, Ua's mother, female; the King of Kaya, male, Ua's father; Kooloo's mother, female; Koon (Mr.) Laeng, male rival for Ua; four servants, two male and two female; a ghost, male; and an elephant, male. The latter was a non-speaking part played by someone who put a sheet over his body, held an artificial trunk, and walked along with Prince Kooloo. Like Mr. Lee's troupe they performed on the ground before a white cloth with only one prop, a stump representing the throne. The troupe quit performing when the lead female got married.

Like the nearby ligeh-lao troupe, the maeng dup dao troupe used Lao instruments, Lao language, Lao singing, and a Lao story although the original stimulus was obviously ligeh-tai. Both genres played extensively but within only a few provinces and never ventured as far west as Kawn-gaen or Chaiyapoom. Informants from the Kawn-gaen area who had direct knowledge of early ligeh-lao and mawlum moo were not familiar with maeng dup dao theatre calling into question any assumptions that these genres, at least beyond the Roi-et area, were the direct predecessors to mawlum moo.

Ligeh-lao in the Kawn-gaen area differed significantly from that of the Roi-et region. Mr. Pim, a script writer from Kawn-gaen, said that ligeh-lao came about 1934 through the efforts of Korat Thai living there. The Northeastern imitation used ligeh-tai instruments and Central Thai stories such as Nang Nak Prakanong, but was never very successful because the language was Siamese and the actors were not completely comfortable performing this alien style.

Mr. Tawin Boot-ta of Ban Lao-na-dee southwest of Kawn-gaen described how ligeh-lao began about 1937. Mr. Gunhah, a ligeh-lao performer from Buk-tong-chai district southwest of Korat city, began teaching new troupes at that time. The troupes were small, about ten members each, and performed on a stage like ligeh-tai before painted backdrops, but their costumes were simpler--black sh ts, jong-graben trousers, and a few ligeh accessories. Their only story was Prince Wetsundawn performed without a script. The singing, which was an imitation of ligeh-tai style partly in Siamese, partly in Lao, was unaccompanied. A kaen was used as people walked about the stage or between stanzas, but it played only Central Thai classical melodies. A transcription of Tawin's ligeh-lao is discussed in detail in Chapter 4.

Mr. Tawin said that ligeh-lao was never very popular and tended to disappear when the authentic ligeh-tai troupes began coming to the area, about 1944 according to him. He claimed that a more important factor in the development of mawlum moo was mawlum rüang rather than ligeh-lao. Lum rüang is a variation of lum pün in which the singer acts out the story by changing costumes or hats and moving about as if to be several characters.[3] Tawin said this genre came from Wiangjun, Laos, about 1932, although as pointed out before there were others performing lum rüang in Roi-et at that time also. Tawin, though the manager of an active mawlum moo troupe, still performs lum rüang drawing from such well-known stories as Nang Daeng-awn, Sung Sin-sai, Sooriwong, and Prince Wetsundawn.

Tawin's brother founded the first mawlum moo troupe, Kanah Indah, in 1952 in Ban Lao-na-dee near Kawn-gaen.[4] At first they played but one story, Nang Daeng-awn, in a fully-written script by Mawlum Sopon from Selapoon district, Roi-et province. Their costumes were like those of lum rüang; they played on the ground but used no painted scenery. Their accompaniment was a kaen wong (kaen "ensemble") of from six to seven kaen in two sizes an octave apart. The singing style was Northeastern lum tang yao accompanied, according to Tawin, in lai soi mode.[5]

The year 1956 saw the beginning of mawlum moo as it is known today when Kanah Indah was invited to perform in Ban Suan-mawn in Wiangjun province, Laos. Tawin was not entirely clear on the matter, but apparently ligeh was already known in Laos and a second mawlum moo troupe founded after Kanah Indah had performed there shortly before. The sponsors requested the Indah troupe perform on a small stage and dress in the ligeh fashion but without socks, a custom in ligeh earlier demanded by a prime minister who abhorred the sight of bare feet. The stage was so small that actors not actually performing had to wait elsewhere. When the troupe returned to Northeast Thailand they continued these customs. At first the stage was very small but later that year it was enlarged to its present size.[6] They also added painted backdrops and reduced the kaen wong to a single kaen. About this time they also added lum dŏi to their repertory, probably dŏi hua non dan (which Tawin called dŏi see poom dŭm) which is similar to lum kawn-sawun from southern Laos.[7] In 1958 electricity became available for lighting and amplification, and mawlum moo has changed little in appearance since then.

.. The second contemporary theatrical genre is called mawlum plun. Plun means "spontaneous," but it is used for its effect rather than literal meaning. Today both moo and plun visually appear to be identical, but the differences are great. Although most informants thought lum plun was younger than lum moo, dating from approximately 1960 or later, lum plun actually predates lum moo by two years. The first troupe was founded in 1950 in Ban Non-kaen, Sang-taw subdistrict, Muang-samsip district, Oobon province (now Yasoton province), according to Pun Silaruk, age forty, who provided the early history of lum plun. Their first story, Gaeo-na-mah (Horse-faced Girl), was performed without a script but based on palm-leaf manuscripts. It was only after the troupe found public approval that they began writing down their parts. At first the troupe was strictly amateur but later trained at least two other troupes, one of which not only still performs but is the leading lum plun troupe in Northeast Thailand today.

This second troupe, Kanah Paw Roogsin founded in 1953 and soon thereafter led by informant Pun Silaruk, is based in Ban Dong-kaen-yai, Sang-taw subdistrict, Kum-kuan-gaeo district, Yasoton province. Mr. Pun was not part of the troupe when it started, for he was pedaling a tricycle taxi in Bangkok at the time, but claims that both troupes were identical. When he returned in 1953 or 1954, he began to improve the troupe's appearance and staging based on the performances of ligeh, lakon (dance drama), and lakon rawng (drama with songs)[8] which he had seen in Bangkok. Movies no doubt influenced him at least as much, however. At first their costumes were ordinary street clothes, although the women wore the more modern grahrong which is similar to Western skirts, but they attempted to decorate themselves with paper hats and a paper horse-face for the title character. Their decorations were influenced by stories illustrated in school readers published by the Central Thai government for the new public schools appearing in the Northeast. As soon as they could afford them, they purchased ligeh costumes. The heavy influence of Central Thai ligeh on lum plun is apparent visually, but popular influences show up in the singing and stories. It is noteworthy that Mr. Pun had never seen ligeh-lao or mawlum moo maeng dup dao.

When the troupe began performing it had no stage but performed on the ground before a plain cloth with light provided by gabawng lamps. By about 1956 Pun said he knew of mawlum moo, but it was more expensive to hire and performed on a stage. Lum moo was known to them as lum wiang in reference to Wiangjun because the language was more formal and conservative. Nevertheless lum plun began using a stage and painted drop cloths similar to ligeh at this time. Because transportation was still underdeveloped, the troupe walked from village to village for performances lasting from 9 p.m. to about 1 a.m. They would wait until they had scheduled about eight performances before setting out because they did not return home until these were finished. Their locale was more than two hundred kilometers from the home of mawlum moo, and given their small performing radius, it is not surprising that the genre remained obscure for many years.

As noted earlier the first story was Gaeo-na-mah. Their second story was See-ton Mano-rah, a story popular in Central and South Thailand. In 1955 Mr. Boon-num Goon-gaeo of Umnat-jarun district, Oobon province, wrote a script based on Koon Chang Koon Paen (names of the lead characters), a story which has since become the mainstay of lum plun. As will be demonstrated later, lum plun and lum moo can perform the same stories, but each genre has its favorites and the attitude with which the story is presented differs somewhat; lum moo is serious while lum plün tends to the comic with its main goal entertaining the audience. From the very beginning lum moo was more professional since the early troupes were lead by professional singers from long established genres, especially lum pün (or lum rüang) and lum glawn. Lum plün on the other hand began as an amateur effort, and professional troupes such as Paw Roongsin notwithstanding, it still remains more amateurish than lum moo.

Contemporary lum moo and lum plün

While in popular usage the terms ligeh-lao and mawlum rüang are still encountered, they refer to contemporary lum moo or lum plün. The total number of troupes, estimated by some to be nearly a thousand, is however unknown. The following material describing the troupes, literature, staging, and economic aspects is based on interviews with forty-two troupes, extensive observations, and data gleaned from various other informants. Much of the information was gained during the 1973 Northeastern Music Festival when ten troupes, five lum moo and five lum plün, competed each night. We later sought interviews with the leading troupes of the region as well.

Ordinary troupes are often organized within one village, even within a family, and usually with monetary gain in mind. A few of the professional troupes, however, were founded by famous mawlum glawn who could attract qualified singers into the organization. The troupe pools its resources to buy costumes, scenery, lighting, and amplification, joins a mawlum association, and waits for engagements to be scheduled. The vast majority of the troupes are only part-time, but a few troupes have become famous enough that their members do not have to farm to make a living. As the dramatic genre became more and more popular, first lum moo, then lum plün, there was a natural proliferation of troupes reflected in the fact that the average age of the seventeen mawlum moo troupes interviewed was 6½ years (ranging from one to twenty years), but lum plün which is now on the rise averaged only four years (from six months to twenty years).

Most troupes have a leader or manager who oversees the schedule, finances, and setting up at performances. In many cases he is the leading male as well, but some non-performing managers cannot even sing, while a few troupes report having no official manager. Troupe size depends on its financial success, the professional troupes being two to three times larger than the humble amateur troupes. Of those interviewed, lum moo troupes averaged 24.4 persons ranging in age from 12 to 57 while lum plün averaged only 19.7 ranging from 16 to 27. The ratio of males to females is usually 2:1 since males play the instruments. It is also true that the more professional troupes are not only larger but better paid, perform more stories, and are better organized.

All stories require certain stock characters and thus troupes have a predictable array of character types. The eight classes listed by one professional troupe manager are:

1. The leading male (pra-ek) and leading female (nang-ek) representing a prince and princess.
2. The second leading male (pra-rawng) and second leading female (nang-rawng), also of aristocratic status; they are

Figure 27. A <u>mawlum moo</u> troupe performing at a temple fair in Mahasarakam.

Figure 28. Costumes vary greatly in this scene from <u>mawlum moo</u>.

also called poo chui.
2. Two older figures, either father and mother or king and
   queen, called paw-payah and mae-payah.
4. The enemy or foil of the leading male, called poo-rai
   or dua-gong.
5. A comedian called dua-dalok.
6. Servants and soldiers, the former called senah or kon-
   chai, the latter dua bra-gawp; the comedian may be a
   servant character too.
7. Miscellaneous figures such as monks, ghosts, and giants.
8. A hermit monk or rusi who lives deep in the forest and
   practices magical arts; the prince goes to him to learn
   secret warfare, protective arts, and so forth.

Leading males averaged twenty-seven years of age ranging from nineteen to forty-six, but leading females only nineteen ranging from sixteen
to twenty-one. Their educational level, as with all troupe members, was
but four years, though all were literate. As noted earlier, married males
appear on stage, but married females are far less common. A few, such
as Chawiwan Dumnun, the former leading lady of the Rungsamun troupe,
however, had been famous before marriage and thus continues as leading
lady of her own troupe. Lead females usually retire upon marriage to
lead the pedestrian life of a village woman. The leading lady of the
prize-winning Oobon Putana troupe who was eighteen in 1973 began her
training when only eleven and completed it at age seventeen. Though
she had only been performing publicly for two years, she was becoming
bored with life on the road and thought she would retire to get married
in five or six years. She studied mawlum moo because she was attracted
to it and her parents encouraged her. The manager of the troupe said
that if parents want their children to become leading singers, they must
pay the manager from one thousand to three thousand baht and the child
will live with the troupe for up to five years receiving no pay while learning texts and how to sing them. There is little actual teaching since the
singer practices privately with a kaen player and only goes to the teacher
when having difficulty. The apprenticeship period for a lessor role is only
a year or two.
   Mr. Tawng-in, age fifty-three (1973), of Ban Lao-kam near Roi-et described how he had trained ten mawlum plun troupes, two of which he
still manages. The troupe first chooses its members, then goes to him
for training. They must pay him two thousand baht for coaching and
rehearsals which last about two months and from five hundred to one
thousand baht for the script depending on whether he writes a new version
or sells them a copy of an earlier one. The members pool their resources
for the training and must secure the other required properties. He stated
that school boys usually paint the scenery. After the troupe has joined
an association and begins to perform publicly, they begin repaying the
members for the debt until, hopefully, the troupe makes a profit. Only
the best troupes can afford their own transportation since motor vehicles
are heavily taxed. The best troupes own busses, the lesser troupes a
truck with seats mounted in the rear, and the poorest such as those trained by Mr. Tawng-in hire a village bus or truck for each performance.
   In comparing lum glawn, lum moo, and lum plun several things become
apparent. A lum glawn singer requires extensive training and mastery of
the poetry and voice rather than good looks to be successful. A lum moo

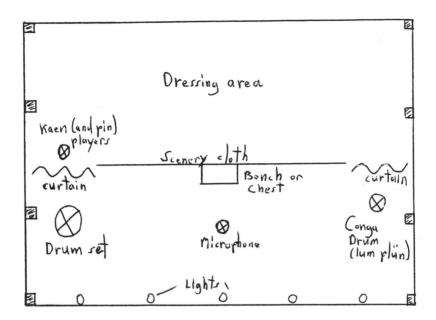

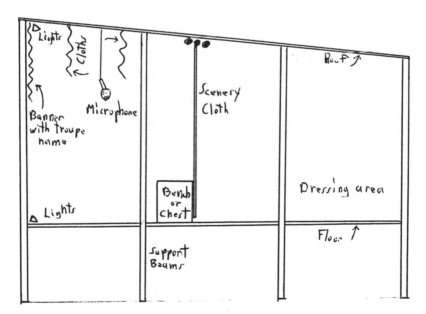

Figure 29. Layout of a stage for either <u>lum moo</u> or <u>lum plün</u>. (Top view above, side view below)

singer requires less training, but the singing style is still rather difficult to do well. As the popularity of lum glawn waned, many lum glawn singers joined or founded lum moo troupes but very few joined or founded lum plün troupes. Of the three, lum plün singers are the least trained, while most lum glawn singers can sing lum moo as well as lum plün. The best of the lum moo singers can perform lum glawn, but very few lum plün singers are of the caliber required for lum glawn. In short, lum plün has become the least artistic and most showy of all Northeastern musical forms. Because it is caught in the maelstrom of popular demand, it must respond to the whims of the public which is increasingly youthful and attracted to Western popular music. More about this trend will be presented later.

Except in quality, the stage and its fixtures differ little from troupe to troupe whether it be lum moo or lum plün. The rule of thumb in rural Thailand is that the gaudiest, most brightly lit, loudest, and slickest troupes attract the greatest audiences and thus increase their fortunes. Artistic integrity as far as the appearance of the stage goes is not a high priority. Troupes today perform on raised stages, either permanent wooden ones usually found in temple courtyards or crude ones erected for the occasion, usually a wooden floor on oil drums with simple wood framing for the drop cloths and sheet metal around the rear area. They average about seven to ten meters long and five to seven meters deep. The scenery cloths divide the stage into two areas, the front for performing and the rear where actors dress and await their entrances. The only furniture other than seats for the instrumentalists is a bench, stump, or chest in the center representing a throne.

The scenery cloths, which are mounted on bamboo poles and may be rolled up and down, are of two basic types though others are found among the more successful troupes. The first is a throne room for the king. Almost without exception the artist's perspective is painfully obvious giving the stage some depth but out of proportion with the actors. The colors are always brilliant, and the insides of the great pillars which line all palace scenes are lighted though the windows open onto the outer side. Secondly there must be a forest scene which might inspire artists to greater variety. One often sees a fountain, stream, mountain, and perhaps in the distance some village huts. Many troupes have a third scene, that of a village or town. These tend to be the crudest and least natural, for artists will mix city and village divided by a receding road complete with center lines, electric power poles, and Coca Cola signs. Other possible scenes include a garden, waterfall, hut, forest temple, or a cloth with the troupe's name and address. Ligeh-tai scenery is virtually identical both in content and artistic level, although it is true of both genres that the best troupes have the most tasteful scenery.

The advent of electricity about fifteen to twenty years ago (between 1958 and 1963) in district towns and larger villages near the highways in addition to the availability of portable generators have changed mawlum moo's appearance greatly. But because troupe managers are unconcerned with subtlety, lighting is used like amplification, to attract the audience, since brighter is considered better. Troupes prefer flourescent lighting, placing the tubes on the front of the stage, around the top, and sometimes vertically along the scenery cloths. There are also usually two incandescent bulbs over the stage; the poorest troupes rely on these exclusively which tells the audience that the troupe is poor indeed. A few troupes use colored spotlights, but except for turning them off and on for a fight

Figure 30. Mawlum moo troupe whose name is emblazoned above the stage.

Figure 31. Village performance of lum plün showing kaen, drum set, and conga drum.

or storm scene, there are few subtle uses made of lighting.

Amplification became necessary when troupes began performing on raised stages far from the audience. The stages are not built to project voices into the open air, and singers are not trained to do so themselves. In order to be heard above the din of a nearby fair, all troupes today place a mcirophone at stage center hung at the actor's eye level. Another mike is usually provided for the kaen (and pin in lum plün) player sitting off stage, and both mikes are mixed and amplified through loudspeakers hung in nearby trees. The volume level is usually the same-- maximum, leading to severe distortion and feedback. Because the stage mike, usually covered with a brightly colored scarf, is fixed, all singing and speaking must take place around it severely curtailing the actors' freedom of action. By way of comparison, Vietnamese theatre, i.e., cai lường and hát bội, also use stage mikes but they are on moveable ropes and follow the actors about.

The area behind the scenery is where the actors and actresses prepare their costumes, apply make-up, perform a brief wai kroo, or sleep and eat between entrances. Actors enter the stage on either side of the scenery cloth and no attempt is made to simulate doors. The musicians are normally on stage right seated on chairs in more or less full view of the audience. The drums featured especially in lum plün are placed on either side of the stage, the Western drum set on stage right, a single conga drum on stage left. Figure 29 shows a typical stage for either lum moo or plün.

The costumes worn by the actors and actresses vary widely; neither consistency nor logic are considered virtues on the Northeastern Thai stage. The leading male and probably the second male as well wear ligeh costumes. These consist of a pair of sateen or silk trousers cut off just above the knees and a collarless shirt worn outside the trousers and falling just below the waist. These will be of one solid color, preferably a bright one such as yellow, green, red, or blue. There is also a glittering headband provided with a feather or silk scarf in back, a scarf around the neck held with a brooch, a necklace of either metal or glittering cloth, a wide belt with a "tongue" hanging in the middle over the stomach, and a similar band around the shoulders. Both the trouser legs and shirt may be finished with embroidered borders. Actors also wear socks with or without shoes, a custom borrowed from ligeh. Michael Smithies' comments on ligeh costumes are also apropos to mawlum moo although the pleats are not worn in the Northeast.

> Fantasy is to be found in the costumes, where imaginative bad taste is allowed to run riot. Never were jewels so gaudy or colours so clashing. The men uniformly wear bouffant breeches (the pleats of which give them constant concern during the performance) held up with brocaded belts and have a fancy throw-over garment something like an undone waistcoat. They wear a flashy earring, a headband as a sign of rank and they all sport prominent Japanese watches with no concern for anachronism. The long off-white lisle stockings are supposed to have been required during the Second World War by the government concerned with proprieties of dress, considering bare feet uncivilised.[9]

Men also wear the latest "mod" styles, formal suits, village clothes, or the

Figure 32. Dancing to the catchy rhythms of lum plün.

Figure 33. Lum plün singing under the microphone.

uniforms of soldiers or police, the latter usually for comedians. In at
least one case, however, a comedian was seen impersonating a woman.
Concerning women's costumes, Smithies continues:

> The younger women wear the latest fashionable styles of
> dockside bars in shimmering sateens and silks. Paste and glass
> ornament every possible part; the few older women, who might
> play regal parts, are dressed more traditionally but with an
> even heavier encrustration of costume jewelry.[10]

Leading ladies in Northeastern Thai theatre usually wear long formal
dresses with either a small head decoration or flower in their hair. Older
women too will wear such dresses, but the younger ones almost universally
wear Western mini-skirts but with less jewelry than in ligeh. Servants
often wear village clothing, however, consisting of a sin skirt and blouse.
The dresses are never low-cut, for this would offend the audience, but
while mini-skirts would not be permitted in villages either, they are tol-
erated on stage.

Make-up is basically the same for both male and female actors. The
face is thoroughly powdered so to appear pale, then the eyebrows and eye-
lashes blackened with mascara, and the lips covered with brilliant red lip-
stick. Some male actors paint on mustaches, but there is no face painting
such as found in Chinese theatre. The pale face is desirable because Thai
(as well as other Southeastern Asians) find light skin more beautiful than
dark skin.

Stories and Scripts

As shown earlier, Brandon believed that the stories used by ligeh and
mawlum moo were the same. Originally this was quite untrue, though
today lum moo troupes tend more and more to play Central Thai stories
which are sometimes played by ligeh as well though in different versions.
The most important difference between ligeh and Northeastern theatre is
that the former does not use a script while the latter does. Ligeh actors
first memorize typical passages but then following stereotypes learn to
improvise their own song texts. That every actor among the hundreds of
ligeh troupes in Central Thailand is a gifted poet is obviously impossible,
but the ligeh ideal is extemporized poetry. Whether ligeh actors are good
poets, bad poets, or rely upon memorized material does not change the
fact that they do not use scripts.

The earliest stories performed by lum moo were of Lao origin, jataka
or local tales. Ligeh-lao usually performed Prince Wetsundawn written in
glawn poetry, but one early troupe interviewed performed only Nang Daeng-
awn. The maeng-dup-dao troupe performed only Tao Kooloo Nang Ua.
Kanah Indah, the first lum moo troupe, began with Nang Daeng-awn but
later used Jumba-seedon when training new troupes. Central Thai literature began to be introduced into the Northeast by two means, government
schools directed from Bangkok and Central Thai movies. Although audiences still tend to prefer the Lao stories and jataka, the deemphasis of
the traditional temple school and an nungsü reading at funeral wakes have
diminished the familiarity of the old stories.

An examination of the stories listed by the forty-two troupes and a
comparison of lum moo and lum plün reveal certain patterns. The seventeen lum moo troupes interviewed played a total of forty-eight different

stories, but the twenty-five lum plun troupes played only thirty-two stories. It has been asserted before than lum plun troupes tend to be less professional, and this is borne out statistically in that the repertory of the lum moo troupes averaged 7.6 stories while lum plun troupes averaged only 2.4. Furthermore, five lum plun troupes played but one story while all lum moo troupes played two or more. In listing their repertory lum moo troupe leaders most often mentioned the story of Galaget, a Lao jataka though only five troupes used it. The other stories which three or more troupes used were also jataka--Took-ka-dah Bung-kum, Tao Gum-gadum, Nang Daeng-awn, Sooriwong, and Seeton-Mano-rah--but the last of these is better known in the Central and Southern regions of the country. The remaining stories, mentioned only one or two times, were either jataka or Central Thai novels.

Lum plun, however, not only relied much more heavily on a few stories, but ones imported from Central Thailand. Twelve troupes out of twenty-five perform Koon Chang Koon Paen, five of them this story alone. Five troupes perform the Siamese literary work Pra Apai-manee by Soontawn Boo, and four troupes perform Gaeo-na-mah, the earliest lum plun story. The remaining stories were mentioned only one or two times and included both jataka and Central Thai novels.

This is not the place for a treatise on either Central Thai or Northeastern literature, both extensive and complicated subjects, but the following information would be helpful in understanding how lum moo and lum plun have come to play such a variety of stories. Koon Chang Koon Paen has been known in Central Thailand for nearly two hundred years and is believed to be a historical novel based on the life of Koon paen, a military officer at Ayootayah born in 1485. The story was set in poetry by a number of writers in the early nineteenth century including Soontawn Boo and published in 1872. It is primarily identified with sepah recitation, a kind of entertainment in which a reciter tells a story in melody accompanied by two pairs of wooden blocks called grup. The story concerns a marriage agreement between the kings of Ayootayah and Lan-sang (the old Lao kingdom) which was frustrated by the King of Chiang-mai and is thus of historical interest to Lao people. H. H. Prince Bidya has dealt with this story in some detail in the Journal of the Siam Society.[11]

Pra Apai-manee was written during the reign of Rama II (1809-1824) by Soontawn Boo (1786-1856), the greatest poet of the Bangkok era (the current era following the destruction of Ayootayah in 1767). M. L. Manich Jumsai believes this story parallels some of the chaotic events in the life of its writer who lost favor with Rama III and was exiled during most of his remaining years. The poetic form was klong and the language Siamese. Both Koon Chang and Pra Apai-manee, when played by lum plun, however, use Lao versions written in glawn.

Both Gaeo-na-mah, the first story played by lum plun, and Seeton-mano-rah, the second, are thought to be jataka, but the third story, Koon Chang, which was first set into Lao glawn by Boon-num Goon-gaeo in 1955, illustrates the strong Central Thai influence on lum plun. Mr. Pun Silaruk, who joined the Paw Roongsin troupe soon after it began in 1953, had lived in Bangkok and seen ligeh and other Central Thai forms. He also mentioned the influence of Bangkok-oriented textbooks, and thus these are the most likely routes by which Central Thai literature penetrated the Northeast.

To illustrate the nature of the Lao stories, brief summaries of two of the most popular stories are included, Galaget and Nang Daeng-awn. Both are sung in <u>lum pün</u>, <u>lum rüang</u>, <u>lum moo</u>, and <u>lum plün</u>, and excerpts of them are sometimes sung in <u>lum glawn</u>. Both stories vary in details from version to version, and these summaries provided by Jarünchai Chonpairot provide only the outlines.

Galaget

A king, Sooriwong Get-dalat, retired to the forest to learn martial and magical arts from a <u>rüsi</u> (hermit). Before returning home he met Prayah Kroot, a kind of bird, who became his friend. The latter sent him to meet a friend, the giant Goom-pon, after which the king returned home. Soon he desired a son, then a wife for the son and prayed to Pra In for these blessings. Pra In heard the prayer and sent a boy named Galaget and a woman for his wife, but she had been born in a city of giants.

It happened that the king had a magic flying horse and warned Galaget not to go near the beast, but one day his son mounted the horse for a trial ride and landed in the city of giants. There he discovered a beautiful young girl picking flowers in her family's garden, but because he was invisible he could ride on the cart with her undetected. That night at midnight when she had gone to bed, he went to talk to her and attempted to make love to her, but she resisted. He said he would leave, but she asked him to stay and become her husband. From then on he slept with her at night and hid in the garden by day.

One day a servant noted that someone was sleeping with the girl and told the king who ordered the man killed. One night the guards succeeded in killing Galaget, but before he died he told his wife to send the horse and his body away on a bamboo boat. Prayah Kroot, flying overhead, saw them floating on the water and took them to a <u>rüsi</u> who nursed Galaget back to life. Galaget then returned to his wife in the city of the giants. During the day he was a chain of flowers on her head and at night enjoyed her in bed. A servant again discovered his presence, but when the king tried to have his men kill Galaget again, the latter turned on them and killed everyone in the town except the king and his wife. His wife begged Galaget to bring them back to life, which he did, and the king realized that this was no ordinary man. The king asked Galaget to rule, but he preferred to return home. The journey was difficult, and he fought many battles with snakes, giants, and elephants, but the giant Goom-pon who had befriended his father attempted to seduce Galaget's wife. They fought but neither could dominate. The giant sent a message to Prayah Kroot to come to his aid, but when the latter arrived he identified Galaget as a friend. Consequently the battle was suspended and all returned home to King Sooriwong.

Nang Daeng-awn

Jukree Mahwong, prince of Gosee and son of King Paranasee, went hunting with his friends and servants in the forest. Having become lost, they made camp and retired for the night near a large pond. Prince Jukree dreamed that under the pond lived a beautiful maiden, a premonition borne out the following day by his retainers. After he returned home he sent an ambassador to seek the girl's hand in marriage. Though the girl was indeed human, all other inhabitants of the underwater city were crocodiles. Over the objections of her family, she accepted the prince's offer and the couple together lived happily for several years.

One day a hunter sighted a white elephant, a sign that Jukree should become king. While he and his men were out capturing the beast, Jukree's six other wives, whom he married after Nang Daeng-awn's arrival, became jealous when the latter gave birth to a son at the same time one of the six did. Fearing that Nang Daeng-awn's son would inherit the throne, they switched her baby for a crocodile and bribed all witnesses with silver and gold. Upon his return the new king was told that he wife had given birth to a crocodile begat by a crocodile husband. Enraged, he beat her and drove her into exile in the forest.

Her trials were severe and she prayed to the god Pra In to help. Hearing her supplications he told her to return to her family where she told them all that had happened. Both the elder and younger brothers moved to the king's city where they lived in the water and devoured anyone who came near. The elder brother, desiring to learn magical arts, retired to the forest. Nang Daeng-awn accompanied him riding on the back of a crocodile, but the brother died causing his sister such grief that she too died. Pra In, sensing that something was wrong and seeing both of them dead, administered a special water which restored them to life. The brother retired to become a rüsi and she to be a Buddhist nun.

At this time there was a giant who roamed the forests looking for food. One day he found a beautiful lotus flower which he gave to his wife. A few days later as she was praying to the gods before the flower a young woman appeared from its petals who became the giant's daughter. He offered to build her a house in the garden, but she overheard some giants plotting to eat her and became afraid to live there. Her stepfather searched through many towns to find female companions for her. One who agreed to come was Nang Daeng-awn.

The king's son, who had been kidnapped and replaced by a crocodile, had been secretly protected by an angel. Growing up, he learned the martial arts. One day he went to the fields where his father's horses were kept and told the servants they actually belonged to his mother, Nang Daeng-awn. A battle ensued and four of the king's generals sent to fight the intruder were killed. Then the king came to do battle with him but neither could succeed. After asking many questions, the king learned the truth. Together they sought out Nang Daeng-awn, fighting many giants before regaining her. Then all returned happily home.

Troupes acquire scripts by three means: (1) new troupes purchase them from their teachers during training. These may or may not be newly arranged versions but they are used exclusively by troupes trained by that teacher; (2) the more successful troupes can afford to hire a professional writer to pen their stories which then become their exclusive property; (3) the poorest troupes sometimes purchase printed scripts published and sold in Kawn-gaen and Roi-et. These scripts, available to anyone for a few baht, are rarely the work of gifted writers.

Almost without exception the script writers were formerly monks during which time they learned traditional poetry and literature. No women are known to have composed poetry or written scripts. Mr. Pim Rudanakonsat, age sixty of Kawn-gaen, is one of the better known writers in Northeast Thailand today. Before becoming a novice in 1928 he completed three years of elementary school. After reaching twenty-one he served for two years as a monk in Korat province, continuing his education in the temple. from 1938 until 1957 he was a public school teacher in Kawn-gaen province but had already begun his writing career in 1932 at age nineteen. He is able to write poetry in both glawn and glawn gap forms and has written texts for mawlum glawn and mawlum moo but refuses to write for lum plün because he dislikes the genre.

Mr. Pim writes his poetry by hand into a ledger book which is at once the draft and finished version. He never keeps a copy of his work, and if another troupe requests the same story, he begins anew. Although Chawiwan Dumnün, who formerly lead her own troupe in Mahasarakam, said Mr. Pim charged four thousand baht for a script which took one week to write, Mr. Pim himself said he charges only one to three thousand baht and that they take one month. He regularly writes for three troupes including the elite Oobon Putana troupe as well as at least one mawlum glawn. In addition he writes scripts for the Thai government which are used on radio and television. The government Information Ministry sends him contracts outlining the subjects and timing of each section. At the time of the interview (1973) Mr. Pim was writing a mawlum glawn text about progress in agriculture, education, and news of the country including the floods that destroyed the rice crop in the North in 1973.

The scripts themselves reveal much about the construction of a mawlum moo play. Following a list of dramatis personae, some scripts such as one penned by Mr. Pim for the Chawiwan troupe, give a list of chapters or sections. These, however, do not constitute acts or scenes, for the performance is continuous from beginning to end. The only "rule" of construction surmised by Chawiwan was that a character must speak following a passage of singing, but even this is not hard and fast in practice. She stated that all sung and spoken material relating to the story including the part for the comedian is written into the script, but troupes may add dancing, dün glawn poems ("walking in the forest"), or the comedian may improvise additional material. Before each portion of text the author indicates the character and whether the passage is sung (lum) or spoken (poot). Mr. Pim notes when dancing is to take place, when lum döi is to be sung, and marks entrances and exits.

The following excerpt from the beginning of the lum plün story Dap Seree-pap (Freedom Sword) by Jarut Grai-gaeo published in Kawn-gaen in 1960 illustrates the form of a script although this story is not traditionally Lao. The spelling and tone system used in both hand-written scripts and published versions is that generally used by singers and Northeasterners. Mr. Pim stated that while he knew the correct and consistent system, he could not use it because the singers would then misinterpret the words.

Dramatis personae

Roong-fah, lead male (pra-ek)
Chaw-fah, second lead male (pra-rawng)
See-fah, second lead male (pra-rawng)
Oon, servant of lead male
Gawng, servant of second lead male
Da-boon, owner of the house
See-nuan, daughter of Da-boon
Da-bio, manager of a cock fighting ring

Roong-fah goes to meet his girl friend in the garden. Roong-fah sings from inside.

Please listen to me, listen to my words. The troupe will now perform a story according to an old folk tale. Other performers will be permit-

ted to imitate this poem later if they like. (He shows only his face
to the audience and sings.) With the curtain open the scene is brightly
lit. Hello, dear girl friends sitting over there. (Roong-fah comes
from behind the curtain, then sits on the bench and sings.) Oh fortune.
I raise my hands and bow my head to pay respect to the god Pra Kanet
and to the Three Gems. Please come and sit near me; prevent trouble
from ruining my singing. May the audience enjoy and praise my voice
and my words.

Now I want to tell you about the city of Saen-wee. Jao Lüan-fah, a
brave and famous king, has ruled Saen-wee with moderation. His subjects are happy. The king has two wives, See-jan and Gaen-gaeo.
See-jan has given birth to a handsome son named Chaw-fah. Gaen-
gaeo also has a handsome son whose name is Roong-fah with whom
many girls fall in love. Everyone in Saen-wee is proud of Roong-fah.

(Roong-fah speaks) My greetings to the audience. My name is Roong-fah.
I am the son of Jao Lüan-fah's second wife. Jao Lüan-fah has two
wives, See-jan who has a son named Chaw-fah, and Gaen-gaeo who has
a son named Roong-fah. I am Roong-fah. I am in love with a daughter
of Prayah See-wiang, my teacher, but I never let her know. Tonight
I shall ask my friend Oon to accompany me for a courting visit.

(Roong-fah sings) I, then, shall get out of the golden bed and look for
beautiful girl friends.

(Roong-fah sings in the fast tempo.) Oh, my friends, I see a pretty girl's
face and I'd like to say hello to her, but she is too far away. I wish
I could win her heart. Oh, I am falling in love with that girl, that
girl (He leaves the stage.)

Oon enters, sits on the bench, and sings.

Now that I've opened the curtain and gotten out of the room, I shall sit
alone. I am here to look for my girlfriend, but no one is here. My
name is Oon. I look like a flour bag on a verandah. I am not really
lazy, but I like to sleep during the daytime. In the evening I put on
my clothes and come out to dance.

(Oon speaks) My name is Oon. I am a close friend of Jao Roong-fah.
Every day he asks me to accompany him when he goes courting. He
hasn't come yet today, so I must wait for him here. (Oon sits on the
bench and waits.)

Roong-fah sings from inside.

I shall reach Oon's house soon, but I must continue walking. (Roong-fah
comes out from the curtain and sings.) Now I have arrived and I
shall call out to him.

(Roong-fah speaks) Hey, Oon, my dear brother, please take me to your
girlfriend's house. I have been thinking of her a lot and my heart is
nearly broken. Can you do it?

Oon speaks.

Of course. I would always do what you ask me, anything for the master.
I'll follow you anywhere, through holes, caves, anywhere you go.

Roong-fah speaks.

Excellent. Let's go.

(Roong-fah sings) Since Oon has decided to go with me, we must leave
immediately.

Oon sings.

You go first; I'll follow you.

(Oon sings in a fast tempo) I am a servant walking along a dirt street.
The dust flew onto a girl's skirt. I must hurry because I have far to
go. Hey, who is your boyfriend? How beautiful you are! (Oon leaves
the stage.)

See-fah sits on the bench and sings.

Oh, this is a bright scene. Please do not leave and go home to sleep. I,
the one who is singing, am See-fah. I am not as beautiful as the other
girls, but if you would like to be my boyfriend, please stay here and
listen to the performance until dawn.

(See-fah speaks) My name is See-fah. I am the daughter of Prayah See-
wiang who is a teacher in Sean-wee city. Every night I go to the
garden to pick some flowers for my father, and tonight I shall go
there as usual.

(See-fah sings) I, a slender girl, after finally making up my mind, shall
leave the golden bed and make haste.

(See-fah sings in a fast tempo) Oh, my boyfriend. When I see your handsome face I would like to say hello, but I am afraid you might ignore
me. If you love me, please send me a letter. I'll await your letter
at my house. (See-fah leaves the stage.)

Roong-fah and Oon come near the bench and Roong-fah sings.

Now I have reached the gate of the garden. She always comes to pick
flowers in this garden every night. Oon, please wait for me here
while I enter the garden to meet my girlfriend. [12]

Of the numerous troupes observed only one performed without a script
as in ligeh. This exceptional troupe, called Kwunjai Wiangnüa, was formed
in 1973 and is based in Ta-düa, a small town along the Maekong a few
kilometers southeast of Wiangjun, Laos. Although no mawlum moo troupes
have been founded in Laos, several including this one have migrated there
because audiences across the river are increasingly interested in lum moo.
The members of the troupe were all veterans of the stage, however, some

for as long as twenty years, and had come from such diverse places as Korat, Mahasarakam, Nawng-kai, and Chiang-rai in the North. Some of them performed old-style lum moo and others contemporary style. Performances were extemporized from the memorized repertory of poems known to each singer but with changes of name and place to suit the story. The director of this troupe, unlike that of troupes using a complete script, was constantly busy assigning parts to actors, instructing them when to enter, and what the next events were to be. The interview was interrupted periodically by actors wishing to know who they were to be next and what the situation would be. Their repertory was therefore vast but more heavily weighted with old Lao stories than many troupes in the Northeast. Lao audiences not only prefer Lao stories as opposed to Central Thai stories, but require them to be played in a more conservative fashion without the artistic violence committed so often in Northeast Thailand.

Musical Performance

While a technical discussion of singing in both non-theatrical and theatrical genres with appropriate transcriptions appears in Chapter 4, the following material will provide an introduction ot the latter subject. The theatrical genres which precede modern lum moo made use of three distinct singing styles. Ligeh-lao and maeng-dup-dao theatre in the Roi-et area used the yao scale sung in tang yao, parlando-rubato meter; the ligeh-lao troupes known to Mr. Tawin in Kawn-gaen province, however, more closely imitated the style of ligeh-tai which is a kind of recitation though using the yao scale. The earliest mawlum moo troupe, Kanah Indah, made use of the same melody as lum pun or lum ruang, these making use of the yao scale but with the addition of a sixth pitch, a b c d e g a. In all cases the tempo was slow and there were noticeable pauses between lines.

Later mawlum moo troupes sang the pentatonic yao scale in parlando-rubato, and continued the pauses between lines, a performance style now called old Kawn-gaen style mawlum moo. These troupes also added dun dong poems ("walking in the forest") whose scale remained yao but the rhythm became metrical. These poems are technically called dun glawn in lum moo and could be added at the will of the troupe since they were rarely part of the script. It was not until the early 1960s that mawlum moo began to change to the vocal style heard today. In 1963 mawlum glawn singer Chawiwan Dumnun, at age eighteen, became the leading lady of the Rungsamun troupe in Oobon. Chawiwan had already established a career at age fourteen and like most lum glawn singers from Oobon used a "sweet" vocal quality combined with a more flowing line and longer melismas. Lum moo had not been particularly favored in the Oobon region until then, but when Chawiwan added her refined Oobon style singing to the Rungsamun troupe, it became an instant success. Since survival depends on popularity, other troupes soon followed suit with the result that the flowing Oobon-style mawlum moo became dominant. Consequently Kawn-gaen style with its pauses and dun glawn poems has become less and less common.

Through the years troupes have sought to add musical variety to their performances by adding new melodies. Besides the dun glawn found only in old Kaen-gaen style, all troupes now use lum doi as well. They are doi tumadah, kong, and pamah, but doi hua non dan is especially characteristic of lum moo. This latter melody, which is related to lum kawn-sawun from southern Laos, is also called dŏi mak-ngiu-dawng-dawn (dŏi "of the kapok pods swinging in the wind"). When a couple is in love they will often join hands and sway back and forth as they sing dŏi hua non dan suggesting the swaying of kapok pods. An earlier name for this melody was dŏi see-poom-dŭm, a term which is now often misunderstood by younger mawlum. It is ironic that while dŏi hua non dan is identified with mawlum moo, its best singers are mawlum glawn. The reason is that the latter are more highly trained than either lum moo or lum plŭn singers. Unfortunately, however, lum glawn singers have no regular opportunity to perform dŏi hua non dan.

Mawlum moo may therefore be compared to the early German Sing-spiel or English ballad opera, a spoken play with singing. The older Kawn-gaen style troupes, at least according to available recordings, used more spoken dialogue than Oobon troupes where dialogue was often short or even missing. Depending on the script, the sung portion may last less than a minute or as long as five minutes. A short monologue or dialogue may or may not follow and then the singing continues. Both lum tang yao and the dialogue keep the story moving, for the occasional interruptions of lum dŏi, dŭn glawn, or popular songs are only rarely part of the story; they are added for the pleasure of the audience. Many troupes now end their performance with a short lum glawn cycle consisting of tang sun, tang yao, and lum dŏi such as would be heard on a thirty-minute radio program.

Lum plŭn offers more variety of rhythm than lum moo but also tends to become a monotonous cycle. Whereas the lum tang yao in lum moo is serious and melancholy, its mood in lum plŭn is rarely serious. Before lum plŭn actors enter the stage they sing a short and highly stereotyped version of lum tang yao from behind the curtain into the microphone used by the accompanists. Almost invariably the poem begins with the phrase "but pah gung" or "but man gung" meaning "open the curtain." For exam-ple, such a line might read, "Now as the curtain opens I see a pretty girl standing before the door. I hope she will stay there until I can get close to her." The actor then enters the stage to strongly accented music sing-ing this second lum plŭn style. The scale remains yao but the rhythm be-comes metrical and the tempo becomes rapid. After the poem the accom-paniment continues while the singer dances fawn style for a minute or so. Such is the musical pattern of lum plŭn, a repeating cycle of lum tang yao, the faster music, and dancing. Dialogue may occur before or after the faster music.

In both genres the comedian may sing, but his part is mostly spoken. He usually speaks in a highly mannered fashion with obvious speech pecu-liarities such as a drawl, falsetto, strident breaking quality, or that of an old man. When he sings his style may parody that of the other singers. The tone is again mannered, often falsetto, and with exaggerated orna-ments.

The instrumental accompaniment for the early genres varied consider-ably. Maeng-dup-dao singing was accompanied by an ensemble of kaen, pin, saw bip and ching, while ligeh-lao singing in both Kawn-gaen and Roi-et privnces was unaccompanied. The first mawlum moo troupe began with a kaen ensemble but in 1956 changed to solo kaen. From the beginning mawlum plŭn's accompaniment has been kaen and pin. A few mawlum moo troupes today combined saw oo (fiddle with a coconut corpus) with the kaen or in one case observed, an electronic organ. In both genres the instrumentalists may continue to play improvisations in lai yai or lai noi modes during spoken dialogue. Both genres have also added percussion

instruments, especially lum plün which now requires a Western drum set
and a conga drum to play during tang sun and may be used to punctuate
the dialogue as well. The instrumentalists sit or stand on stage in full
view of the audience. When there is a drum set, it is also on stage right
in front of the kaen and pin; the conga drum is on stage left. The instrumentalists, who are always male, are notoriously nonchalant while playing,
often puffing on a cigarette hanging loosely from their mouths.

Whereas ligeh is basically an acting tradition requiring effective dramatic action, mawlum moo and mawlum plün grew out of singing traditions, and the acting tends to be rather amateurish. As noted earlier,
action centers around the microphone hung in the center of the stage,
stifling any possibility of dramatic dialogue. Actors who are not speaking
or singing usually stand around expressionless until their next line or poem.
Stylized fight scenes are rather rare and performed without the skill of
Chinese theatre after which they were probably modeled. In lum plün the
action centers around the dance while in lum moo action occurs during
dialogue.

Lum moo and lum plün's rise to popularity brought with it the necessity of keeping up with fashion. Older people still enjoy lum glawn, but
the younger people now flock to lum moo, plün, and Westernized competition such as rum wong and popular music troupes. There is no doubt that
Western popular music and its Thai imitations have completely captivated
the young people of Thailand both in cities and villages. Beginning in the
late 1960s a few troupes, in order to lure greater audiences, began adding
the drum which when played with lum döi, dün glawn, and lum plün gave
the audience a modernized beat like that of pleng look-toong (popular
songs). During this same period an English rock band called The Shadows
led by Cliff Richards visited Thailand and created a sensation similar to
that caused by the Beatles in the United States about five years earlier.
Soon thereafter the word "shadow" became synonymous for rock band in
Thailand. In the early 1970s the leading troupes began adding rock band
concerts before the plays to attract audiences. Today only the poorest
troupes fail to entertain audiences for up to an hour with Western instruments and dancing girls in mini-skirts or hotpants who endlessly repeat a
simple routine accompanied by castanets. The Rungsamun troupe, for example, which was the elite lum moo troupe of the late 1960s, split into
three troupes in the early 1970s, the current Rungsamun troupe, a second
lum moo troupe headed by Chawiwan Dumnün, and thirdly a slick popular
music group which now takes the latest in Bangkok musical fashion to the
remotest of villages.

The manager of the well-known Oobon Putana mawlum moo troupe
said that he added a "shadow" in 1971 because audiences demanded it.
Audiences require their entertainment to be "modern," and anything
Western, brightly lit, and loud is considered modern. Troupes seek to
impress audiences with powerful amplifiers, a variety of Western instruments, beautiful girls in chic Western clothes, and the latest popular tunes
from Bangkok and abroad. It is even necessary for pop singers to sing in
English when doing American or British songs. Furthermore, these instruments and songs are now intruding into the play itself. Several prominent
troupes were observed adding popular tunes to the story though the texts
were not related to the script. It must be admitted, however, that few
popular ensembles heard in Northeast Thailand displayed much understanding of Western harmony.

Theatrical genres in Northeast Thailand began less than thirty years ago but during this short period have undergone rapid and continuous change. The rate of change has accelerated dramatically since 1970 with the introduction of Western popular music into rural Northeast Thailand. Troupes scrambled to keep up with each other in the latest fashion; a leading troupe discovers an innovation, and all others must then follow suit or lose their fickle audiences. Things Western and modern are good; things Lao are bad. The intrusion of popular songs into the actual story is the most disturbing change today, and this development which began only about 1973 is having a profound effect. A few troupes have already replaced the kaen with an electronic organ. It seems quite possible that sometime in the future there will be "mawlum moo" troupes performing only pleng look-toong, the popular tunes which plunder traditional material. Of the two major genres, lum plün appears to be the most popularly oriented. A number of lum moo performers and writers spoke of their refusal to be associated with lum plün, and yet this genre is crowding out lum moo because it is cheaper to hire and provides the catchy rhythms demanded by today's youth.

Economic Considerations

Lum moo and lum plün are performed for the same occasions as lum glawn, primarily Red Cross and temple fairs, tumboon (merit-making parties) celebrating ordinations or festivals, and special occasions such as the Northeastern Music Festival or New Year's Eve. A French Catholic priest also told me that Christian Lao living near Oobon and also in Tarae district, Sagon-nakawn province have lum moo for Christian festivals even though the stories are often Buddhist jataka. Performances begin about 9 p.m. with popular music before the story begins. Although a troupe can tailor its performance to the sponsor's requirement, shows ordinarily last all night ending about dawn. The troupe sleeps by day, often in the bus or truck on the way to the next engagement, and the crew sleeps during the show. Life with a successful lum moo troupe is demanding, but most of the participants are young and do not mind; for a few years it is a pleasant diversion from the austere life in a village.

Lum moo and plün enjoy greater popularity in Roi-et, Mahasarakam, Galasin, Kawn-gaen, and Oodawn provinces than in the others. Lum glawn is still more popular in Oobon province, parts of Kawn-gaen, and neighboring Chaiyapoom province, however. It has proved impossible to determine exactly how many troupes are actually playing in the Northeast today, but some estimates run as high as one thousand. The number of small lum plün troupes, mostly of a very amateurish sort, is proliferating. The manager of the Oobon Putana troupe estimated there were only fifty professional troupes.

Of the forty-two troupes interviewed, thirty-eight came from only three provinces, Mahasarakam (twenty-two), Roi-et (eight), and Galasin (eight). These figures must be qualified because many were attending the music festival in Mahasarakam which naturally attracted mostly local troupes. The distribution of mawlum associations, which proliferated at the same time that lum moo and plün became popular, also reflects the above conclusions, though. Of sixty-eight known associations, forty-three are in five provinces, Kawn-gaen, Mahasarakam, Oodawn, Roi-et, and Galasin. The four provinces heavily populated by upland peoples, namely Nawng-kai, Sagon-nakawn, Loi, and Nakawn-panom, have together only thirteen while the Khmer provinces, Soo-rin, Sisaget, and Boori-run, have only three among them.

Each of the forty-two troupes was asked where they had given performances. Nor surprisingly all had performed in Mahasarakam province. The next most commonly mentioned provinces were Galasin, Roi-et, Kawngaen, Chaiyapoom, and Oobon. Seven troupes had played in Boori-rum and Korat and five in Laos, but very few mentioned the remaining provinces. Surprisingly a few troupes mentioned Central Thai cities and provinces including Bangkok, Brajin-booree, Ayootayah, Nakawn-sawun, and Petchaboon. This is not difficult to understand because of the large number of Lao living in Bangkok as temporary workers or elsewhere who descended from the early nineteenth-century population exiled from Wiangjun.

The cost of hiring troupes depends on two factors, their reputation and the distance travelled. Because troupes charge higher fees for performing greater distances from home, organizations and individuals are inclined to hire nearby troupes unless a specific troupe is desired. One informant, asked why lum plün had become so popular stated that it required fewer people, less training, and was thus less expensive.

A large number of troupes interviewed, especially lum plün reported equal division of money after expenses because troupe members were related or from the same village. The professional troupes, however, pay actors according to their importance. The manager of Oobon Putana said that he divided his personnel into four groups: first class, leading characters; second class, secondary leads; third class, comedian and musicians; fourth class, king and queen figures and miscellaneous characters. A smaller lum moo troupe from Galasin province reported that leads received 120 baht each, king and queen figures seventy, and all others fifty baht for a night. The range for individuals in another troupe varied from thirty to eighty. In lum plün the range was most often from fifty to one hundred baht. In comparison to lum glawn singers who earn equal fees but have fewer people to pay, theatrical people have very modest incomes. Since troupes do not perform year round, even the leads of all but the best troupes must return home to farm during the rainy season when performances cease. The lowly actors and musicians who receive but fifty baht a night are only marginally better off than such humble people as tricycle taxi drivers making from twenty to thirty baht a day. The leads are relatively well paid if they receive one hundred baht or more a day, but this is still very modest compared to that received by even the lesser-known lum glawn singers.

For many young people the bright lights and excitement are enough to lure them from the village into a troupe, and while the monetary rewards are slight, the work is more pleasant than farming. Thus it is common for the youth of a village to form a troupe however amateurish and sally forth into the world of entertainment for a few years before taking up the less exciting career of a farmer. The training required of a lum moo singer is still modest compared to that of a lum glawn singer, but it is possible to form a lum plün troupe and acquire training within a month or two. Theatrical performances, because they lack the element of competition, do not require quick-witted singers with an extensive repertory of poems. Most lum moo and lum plün singers can perform only those styles and parts in perhaps only a single play. But the attractions remain, and as a result lum moo and lum plün remain vigorous expressions of Northeastern traditional culture.

NOTES

1.   For further information on Central Thai instruments, see Dhanit Yupho, Thai Musical Instruments, or David Morton, The Traditional Music of Thailand, both listed in the bibliography.

2.   Brandon, Theatre in Southeast Asia, p. 70.

3.   See Chapter 2, p. 42.

4.   Kanah means "troupe."

5.   Lum tang yao is normally accompanied by either lai yai or lai noi depending on the singer's voice range. The use of lai soi is therefore unusual and contradicts the arrangement of the scale.

6.   See Chapter 3, p. 83.

7.   Doi hua non dan will be discussed with transcriptions in Chapter 4.

8.   Lakawn rawng is spoken drama with popular or classical songs attempted in Central Thailand, but it has not become popular.

9.   Michael Smithies, "Likay: A Note on the Origin, Form and Future of Siamese Folk Opera," Journal of the Siam Society 59-1 (1971):41-2.

10. Ibid., p. 42.

11. H. H. Prince Bidya, "Sebhā Recitation," pp. 1-22.

12. Jarut Grai-gaeo. Dap-seree-pap [Freedom Sword] (Kawn-gaen, Thailand, 1960), 1: 5-7.

IV.

The Technique of Singing

Poetry

The two previous chapters, which dealt with nontheatrical and theatrical singing genres, purposely avoided introducing technical details, and thus no musical examples were provided. The subject is best approached as a unit since similar problems prevail in all genres. Chapter 1 includes a brief introduction to Lao glawn poetry but only as encountered in written literature. Its inclusion there was necessary because references to glawn poetry are made in Chapters 2 and 3. The present chapter attempts to answer the question "How does a mawlum sing the text?" The goal, in addition to seeking fundamental principles, is to explicate the techniques of several representative singers from each performance style and genre.

The poets who provide mawlum with texts use three poetic forms: ordinary glawn (called glawn yün in Laos), glawn gap (glawn dut in Laos), and glawn see (gawn see in Laos), the latter encountered only in introductions to lum tang sun (metrical style). Furthermore, sung poems often include additional stereotyped phrases at certain points or such phrases may be added spontaneously by singers. Kawn-gaen style singers often insert short sections of prose either from the written text or improvised for the occasion. It is these often topical prose sections spoken like poetry which may lead observers to the faulty conclusion that mawlum improvise their poetry.

Ordinary glawn and glawn lum--that composed specifically for singers--are written in four-line stanzas called bot. The individual lines, called bat, each have names--wak sadup, wak hup, wak hawng, and wak song--but because singers do not ordinarily use these terms, I shall refer to them as the first, second, third, and fourth lines. Each line consists of seven basic syllables which separate into two phrases (wak) or hemistich having three and four syllables respectively. Multi-syllable words, however, may bridge the caesura, a technique called yut dipung. Any of the initial six syllables may be followed with an added syllable, however. While this implies that a line might theoretically consist of up to twelve syllables, in fact it is rare to encounter lines of more than nine or ten. Poems also admit prefixes (kum boopabot) and suffixes (kum soi) normally consisting of two syllables each. Certain performance styles such as lum tang yao (parlando-rubato) permit both, but <u>lum tang sun</u> (tempo giusto) ordinarily admits only prefixes.

There is, moreover, a tonal scheme which is followed rather closely by poets, requiring certain written tonal signs over specific syllables in spite of the fact that the tones produced differ considerably from consonant group to consonant group and dialect to dialect. Line 1 requires <u>mai-to</u> (√) over the third main syllable; line 2 requires no tonal sign to be placed over the third main syllable but <u>mai-to</u> over the seventh; line 3 requires <u>mai-to</u> over the third syllable and either <u>mai-ek</u> (') over the seventh or that syllable to end with a hard consonant such as p, g, or t; line 4 requires <u>mai-to</u> over the third and fifth syllables and no sign over the last:

Line 1	____	____	√	____	____	____	
Line 2	____	____	-	____	____	____	√
Line 3	____	____	√	____	____	____	' (b,g,d)
Line 4	____	____	√	____	√	____	-

For singers, especially in <u>lum tang sun</u> (metrical), one of the most important aspects is rhythm. In a little known article written in English but published in an otherwise Thai-language collection, James N. Mosel best explains the rhythmic quality of Thai (and by extension Lao) poetry using the term "demarcative rhythm."

Thai of course is unable to produce the stress-type of metric foot because the Thai language has no marked stress; each syllable is given about equal stress, or at least stress differences are non-phonemic. . . .

We see, then, that the two approaches to producing a metric foot, either through using vowel length or stress cannot be successfully applied to Thai. The metric foot based on stress is totally impossible in Thai, while the foot based on vowel length, as attempted in <u>chan</u> verse, is laborious if not awkward because of the dearth and unpleasing sound of short-vowel syllables in Thai.

The second way of creating rhythm in language is to abandon counting in terms of some one kind of sounds (such as short vowel or stressed vowel) and to count in terms of the total number of syllables only. This kind of poetic rhythm is known technically as demarcative rhythm. One simply courts syllables, without regard to any unit of time (such as vowel length) or other quality of the syllable (such as stress). . . . Demarcative rhythm therefore tends to require rigorous rules as to the place of the caesura and the division of verse into sections, lines, and stanzas. And furthermore, as we shall soon see in the case of Thai, because demarcative rhythm is more difficult to apprehend than foot rhythm, it is frequently necessary to strengthen and give added emphasis to the caesura by means of other phonetic devices (such as tones and rimes).[1]

When Lao <u>glawn</u> poetry is sung in <u>lum tang sun</u>, which has a steady beat in a duple framework, the downbeats tend to give certain syllables in each line stress which Mosel stated is not, strictly speaking, a part of Thai poetry. In order to avoid the word "stress," I shall use "accent" which shall imply stress in a lesser degree, a concept that is not foreign in <u>lum tang sun</u>. If the line consists of only the seven basic syllables, the accents fall on the first, third, fifth, and seventh syllables with a rest after the final word. Translated into rhythmic musical notation, each of these four accents amounts to a sub-beat within within a 4/2 measure. Lao poetry, however, like much Southeast Asian music, is end-accented, i.e., the greatest accent falls on the final syllable of the line. The second half of the fourth beat, that reserved for a prefix or rest, is actually the beginning of the next rhythmic unit; in transcriptions, however, the lines will be kept intact for clarity.

Figure 34. Rhythmic divisions in a single line of <u>glawn</u>.

The extra syllables which may be added after any word borrow either one half (equal division) or one fourth note value (dotted pattern) from the main word. Prefixes, which consist of two syllables, are placed as upbeats to the line and borrow the final beat (normally a rest) from the previous line:

First beat	Second beat	Third beat	Fourth beat
1 1a 2	3 3a 4	5 5a 6	7 7a (prefix, beat to next line)
o o o	o o o	o o o	o o
♩.♪ ♩	♩.♪ ♩	♩.♪ ♩	♩.♪ ♩.♪

(Figure 35 continued on next page.)

First beat	Second beat	Third beat	Fourth beat
1 ⋮ 2 2a	3 ⋮4 4a	5 ⋮ 6 6a	7 ⋮(prefix, ⋮beat to ⋮next ⋮line)
o ⋮o o	o ⋮o o	o ⋮o o	o ⋮o o

Figure 35. Rhythmic divisions in a complex line of glawn.

Bang-kum's epic poem, Sung Sin-sai, which exemplifies glawn poetry at its best, rarely consists of more than ten or eleven syllables per line including the prefix; the basic seven-syllable line is probably more common than are the more complex forms. The poetry, however, avoids degenerating into mindless sing-song rhythm because words vary greatly in length and in number of syllables since a two-syllable word such as müa counts as one. The following stanza from Sung Sin-sai illustrates a glawn stanza with a number of extra syllables.

Mee hang poo bet poon │ ken kat pong ga sut

2/4

Jing koi jum kah kio │ kao hao pai pee

Müa nun kawn ta win toi │ taem ta wai nop nawp

Müan dung boon baeng sun │ boo han kawng kawt gun

(Please note that the vertical slashes in the poetry indicate the caesura while those in the rhythmic notation indicate metrical divisions.)

In traditional literary poetry, ordinary rhyme (sumput sara--"vowel rhyme") plays an insignificant role while alliteration (sumput ukson--"consonant rhyme") gives the lines a euphony that the Lao immediately associate with poetry. Alliteration occurs most commonly in groups of two or three words, while groups of four or more syllables are considered unusual, even cacophonous unless used for special effect. Sung Sin-sai is also replete with an alliterative rhyme combination called suppa-gawt in which the fifth and seventh words are identical in sound but not tone, the latter giving them quite separate meanings. The following verse from Bang-kum's epic illustrates both ordinary alliteration and suppa-gawt:

Line 1   Ling hen mai lao lom lian hawm kao hawm

Line 2   Poo tawn lut liap pa nawng num nawng

Line 3   Hen pah guang kao kum koi kum

Line 4   Doi nun in daeng dung kao hüang hoong hüang[2]

(Note: Two lines under a syllable indicate alliteration, and extended lines show rhyme.)

The following verse with lines from the preceding and following stanzas added is taken from a poem sung by Mawlum Boonpeng and illustrates the rhyme typical of glawn lum though perhaps in unusual abundance (When the final syllable rhymes with one in the following line, it must occur on either the first or second accent.).

Line 4   . . . püi yaem gaem see

Line 1   Dawk mai nee mee yoo nai dong

Line 2   Mee gah long gah lao kae kao kae kawm

Line 3   Jawm jai nawng mawng dün plün sün

Line 4   Kün kok hawm dawk mai pleng lawng glawm jai

Line 1   Yam müa glai nawng. . . . [3]

Though following a text, singers are inclined to add words or phrases to the lines which often have little or no meaning but which make the line smoother or extend a prefix into a full phrase. These euphonic words (kum soi) are often found in prefixes and suffixes where they are integral to the written line but of an exclamatory, interrogative, or supplicatory nature. The most common prefixes include but nee ("now"), denun ("henceforth"), and müa nun ("at that moment"); common suffixes include gawn laeo ("first"), jing laeo ("surely"), and de-naw ("I beg you"). Singers are also much inclined to add the phrases, jung wah, la maen, la maen wah, and sala dü which have no easily translatable meanings, as well as nang oi sao and nang oi nang meaning "Oh my sister"; they also may add syllables such as si (future tense auxiliary), ga, and la between words. The syllable dü in sala dü is a corruption of sala nü ("let it be") and must be pronounced with the latter's tone--high falling--rather than the mid tone of dü as written.

Glawn poetry is used throughout Lao-speaking areas. Today's writers tend to use more rhyme than earlier writers, but the form is otherwise little changed. Glawn is used not only in written literature but in pa-nyah (ritual courtship), all forms of mawlum, tet lae (the monk's entertainment singing), and in Northeastern shadow puppet theatre (nung bra-mo-tai). All singers, whether literate or not, must understand the structure of glawn, know how to divide the lines into accents or beats, where to place the prefix, and how to distinguish each line. Singers who use poor quality poetry or whose rhythm is mediocre cannot be successful in their careers.

A second form of poetry which mawlum, especially Kawn-gaen style singers, use is called glawn gap or gawn dut. A listener unacquainted with the technical aspects of Lao poetry would probably not be able to distinguish ordinary glawn from glawn gap although the latter form consists not of stanzas but continuous lines interlocked with rhyme. The glawn gap used by mawlum is not to be confused with a simpler form of gap as in gap süng bung fai, the responsorial song sung by drunken revelers at the rocket festival (boon bung fai).[4] Glawn gap, like gap süng bung fai, consists of lines having seven words or syllables, the last of which rhymes with the third of the following line. In practice singers often add the syllable ga between the third and fourth words. There is no tonal pattern except that rhymed pairs must have the same tone sign. Glawn gap differs from gap süng bung fai because it has a greater number of syllables per line.

As in glawn, a line of glawn gap divides into four accents requiring therefore at least seven syllables and thus can be notated in one 4/2 measure, the last beat of which is a rest. As in glawn, the final syllable has the greatest accent and the following half beat is the beginning of the next line. The final syllable of the line (fourth beat) should rhyme with the word or syllable falling on the second beat of the following line. Prefixes similar to those of ordinary glawn may intercede and are given an upbeat borrowed from the end of the previous line. Any two adjacent accents may also be separated by a euphonic phrase which interrupts the beat.

Jung wah fung dü jao puak tan sot tah

Kon rao get mah hai ra wung hai mak

Ra wung müa ra wung bak müt suan tung gai

Bak baw dee chip hai tum pit dai tot

Glawn gap may be used throughout a mawlum's poem, in a contrasting section for variety, or in introductions. Glawn gap, however, is not the preferred form and constitutes but a small part of Lao literature.

A third form of poetry encountered in mawlum texts is called glawn see (glawn "four") which is found only in the introductory portions of lum tang sun. Glawn see also occurs in continuous lines rather than stanzas but has only two accents per line, one of which always falls on the final word. A line of glawn see consists of at least three syllables, but allows up to two syllables preceding each accent for a maximum of six. Glawn see is best known through a traditional custom called sok (from chalok or salok), a method of predicting luck based on the length of an object. Sok poems are recited as participants place their hands around a pole and alternate upwards saying a line for each hand. When they come to the pole's end, the last line of poetry is used to determine the future. Glawn see may include rhyme at the ends of phrases, or the last word of a phrase may rhyme with the first word of the following phrase. The following example taken from the introduction to a lum glawn poem, however, does not display rhyme.

Ao dawk mai ban kum

La mah boo sa tam

Ga ta wai glawn lum

Hong mah rup ao pon

Mawlum glawn

Lum tang sun

Although lum pün is generally considered to be an older genre than
lum glawn, the clear separation of lum tang sun (tempo giusto using the
sun scale) from lum tang yao (parlando-rubato using the yao scale) in the
latter facilitates an easier understanding since these two rhythmic forms
are often mixed in lum pün. Furthermore, Oobon style lum tang sun,
which is less complicated than Kawn-gaen style, will be dealt with first.
As explained earlier, the differences between Oobon and Kawn-gaen styles
are only clear among those singers whose styles can be characterized as
"pure Oobon" or "pure Kawn-gaen," but most contemporary singers tend to
combine elements of both making the distinction less valid. These cases
often require a native speaker with some knowledge of lum to make the
distinction. On a personal level, I have come to appreciate the differences
only with great difficulty and when certain obvious factors to be explained
later are present.

The term sun literally means "short, brief, concise, succinct."[5] The
concept results in syllabic text setting. Lum tang sun, therefore, implies
both mode (sun scale) and rhythm. Lum tang sun poems consist of two
parts, the introduction and the body. The introduction in turn breaks into
three parts, the first and third of which are similar. Many refer to this
opening section as the "oh la naw" because the opening words are these.
"Oh la naw" derives from the greeting, "oh naw nawng oi" meaning "oh,
my dear." "Nawng oi" refers to the other person in a polite way while
"naw" is defined as "a final exclamatory particle."[6] It is a gentle way of
telling the audience to give its attention since the poem is about to begin.

As discussed briefly in Chapter 1, the sun scale used for singing lum
tang sun in lum glawn is a pentatonic scale consisting of the following
intervals: whole step, minor third, whole step, whole step, and minor third.

The kaen may accompany this scale in any of three modes or positions,
sootsanaen, bo sai, or soi depending on the singer's range. Soi is, however,
rarely used, and while bo sai was formerly the most common, sootsanaen
has become so today. Regardless of actual pitch, transcriptions will always
be notated using the following pitches according to the accompanimental
mode to facilitate comparison.

Example 4. The pitches of the sun scale expressed in the three kaen
modes to be used in transcriptions: (1) sootsanaen, (2) bo sai, (3) soi.

A complete explanation of the kaen modes will be found in Chapter 6.

Material regarding lum tang sun is based on five transcriptions as well as examinations of additional poems and aural analysis of other recordings. The excerpts transcribed here (see pages 109 to 132) include three representative samples of Oobon style and two of Kawn-gaen style. They are:

A. Oobon style
   1. Mawlum Boonpeng (female); six full stanzas (twenty-four lines) from a poem entitled "lum plun" after one of the two major Northeastern theatrical genres (Example 5)
   2. Boonpeng; the introduction and 2½ stanzas of a poem entitled "glawn gio" (courting poem) (Example 6)
   3. Ken Dalao (male); the introduction and 3½ stanzas (nineteen lines), five later lines which include an interlude for kaen, and the final two stanzas (eight lines) including the cadence. The title of the poem is "Poo bao gae poo sao sum noi, glawn gio" (An old man courts a young girl) (Example 7)
B. Kawn-gaen style
   4. Choompon Nonta-luchah (male); forty-six lines with introduction of a glawn gio poem in glawn gap form (Example 8)
   5. Plunpit Gaw-kum (female); thirty-three lines of a glawn gio poem including a change of mode technically called see tun dawn which changes to a dun dong ("walking in the forest") poem (Example 9)

Please take note of the following: (1) the line number of the glawn stanza is given in a circle; (2) vertical lines in the text indicate prefixes and caesura; (3) words in parenthesis were added to the structure of the line; (4) letters underlined with two short horizontal lines and a vertical slash indicate alliteration, two longer lines under a word indicate rhyme with a word in another line, and connecting lines indicate rhyme within the line. The pitches indicated are relatively clear without portamento. Northeastern Thai musicians assert that excellent singers match the pitches of the kaen clearly. The tuning of the kaen is described in greater detail in Chapter 5. Until then, suffice it to say that semi-tones approximate one hundred cents and whole-tones two hundred cents.

Assuming for discussion the use of sootsanaen accompaniment, lum tang sun opens with a brief improvised introduction on the kaen using figures characteristic of sootsanaen. The introduction's length varies from six to about sixteen 2/4 measures, then cadences on the finalis, g. Sometimes near the cadence the mawlum will audibly match pitches with the kaen's finalis to clear his voice and establish the pitch. The "oh la naw" almost always begins a fifth or sixth above the finalis (on d or e), rarely ascending higher than this. The first two syllables, "oh la," are sung to one or two notes each, but the "naw" receives extended vocalization that gradually descends with trills and other embellishments to the note above the finalis, then finally to the finalis itself. The kaen accompaniment during the "oh la naw" is always softer than during the introduction. In some cases the player merely holds the finalis sonority. If he plays patterns, he needs to join the singer only on the last two or three notes. The "oh la naw" is then followed by a short interlude on kaen similar to the introduction.

The middle section opens with one of many stereotyped phrases which

(Example 5 continued on following page.)

Example 5. Lum glawn (tang sun) "lum plün" sung by Boonpeng.

(Example 6 continued on following page.)

(Example 6 continued on following page.)

Example 6. Lum glawn (tang sun) "glawn gio" sung by Boonpeng.

(Example 7 continued on following page.)

(Example 7 continued on following page.)

(Example 7 continued on following page.)

(Example 7 continued on following page.)

(Example 7 continued on following page.)

(Example 7 continued on following page.)

Example 7. Lum glawn (tang sun) "glawn gio" sung by Ken Dalao.

(Example 8 continued on following page.)

(Example 8 continued on following page.)

(Example 8 continued on following page.)

(SPOKEN)

(19) AO LAEO PAN BAI LAEO MÜA NÜNG MAEN BAW PAW MAE PEE NAWNG

(20) BUT MÜA SAWNG DAW RAWNG GUN SIN MAH

(21) POP GUP PAI KOON PLÜN PIT KÜA GAO

(22) AO LA MÜA WAN NEE DAI GIO GUN BAI NAE

(23) MUK GUN LAI DÜP YOO WAH NUN TAO

(24) PIM GUP PÜN NEE KIT NÜK NÜK MIK MIK NAE YOO

(25) MÜA LUM BEN GA DI GA DUNG SAH NAE JUK NOI HAH NEE AO

RHYTHMIC VALUES SOMEWHAT FREE

(26) JUNG WAH | FUNG DÜ JAO PUAK TAN SATTA TAH

(Example 8 continued on following page.)

(Example 8 continued on following page.)

Example 8 continued on following page.)

(Example 8 continued on following page.)

Example 8. Lum glawn (tang sun) "glawn gio" sung by Choompon.

(Example 9 continued on following page)

(Example 9 continued on following page)

(Example 9 continued on following page.)

WAO WAO HAWNG GAI SUN (24) BAT TEE NUN JAK LAWNG SOM

LUANG (25) MOO JUANG JUN HAWM YOO DONG PONG MAI (26) DÜ LA DÜN DAM

KAO BAI HUNG BAN BAN BENG (27) DÜ LA KENG MAK MAI MÜI PRAWM PRUM

BAN (28) DAWK YOO BAN BAN YIANG DAO RÜANG (29) TUNG DÜAN

JIANG GAE JAWM GA YAWM GOOM (30) JUNG WAH KOOM KOOM

NEE NAH REE SA MUNG AO LA NAW BAT NEE LONG WAI WAH GLAWN

(32) SA NEH LEN DE LIANG NAWNG NAE NAH

KAEN   (FINAL WORDS OMITTED)

Example 9. Lum glawn (tang sun) Kawn-gaen style sung by Plünpit.

may be extended into full poetic lines through repetition and use of euphonic words. Virtually all phases begin with gaem meaning "cheek," then
adjectives describing them. The following list includes those most often
encountered, but gaem bah lah is the most popular: gaem bah lah ("big,
pink cheeks"); gaem bee lee ("small, pink"); gaem awn awn ("soft"); gaem
mai mai ("young"); gaem um tum ("purple"); gaem awng dawng ("small,
fresh color"); gaem ong dong ("big, fresh color"); gaem bing sing ("small,
proud of beauty"); gaem bang sang ("big, proud of beauty"); gaem bun wun
("big and beautiful from a distance"); gaem bin win ("big, proud of beauty");
gaem baen waen ("small, thin cheeks"); gaem boi loi ("small cheeks"); gaem
baeng saeng ("small, proud of beauty"); gaem uan suan ("chubby cheeks").

   A few examples in expanded form taken from actual performances include: "gaem oi gaem bah lah kun gaem oi bah lah" (Boonpeng); "un tum
gaem oi um tum" (Sai-tawng); "la gaem oi gaem bun wun nawng bun wun"
(Ken). Exceptions to the above may be found from time to time, especially
in poems deviating from the usual glawn gio ("courting poem") routine.

   The remainder of the introductory poem is in glawn see, glawn gap, or
a combination of the two. In many kawn-gaen style introductions there
are also short prose passages. The last word of this introductory poetry
should have a mai ek (') tone mark or the last two lines when combined

should constitute a complete fourth line of glawn poetry. To complete
the passage there must then be an ending phrase consisting of three words,
the last of which has a mai toh (√) tone mark causing the voice to sing
a falling interval or lower pitch. If the word does not have mai toh, the
singer must execute the word as if it had one. This ending phrase is often
sung melismatically and leads then to a cadence on the finalis.

The final "oh la naw" is both preceded and followed by kaen interludes
similar to those described earlier. The ending of this phrase may be extended slightly, however. Many singers use "nuan oi" meaning "cream-
colored" and implying "cream-colored cheeks," or "nang oi" meaning
roughly "oh woman." Mawlum Ken's final words are often "sui laeo,"
meaning "ah, beautiful," a phrase that has become his trademark.

As explained earlier, the first "oh la naw" begins a fifth or sixth above
the tonic (on d or e in sootsanaen mode) and gradually descends by way
of trills, melismatic passages, and sustained pitches until the finalis, g,
is reached. Converting all pitches to sootsanaen mode for comparison,
the three introductions transcribed reveal surprising consistency in range
and starting pitch. The starting pitch of the first "oh la naw" is always
lower than that of the second. Furthermore, the range is greater in the
second "oh la naw" than in the first, removing it further from the finalis
or point of relaxation and thus creating greater tension. Figure 36 compares both starting pitches and range among the singers whose introductions were transcribed:

Singer	Initial Pitch (1)	Range (1)	Initial Pitch (2)	Range (2)
Boonpeng	e'	g-a' (9th)	g'	g-c" (11th)
Ken	e'	g-e' (6th)	g'	g-a' (9th)
Choompon	d'	g-e' (6th)	a'	g-c" (11th)

Figure 36. Comparative chart of initial pitches and ranges of the "oh la
naw" among three mawlum singers.

The poetry framed by the two "oh la naw" is rarely sung in measured
accents but is closer to parlando-rubato or even speaking. The range is
restricted to the lower notes, a, c', d', e', or rarely the octave g' but
may use as few as the lowest three. The finalis, lower g, is avoided until
the cadence.[7] The style may be semi-melodic as in the case of Boonpeng
and Ken (Examples 6 and 7), or it may be recited in a nonmelodic fashion
as by Choompon (Example 8). Choompon's introduction, perhaps because
it opens with Pali proverbs, is sung in a style resembling Pali chant, but
the same style prevails when the Lao poetry begins. The kaen accompaniment rarely matches the signer's part either melodically or rhythmically until the cadence is approached, at which time the kaen must follow
the singer.

The subject matter of the introduction varies greatly. If the introduction and main poem were written together, the former provides the audience with a preview or summary of the latter. If the main poem lacks an
introduction, the singer may borrow one from another poem whether appropriate or not. The subject of the introduction might be religious
doctrine and that of the main poem love. Introductions often pay respect
to the Buddha, the singer's teacher, or may include bawdy jokes. Informants indicated that the introduction often reveals whether the singer will

use bawdy jokes in his main poem or avoid such humor. This section of the gap after the first "oh la naw" must include at least two lines of poetry, but for some it can be much longer, up to sixteen or more lines.

The terms Oobon style, Kawn-gaen style, and Chaiyapoom style are used freely by singers and audiences alike. The Lao term for style is baep or wat (e.g., baep Oobon) and means "model, type, style." [8] While most informed listeners and trained singers use these terms, they do not as readily define or delimit them. A generation ago when transportation was almost nonexistent and singers rarely travelled further than the next province, differing manners of text setting developed in relative isolation. Today this is no longer true because singers travel freely, listen to records and the radio, and may study with teachers from outside their home province. Oobon boasts the best mawlum glawn singers and even claims to be the birthplace of mawlum glawn, but Oobon's location is not central. Consequently many well-known singers and troupes from that province have gone to live elsewhere. Younger singers tend to mix the styles today making the distinction less clear.

As far as can be determined, the differentiation was formerly quite valid. Old Kawn-gaen mawlum glawn was a contest of knowledge usually between two males since females lacked access to education in temple schools. The term used to define the type was mawlum jot or jot gae. The subjects were religion, literature, geography, and history. Oobon singers, however, usually sang of love (glawn gio) and performed in pairs, male and female.

To a sensitive listener there are fairly obvious differences between the two styles even today. The tempo of "pure Oobon" singing is much slower than Kawn-gaen, and the vocal line of Oobon is more melodic than that of Kawn-gaen where the inflections of speech sometimes cause it to sound jagged; indeed, the most obvious difference is the recitative manner of delivery that dominates in Kawn-gaen as opposed to the more flowing, lyrical manner which characterizes Oobon singing. The manner of setting the poetry's accents is also different, though this distinction is less obvious to someone not acquainted with the poetry. When an Oobon singer performs a dun dong poem ("walking in the forest"), the melody remains as in "glawn gio," but Kawn-gaen singers usually "modulate" from the sun scale to the yao scale which is considered more emotional than the sun scale. The kaen too must change mode, from lai sootsanaen to lai noi. An example of this phenomenon may be seen in Example 9. Distinguishing the two styles according to accompaniment was also formerly possible when Oobon style used bo-sai almost exclusively (according to older informants), but today Oobon singers use sootsanaen as often as Kawn-gaen singers.

The poetry, besides differing in subject, often differed in form since Kawn-gaen singers were more inclined to use glawn gap while Oobon singers use glawn exclusively (except for the introduction). The poly-syllabic words of Pali or Sanskrit origin which naturally dominated texts about religion and other learned subjects were difficult to fit into the glawn rhythms or tonal scheme, and, in fact, prose was sometimes necessary to explain something that simply would not fit into a poetic line. As a result Oobon poetry was not only easier to write than Kawn-gaen poetry, but easier to sing.

Many of these differences have been diluted today, for Kawn-gaen singers now sing glawn gio too but in their own way. Because Kawn-gaen style was formerly more popular than Oobon style, it could afford to maintain its identity, but in recent years Oobon style has become far more popular, and Kawn-gaen singers have tended to alter their singing habits to meet popular demand. The term Chaiyapoom style was used by many singers to denote Kawn-gaen style singing that imitates Oobon style, that is, emphasizes love as a subject; it is also more inclined to smooth melodic lines with regular accents and less inclined to competitiveness, didactic subjects, and use of prose. Chaiyapoom province is south of Kawn-gaen, borders the mountainous area of the Central Plain in Petchaboon province, and is apparently an important area for mawlum according to the distribution of mawlum associations, but Chaiyapoom style singers do not necessarily come from this region. The term appears to be one of convenience to denote a newer style mixing Kawn-gaen and Oobon characteristics.

The poem proper begins soon after the second "oh la naw" and a brief kaen introduction. The first line is, however, not part of the glawn poem but a phrase of at least two accents (four syllables) or one line of glawn see which merges with the beginning of the poem. The phrases are stereotyped and difficult to translate literally but simply tell the audience the poem is beginning. Boonpeng's phrase in "lum plun" is longer than usual but divided into three phrases of two accents each:

maen wah dü nai / maen wao taw nee / maen paw soo gun fang

"Maen wah" and variations beginning with "maen" mean little more than "yes" or in the language of contemporary popular music, "yeah." The term dü is a corruption of nü and simply "an affirmative, emphatic, suffix" according to Kerr.[9] The three phrases loosely translated mean:

Yessir, mister / yeah, gather here / yeah, now let's get together

Boonpeng's phrase in another performance called glawn gio, "maen wah dio nee," simply means "yes, now." Mawlum Ken uses "la maen wah dü nang" or "yes, my dear." A singer named Jumbee sang, "ao dü nang oi nang," which translated into contemporary American English, might be "OK, my dear." Sai-tawng began with "ao nü fung ao nü" or roughly "OK, now listen."

The main poem then begins, either on the first or third line of the glawn stanza. The pattern then varies little except that half stanzas of either the first and second lines or third and fourth lines may come between complete stanzas, a characteristic found in written Lao literature as well. In Kawn-gaen style there is the possibility that a prose line may be inserted when the thought is unavailable in poetry, and in either style there may be a section of glawn gap, a characteristic of, for example, Mawlum Ken's poetry. When the poem is finished, the singer will indicate to the kaen player whether he wishes to continue or stop by how fast he sings the last line. Assuming he wishes to continue into a new poem, he sings the last line at full tempo and the kaen continues without break playing a short interlude. The new poem then opens as did the first one with a phrase such as "maen wah dio nee," but it is then immediately followed by a "changing phrase" which tells the audience essentially, "enough of this, now let us walk in the forest" (dun dong) or "enough of this, let us have a variety of poems" (betdalet), or whatever the next poem is to be. The changing phrases often begin with one of the following: paw krao laeo, laeo taw nee, wao taw nun, paw wah laeo, laeo but nee, paw

glao laeo, or wao num nee. Such changes occur rather frequently in
recordings I made because singers performed several favorite poems, the
last of which was usually dŭn dong.

When the singing is to stop or the singer is tired, the poem must have
an ending phrase which like other such phrases is highly stereotyped. The
most common is see nah nuan (cream-colored cheeks), but variations include nah [rising tone], nah [high-falling tone], nuan (same meaning), nah
nuan nuan, see nah wah (wah has no meaning but rhymes with nah), saneh
len de (lovely fragrant flowers) or see nah choom (good paddy field).[10]
If the phrase involves nuan, the next word should rhyme and is usually
suan meaning "to embrace" but literally "to shovel, scoop up with a flat
tool."[11] This means the singer is tired and needs the support of two
strong arms. If the phrase involves choom, the following word should also
rhyme and is usually doom meaning "cover from the cold." It means the
singer is cold and wants to be covered with a blanket or held tight in the
partner's arms. If the phrase ends this way, it should rhyme with the last
word of the line. In fact, however, both audience and singer disregard
accuracy and meaning after the initial phrase has been spoken, and many
singers either mumble, slide through, or even omit the words coming after
it.

A performance of a single lum tang sun poem by a mawlum glawn
thus consists of two basic divisions, the introduction (gap) and the poem,
with the former breaking into three parts, the first and last of which are
similar, forming an A B A' pattern. The complete outline follows:

A. Introduction
    1. "A" section
        a. kaen introduction
        b. first "oh la naw"
    2. "B" section
        a. kaen interlude
        b. phrase manipulating gaem and two other words such
            as gaem bah lah
        c. introductory poem in glawn see at least two lines long
        d. ending phrase of three syllables, the last of which has
            a mai-toh tone mark
    3. "A" section
        a. kaen interlude
        b. second "oh la naw" starting at a higher pitch and often
            having a short ending phrase
B. Main poem
    1. Opening
        a. kaen interlude
        b. introductory phrase
    2. Main poem
    3. Closing phrase

Mawlum Boonpeng's poetry is among the most artistic heard in the
Northeast region today. Because women do not customarily write poetry
even though many are capable of it, she acquired her poems from a male
teacher. The transcript entitled "lum plŭn" (Example 5) includes only the
second poem and was of course separated from the first by a short kaen
interlude. The excerpt opens with the third line of the stanzas incorporating "paw krao laeo" and words telling the audience that she will sing

a dŭn dong poem, but after only two lines she begins a new poem with a similar phrase, also using the third line of the stanza. Apparently after she began she decided to sing a different poem for us and simply started over.

The poem is saturated with alliteration, interior rhyme, and gap rhyme (the last word rhyming with a word in the next line.) Line 6 ends with the phrase "dao dan dong" with three alliterative d's which is immediately reversed in line 7 as "dong dan dao." Lines 15 and 16 are in Central Thai and are thus pronounced with those tones even though the double consonants are reduced to single and chun to sun according to Lao usage.   Scattered lines of Central Thai occur in many other poems too. Because of the effect on the singing, it is worth noting that Boonpeng's first and second lines lack prefixes while the third and fourth lines have them almost without exception. Such regularity is not a common feature in other examples observed although second and fourth lines do commonly end with a rest, especially the last which marks the end of the stanza. If the first line beginning the next stanza has a prefix, it is rhythmically handled in a different way. In the excerpt cited, only a few lines have more than seven syllables not counting the prefixes. Setting such poetry into rhythmic accents is relatively simple since each syllable requires but one quarter note. Each line therefore requires four 2/4 measures with or without an upbeat divided into two eighth notes.

The most striking feature of Boonpeng's singing is her use of syncopation. Syncopation occurs in eight of the twenty-four lines, but most commonly in first and third lines. Four lines have syncopation within the first two full measures, and four have it in the prefix. In the latter case the final syllable of the line receives an eighth note instead of the usual quarter, and the first syllable of the prefix receives a quarter followed by an eighth. Examples of the first type may be found in lines 7, 15, 19, and 24, while examples of the second occur in lines 6, 10, 18, and 22. Because the short notes which generate the syncopations do not necessarily occur on short vowels, there is no rational explanation for the phenomenon; it is simply a part of her style.

The overall shape of a mawlum's melody might be described as undulating since intervals larger than a fourth are normally followed by an interval or step in the opposite direction. David Morton also speaks of this characteristic in his study of Central Thai classical music.

Thai melodies are typically conjunct within a phrase unit.
It is to be understood that "conjunct" here means passing to
an adjoining pitch in the Thai pentatonic scale or mode, which
may be indicated in ciphers as 123 56 (1); what the Western
ear may hear as gaps between 3 and 5, 6 and 1 are not gaps
in the Thai musical sense. . . . Leaps to a pitch two steps
away in the Thai pentatonic scale and are not uncommon, the
melodic line turning after the leap and proceeding in the
opposite direction.[12]

Although mawlum singers commonly sing intervals of a fifth, even intervals of a seventh, such as from low a up to g' or vice versa are not unusual. Such leaps are nearly always followed by a pitch in the opposite direction. The overall range of Boonpeng's singing is an octave and a fourth, from g to c' in notation.

The term lum implies that there is no fixed melody, but rather that the singer generates the melody based on the word-tones. This way of realizing melody is not restricted to Northeast Thailand by any means, but studies explained exactly how it works are few and far between. This principle, as found in certain Chinese theatrical styles which use "aria types" as the basis of melodic realization of text (also called "system operas"), such as jing xi (Peking opera) and much of Cantonese theatre, is now being studied.[13]Determining exactly how mawlum realize the melody has proven extremely elusive and would probably require a substantial study beyond the scope of this book. While there is no doubt that lum is constructed in a logical and predictable way, isolating the invariables from variables, both of which are known instinctively to singers through life-long exposure to the language and music, may require far more extensive transcription and computer analysis. Preliminary analysis has not demonstrated a fixed system of realizing each tone on, above, or below an imaginary monotone center. If there is an underlying fixed structure of more than one pitch, with word tones behaving differently according to each, then the problems become much greater. There is also the likelihood that the underlying structure may vary from genre to genre, from "school" to "school," and even from person to person. Obviously, since the tonal system varies slightly from one province to another, this is another factor.

Nonetheless, in the case of Boonpeng, the fourth line of the stanza shows definite patterns. While the upbeat prefix is the same in only two cases, and the following two full measures are never exactly the same though very similar, the last two measures are virtually the same in all cases providing the listener an obvious way to hear the end of the stanza.

Example 10. The fourth lines from six glawn stanzas in Boonpeng's "lum plün" poem, example 5.

It will be noted that lines 11 and 15 make use of the pitch f which is not part of the scale. To a very limited extent Ken also uses this pitch. Boonpeng uses this "sour note" (siang som) in the first lines of the stanza. Her accompaniment is unfortunately too difficult to hear to be transcribed, especially because it tends to follow the singing line, but one characteristic apropos to the use of "sour notes" is easily noted. In sootsanaen, players sometimes alternate the usual pitches with f for short periods of time, an effect which to Western ears produces a dominant seventh effect that demands resolution.

Example 11. Excerpt from sootsanaen (Oobon style) played by Tawng-koon.

No kaen player would ever use the f in a cadence, and it may be assumed that to Lao ears the effect is also tension producing. Boonpeng's accompanist uses this harmonic effect whenever the first line of poetry returns whether the singer uses the f or not. The duration, however, is inconsistent, for it may last well into the second line though the singer is then emphasizing the triad c-e-g. In line 5 the player began using the f effect because he assumed Boonpeng would begin a new stanza, but as noted earlier she abruptly changed poems and again began on the third line of the stanza. The kaen player also used this effect elsewhere without obvious reason, but all singers who commented on accompaniment techniques stated that the kaen player is not required to follow the singer melodically (or by extension harmonically), only rhythmically.

Ken Dalao is probably the best-known mawlum glawn in Northeast Thailand, both through personal appearances and records. While he is somewhat notorious for his bawdy and often explicitly sexual texts, no one denies his complete mastery of singing. Ken claims to write his own poetry, but in fact some of it evidently came from others. The poetry is stylistically similar to that of Boonpeng, but there is less alliteration and interior rhyme. Only two lines in the excerpt (Example 7) have parenthetical phrases, lines 11 and 179. The first of these is three syllables, but the second is five. The first two syllables of the latter are sung as an upbeat and the remaining three as downbeats finally leaving an open upbeat for the regular prefix.

Of twenty-three regular lines of poetry, fifteen are set in the usual fashion of four 2/4 measures with or without an upbeat. Five, however, give the prefix two full beats resulting in five 2/4 measures. Lines 184 and 185, however, are irregular. The first of these results from a syncopation at the end of line 183 leaving but an eighth note for the prefix. Consequently the second syllable of the prefix coincides with the downbeat throwing the first two accented words onto weak beats. The third accent, on mawn, returns to normal. Line 185 begins with two full beats for each syllable of the prefix, but the third accent on tang is misplaced on an up-beat note throwing the rest of the line out of rhythm. The following line, though, is the closing line and thus the irregularity disappears as it merges with this also irregular line.

Ken's vocal range, in sootsanaen pitches, extends from g to a, a ninth, whereas Boonpeng had a slightly greater range, from g to c'. I shall con-sider the actual voice ranges in a later paragraph. Ken, unlike Boonpeng, emphasizes the lower a resulting in a generally lower tessitura. His fourth lines were not patterned as were those of Boonpeng, but one of them, line 180, was coincidentally identical. Certain melodic intervals such as a to d', c' to a, and g' to e' are quite common, but with only seven pitches available melodic figures are bound to repeat. In spite of these, the vocal line is not predictable, not a fixed melody, and can only be understood in terms of the lum principle.

In 1972 the government-owned TV 5 television station in Kawn-gaen sponsored a mawlum glawn contest for little-known singers. Finally a male and female were chosen and presented trophies. Far more than re-ceiving a mere trophy, the winners became famous overnight, could sub-stantially increase their fees, and became the singers to imitate in the eyes of budding amateurs. The winners were Mawlum Choompon Nonta-lüchah (male) and Mawlum Plünpit Gawng-kum (female), both Kawn-gaen style singers. Transcriptions of their singing are thus representative of the best heard in the Northeast today.

The extended transcription from a performance by Choompon (Example 8) including introduction and accompaniment, is set in glawn gap poetry whose form is interconnected lines rather than stanzas. The last syllable rhymes with the second accented syllable of the following line in a line consisting of four basic accents with at least three other syllables for a total of seven. There is virtually no interior rhyme or alliteration, how-ever. Lines 32 and 33, which show a decided break in the pattern, may reveal a memory slip repaired on the spur of the moment, for the last four syllables of line 32 and line 33, if joined together, constitute not only a complete line, but a complete thought, the other words being filler.

The second "oh la naw" is followed not with a poem but eight lines of prose which is spoken and unaccompanied. The poem begins at line 26 but without a regular accent until line 31 when the kaen finally joins, although it played a few notes in lines 27 through 30. Lines 31 and 36 are in a steady rhythm and conform to the rules found in glawn whereby a line without a prefix (or in glawn gap without upbeat syllables) begins on the downbeat and ends after four 2/4 measures. Line 32, however, become irregular again with the kaen playing stereotyped phrases at the end of each line until the end of line 45 when the regular accent returns.

The beginning of the poem, lines 26 and following, indicate an uncer-tainty regarding pitch and thus scale because the end of line 26 and begin-ning of line 27 outline an f-a-c triad whereas line 28 seems to outline a d-f-a triad though all presumably remains in the sun scale. There is also inconsistency with regard to note durations, and these are transcribed only approximately. In line 30 the second word, sawng, is as long as jai and jao, but given a short note. While jai sawng together constitutes an up-beat phrase to the main accent, jao, they are given long-short values. Conversely, the word pit in line 29 is a short vowel but receives as much duration as tum and dai, long vowels.

Distinguishing Oobon from Kaen-gaen or Chaiyapoom styles depends upon certain obvious characteristics being present although sensitive native speakers can make the distinction on the basis of far subtler factors such as the accent of the poetry. The introductory section of Choompon's excerpt is not markedly different from that of Boonpeng as far as technique is concerned. When the singer begins the unaccompanied section in speech-rhythm, however, there is no doubt that the performer is Kawn-gaen style. The presence of a transient modal shift between the sun and yao scales (sootsanaen and noi on the kaen), indicates not only a dün dong poem but Kawn-gaen style as well.

Finally, Example 9 was recorded by female Mawlum Plünpit, the other winner of the TV 5 contest. In Plünpit's excerpt there is a relatively long kaen interlude before the dün dong during which the player changes mode from sootsanaen to lao noi, and the remainder of the poem is sung using the yao scale but in tempo giusto. The poem here is also dün dong and the form ordinary glawn; there is little gap or interior rhyme, but alliter-ation is used extensively, especially for special effect in dün dong, as shown in the following passage:

ja nawn poom mai nawm naem num naem

goonah naeo nok num nee naeo mai

ga mawm maeo mao siang maeo hawng mao

lawah den dai kao kong kap koi kio

The transcription begins with the third and fourth lines followed by a prose sentence, then first and second lines of another stanza, another prose line, then the third line. The kaen then plays an interlude after which the sing-er begins with four lines of prose, then five full stanzas and a closing line. One unusual characteristic is that many lines have one-syllable prefixes.

The section preceding the mode change reveals that ordinary lines are set in the usual fashion except line 5 which is the second line. The latter divides into three sections: (1) tah fung dü; (2) tai isan; and (3) tai glang tai dai ("please wait to hear, Thai of the Northeast, Thai of the Central Plain, Thai of the South"). The prefix is three syllables instead of one or two (tah fung dü), the singer giving these two full measures, the second for the word dü and a rest. The section immediately following the kaen interlude describes a monkey climbing in a tree and dancing. The exces-sive alliteration, short melodic phrases, and patterned repetitions almost approach tone painting of this apparently humorous scene.

The dün dong poetry sung with the yao scale, a technique called see tun dawn, is set normally in seven of the twenty lines examined. The three exceptions, lines 15, 19, and 30, are easily explained. Line 15, be-sides being preceded by a phrase la wah den sung thrice, is abnormal in that it has only six syllables, but the total effect is six 2/4 measures with upbeat. Line 19 is normal except that the last four syllables are a repe-tition of syllables from the second hemistich. Lines 30 and 31 are normal in structure but sung in an unusual rhythm, for the second hemistich loses the accent, becoming free until well into the first hemistich of the fol-lowing line. Line 32, the ending phrase, returns suddenly to the sun scale and sootsanaen accompaniment. As is normal, the last few words are lost because the singer mumbled them, or to put it another way, slid headlong into the cadence without the slightest hint of a retard.

Before discussing word-tone and melody, two secondary matters, vocal quality and tempo, shall be dealt with. The first of these includes the voice ranges of the singers. Since the maximum range encountered in the transcriptions was a mere octave and a fourth (g to c'), it is obvious that mawlum do not require an extended range. Using their mid-range exclusively, they do not need vocal exercises to develop and maintain the extreme registers. The transcriptions are notated according to the accompaniment without regard to actual pitch, but using actual pitch, the singers' voice ranges become clear. The range of four singers in addition to those transcribed have been included. For each singer the lowest note should be comfortable though near the bottom of the range. All four females tend to have low voice ranges; none heard here or elsewhere exploited the higher range of their voices as is common in the West. The use of male falsetto was not encountered.

Singer	Notated Range	Approximate Western Range
Sai-tawng		mezzo soprano
Plŭnpit		contralto
Boonpeng		contralto
Kumboon		contralto
Jumbee		tenor
Choompon		tenor

(Figure 37 continued on following page.)

Singer	Notated Range	Approximate Western Range
Sui		baritone
Ken		baritone

Figure 37. A comparison of voice ranges of eight singers.

The study of mawlum singing does not, as far as is known, entail voice culture. The training concentrates almost exclusively on learning the poetry with correct accents, creating a beautiful melody from the word-tones, and enlarging the poetic repertory. Little or nothing is said of projecting the voice, breathing, or general vocal quality, although a singer whose voice is unpleasant to hear cannot become famous. The tone quality desired is said to be "sweet," but virtually no singer encountered exhibited vibrato or other characteristics usually described as desirable in a Western trained voice. The tone is slightly nasal but not to the extent heard in, e.g., Chinese theatre; it is ideally in tune with the kaen, neither flat nor sharp and sung crisply on pitch. The tone quality might be compared to that of American country-western or bluegrass singers or rural church congregations from the south, and especially Sacred Harp singers.

Singing tempos depend on two factors, the generation of the performer and the style, i.e., Oobon or Kawn-gaen. The correlation with age is not nearly so exact as will be encountered in regard to kaen solos in Chapter 6, but in general, younger singers' tempos are faster than those of older singers, and Kawn-gaen singers' tempos are faster than those of Oobon singers. The following table (Figure 38) of singers' tempos includes not only the singers previously transcribed, but others recorded in Mahasarakam and Roi-et provinces.

The average for the Oobon singers, including those of the Chaiyapoom style, is 109 within a range of 96 to 116. Kawn-gaen singers averaged 122 extending from 110 to 138. According to older informants tempos increased in recent years, and those of Choompon (127) and Plunpit (138), who represent youthful Kawn-gaen style, are among the fastest encountered. In the case of Plunpit the quarter note tempo would be 276, and if there are no extra words in each line of poetry, her rate of delivery is at least 4.6 syllables per second, truly remarkable. Even Mawlum Ken, whose tempo is considered fairly slow for today, delivers at least 3.4 syllables per second.

It might be assumed that the lum principle, with melody generated from word-tones, indicates complete coordination between these two elements. Detailed examination of the excerpts transcribed indicates, however, that coordination is neither one hundred percent nor do specified tones always generate specified melodic patterns. In deciding whether melody and tone cooperate or conflict, several compromises must be made. Lacking a set of rules enumerated by the singers, I have decided to accept

(A) Kaen-gaen style singers

Singer	Age	Tempo (beats per minute)
Tawng-luk	38	120
Som-gian	32	110
Tawng-awn	23	116
Somjit	23	132
Plünpit	23	138
Choompon	22	127
Lian-tawng	20	108-112
Sombut	19	120
Kumpun	19	120
Sai-tawng	18	114
Som-tawin	18	126-132

(B) Oobon style singers

Singer	Age	Tempo (beats per minute)
Som-sah	48	114
Ken	43	102
Boonpeng	ca. 40	108-116
Kumboon	38	116
Jumbee	ca. 30	100
Sai-tawng	?	96

Figure 38. Table of comparative tempos among Oobon and Kawn-gaen style singers in Northeast Thailand.

contour tones sung on a single pitch as coordinated if the following pitch is lower or higher according to the word-tone. In other words, if a high-falling tone is sung on g' alone and the following pitch is d', the word-tone is considered to be coordinated with the melody since there is no conflict. In the case of level tones, however, it is sometimes difficult to say which are coordinated and which are not.

George List, in a study of speech melody and song melody in Central Thailand found that coordination there varied from one hundred percent in a lullaby called "Boat and Rain" to only fifty-nine percent in a popular song based on a traditional classical melody.[14] Even literary recitation of a klong poem was coordinated only seventy-eight percent and recitation of the alphabet seventy-nine percent. If coordination is not present, however, the word is not automatically incomprehensible or changed in meaning, because it will be understood in context, or native speakers will know that the syllables sung to certain "incorrect" tones has no meaning and therefore must be something else.

An examination of Boonpeng's "lum plün" reveals the basic pattern encountered in all examples. In Oobon dialect words having a mai-ek (') tone mark in ukson glang and ukson tam are spoken on a mid tone rather than the mid-high as in Roi-et, but the tones are otherwise the same (see Figure 3 on page 10). The low tone occurs on three pitches, c, d, and e and also to an interval, c - a. The mid tone for words other than those having mai-ek is sung to a great variety of pitches--c, d, e, f, and g--as well as to any of seven intervals, most prominently e - g and c - d; in fact sixty-five percent were sung to intervals and only thirty-five percent to single tones. A pitch-tone word sung to an interval would seem to be confusing, especially with this frequency, but is usual in lum. The mid-high tone is sung to g while the mid-rising tone is sung to c̠, d̠, or g. Without regard to interval combination or relationship between high-falling and low-falling, ninety-four percent of the rising tone words, ninety percent of the high-falling tone words, and seventy-four percent of the low-falling tone words were coordinated. Line 8 from Example 5 provides an excellent and rare example of one hundred percent coordination. The tone numbers are those of Figure 3 on page 10 and will be followed through this section.

Example 12. Line 8 from Example 5 sung by Boonpeng showing one hundred percent coordination between word-tone and melody.

Line 25, however, illustrates lack of coordination where several falling tone words are sung to rising intervals.

Example 13. Line 25 from Example 5 showing lack of coordination.

The statistics regarding Ken's singing are much the same. The low tone was sung to c̠, d̠, e̠, or a̠, and the mid tone without mai ek to a single pitch only forty-six percent of the time while fifty-four percent were sung to intervals. The mid tone with mai-ek was sung to c̠, d̠, or e̠ ninety percent of the time and to other pitches or an interval only ten percent of the time. The rising tone was sung correctly fifty percent of the time, the high-falling tone eighty-three percent and the low-falling tone seventy percent. The introduction, however, showed somewhat greater coordination, for all contour tones were coordinated correctly except for one low-falling tone word. Lines 17 and 18 of the poem, however, reveal a purposeful lack of coordination generated by a desire for momentum and repetition. (Example 14)

It is perhaps premature to treat kaen accompaniment techniques at this point because kaen playing is yet to be explained in Chapter 6. Still, the basic technique is best dealt with here. As seen in Example 7 by Ken the kaen's role in providing an introduction and interludes during the gap is very important. When the singer enters, however, the kaen usually reduces its dynamic level, sustaining "chords" as during the "oh la naw" or playing figures as during the poetry coming between the two "oh la maw." In the latter case the singer and accompaniment are not necessarily together but rejoin only at cadences. The kaen is often silent or holds a

Example 14. Lines 17 and 18 of Example 7 sung by Ken.

sonority as the mawlum begins the body of the poem and attains a steady
tempo.

Two basic techniques for accompaniment of the main poem emerge.
The first is to play in unison with the singer. The player may deviate
from the singer's line and play passage of heterophony too as seen in
portions of Ken's excerpt. If the kaen player is able to play in unison
with the singer, this begs the question of how predictable or how consistent is the singer's line? The better mawlum have their own accompanists
who travel with them and have become very familiar with certain poems
and the overall singing style. It is not impossible that the melodies have
become so patterned for certain poems through repetition that the accompanist can remember them. This may be true enough though the same
words or phrases within a poem are sung to a different melodic phrase, a
fact observed many times such as in Ken's poem (Example 7) when lines
13 through 16 all begin with "ot sah," but only two of the four are sung
to the same notes.

The second technique is for the kaen player to repeat two-measure
patterns over and over with little variation. This is especially possible
in Oobon style where melody and beat are continuous, though the player
must watch for lines of five measures and adjust to them. Such patterns
may be observed in Ken (Example 7). I have heard them used by other
accompanists, some not recorded, with even greater consistency. Mawlum
Bunlung's accompanist is inclined to repeat patterns(1) and (2) as seen in
Example 15 three times followed by pattern (3), this equalling two lines of
the stanza.

Example 15. Accompaniment patterns used by Mawlum Bunlung's kaen
player.

There is no need for the singer and kaen player to match pitches for both are in the same scale. If the kaen player failed to follow the singer at the cadence, however, the result would be open to criticism. Similar patterns that have been heard over and over include the following

Example 16. Examples of patterns played in the kaen accompaniment.

In Kawn-gaen style when the singer begins a dǔn dong poem or uses see-tun-dawn technique, it is the accompanist's duty to change mode temporarily. He does this by changing the finger-held drones that accompany each kaen mode quickly and in rhythm rather than unplugging and plugging the drones with bits of beeswax (kisoot), the method followed in solos. The singing may signal the player to change mode by touching him or even saying or singing "yao kaen yao," which means to speed up.

Lum tang yao

Lum tang sun comprises approximately the first eight hours of a full mawlum glawn performance, from about 9 p.m. to 5 a.m. Lum tang yao, however, consists of but one poem per singer and lasts only fifteen or twenty minutes, coming at dawn when the performance is about to end. Though very short, it is highly concentrated in meaning; some in the audience may be brought to tears as the singers, now lovers (for stage purposes), must part.

The word yao (nyao in Lao pronunciation) means "long in reference to length, time."[15] In musical terms it means text sung melismatically, and implies parlando-rubato. Lum tang yao is closely related to an nungsǔ, the speech-melody reading of palm-leaf manuscripts at funeral wakes where, depending on the reader's skill, it might be very plain, almost like Pali chant, or if the reader possesses a good voice, the "reading" might become melodic with extended vocalizations. The scale for both lum tang yao and an nungsǔ is always the yao scale whose prominent minor third is considered plaintive by the Lao. The accompaniment on the kaen will be either lai yai or lai noi. The term lum tang yao is said to be a relatively recent one, for older singers and informants merely used the term an nungsǔ pook (reading a palm-leaf book") when referring to lum tang yao in lum glawn. The differences are in many ways superficial, for the addition of kaen accompaniment with a good an nungsǔ reader would result in a performance barely distinguishable from mawlum glawn. What an nungsǔ reading lacks is an introduction, called "oh nungsǔ." Technically, the poetry of lum tang yao is otherwise identical to that of lum tang sun although the glawn gap form used by some Kawn-gaen singers has not been encountered.

The transcription included to illustrate this section is by Mawlum Boondah of the Soontara-pirom troupe in Bangkok (Example 17). The distinctions between Oobon and Kawn-gaen styles so prominent in lum tang sun disappear in lum tang yao, although in mawlum moo theatre where lum tang yao is used almost exclusively, there were formerly slight differences.

Lum tang yao poems typically open with "oi," "oh laeo put oi," or "oi la naw" which is usually sung to an extended vocalization but is sung to a single note by Boondah. If the poem is a nitan (story), the singer begins immediately with the prefix "but nee" (now). The more common type poem is about love and begins with lines in either ordinary glawn or glawn see first invoking the sound of thunder: "fah oi, fah hawng huan" ("oh thunder, thunder rumbling"). The sound of thunder has deep emotional meaning to the Lao whose lives depend on the rain which causes the rice to grow. The distant sound of thunder invoked at night in an already emotional setting suggests the rainy season, the coming of a nocturnal downpour, the renewal of life. In Western terms thunder has some of the same connotations as spring. The "thunder" phrases in the poem, however, have become so routine and sung so perfunctorily that the emotional aspect is lessened. The introductory lines usually end with the phrase "la naw" or "la nah" sung to an extended vocalization, but in Boondah's example the vocalization is partly to "lai" with [la] "nah" coming near the end.

Boondah's excerpt (Example 17) illustrates the most usual way to begin the body of the poem. After two lines (5 and 6) which follow the introduction but which are not part of the glawn poem, the body begins on line 7 with the phrase "müt dae lum tang sun" (sometimes "müt pit lum tang sun") meaning roughly "now that we have finished lum tang sun."

The extended vocalizations are intended to heighten the emotional atmosphere of the poem, but their placement generally follows a pattern. If the first "oi" is not sung to a vocalization, the last phrase of the introduction must be. The last phrase of the body of the poem is similarly sung to a melisma, but whether any occur within the body will be determined by the singer. Boondah's poem totals forty lines, and melismas are sung on the twenty-fifth and final lines. These are not sung to heighten individual words and thus are not examples of text painting; they come at the end of a particularly meaningful line and serve to emphasize this to the audience, permitting a moment of contemplation. Their shape, unlike those of lum tang sun which are descending, tend to have at least two highpoints, the second just before the final descent to the finalis. As seen in lines 4 and 25 of Example 17, the vocalizations are usually approached by an ascending line immediately following a held cadential tonic note. The approach to the vocalization is highly patterned and can be recognized at once by the listener.

Before the advent of lum döi, which now completes a mawlum glawn performance, when lum tang yao ended, the audience went home. The final note of the evening was not the finalis, however, for it was custom that after holding the finalis (d in lai noi, a in lai yai), the singer ended on a short note one whole step below the finalis while the kaen continued to hold the finalis sonority. This may still be heard on some forty-five r.p.m. recordings where there is not time for lum döi. An alternate ending, however, is more common. The singer performs the last line of the lum tang yai in döi rhythm which is in tempo giusto. This type of ending, while common on the radio and records, is rarely heard in public performances.

(Example 17 continued on following page.)

(6) WAH JUNG DAI GAO BRA MUAN SEE

(7) MÜT DAE | LUM TANG SUN | HUN LONG YAO JAO TANG LAWNG

(8) SAWNG KON | HAO PEE NAWNG | MAH LUM GIO KAO SAI GUN

(9) WAH JUNG | DAI DE NAWNG | TAWNG GRA DING PUA MAK HING

(10) SI BAW | KIT LUM SING | NUM AI NAE BAW NAW

(11) LÜA HAENG | PEE MUN LOT HANG NAH JAW | GRA SONG WAH SI YING NOK

(12) SONG MAH | DON DAWN BLA | HAI PEE CHAI LONG SON

(13) (NEE LA NAW) PÜN WAH | GON GLANG LAED | SONG MAH DUN DUN BAWNG

(14) HAWNG SI | NEE JAK HUI | KUI SI ÜN SUNG NGUA

(15) TAW GLÜA | GLAI DUM SOM | BLAH TOO KEM SI GLAI JAED

(Example 17 continued on following page.)

Example 17. Lum tang yao sung by Boondah.

The form of <u>lum tang yao</u> is therefore:

A. Introduction
    1. "oi" or a phrase incorporating "oi" sung to either a single
        note or a vocalization
    2. A phrase incorporating "fah" (e.g., "fah oi fah") invoking
        the sound of thunder, or if a <u>nitan</u> poem only "but nee"
    3. Ending phrase such as "la naw" or "la mah" sung to an
        extended vocalization

B. Body of poem
    1. Introductory lines in prose or <u>glawn see</u> which lead into
        the <u>glawn</u> poem
    2. First line of poem often incorporating "mǖt pit lum tang sun"
    3. Main body of poem with optional vocalization
    4. Final vocalization ending the poem
    5. If <u>lum dǒi</u> is to be sung, a line linking the two sung in
        metrical rhythm; formerly the performance ended here
        and the final pitch was a whole step below the finalis.

Unlike <u>lum tang sun</u>, whose form is more consistent, <u>lum tang yao</u> may
vary somewhat within this general outline. Much in the introduction would
be added by the singer since the poet rarely writes these stereotyped
phrases. Some singers leave out much of the introduction, but others such
as Ken, might extend it to nearly twenty-five lines. The invocation of
thunder is not always used, neither is "mǖt pit lum tang sun."
    The range of most singers encompasses one octave though some may
rise above the octave of the finalis by a third (<u>f</u>" in <u>lai noi</u>, <u>c</u>" in <u>lai yai</u>).
These are rare, however, found normally within vocalizations and less
commonly within the poem. With such a narrow range, the melodic motives will obviously be fewer in number than in <u>lum tang sun</u> where the
usual range is greater. That the overall shape of the melody is undulating
because intervals are followed by a change of direction applies to <u>lum tang
yao</u> as well as to <u>lum tang sun</u>, but the intervals in the former tend to be
greater. The falling seventh (in <u>lai noi</u> from <u>c</u>" to <u>d</u>") is common, especially at the ends of lines whose word-tone is low- or high-falling.
    Tempo is a difficult matter to determine because the singer is in par-
lando-rubato, but the tempos of the <u>kaen</u> introductions are always relative
to the tempo of the singing although the two do not observe regular accents together. Of fourteen singers including the one illustrated here, the
tempos varied from ♩ = 110 to ♩ = 152, but the vast majority were between
130 and 140, and the average was 134. At this tempo the words are delivered with great haste which seems to contradict the statement that in
<u>lum tang yao</u> the emotional quality of the text is savored. Older singers
did not sing so rapidly, and in fact many Oobon singers tend to the slower
tempos also. The singing is always faster than <u>an nungsǖ</u>, however, which
itself might be slower than ordinary speech.
    Whereas in <u>lum tang sun</u> the four accents of the line fall at regular
intervals, and prefixes are handled according to rules, in <u>lum tang yao</u>
the accents nearly disappeared because there is no regularity of beat.
Even though the singer must bear in mind proper division of the lines into
prefix, first phrase, and second phrase, he rarely reflects these in his
rhythm. Except in the introduction and vocalizations where the range of
note values may vary from sixteenth to whole notes, the range of values

was mostly limited to eighth and quarter notes with occasional sixteenth and half notes. The distinction between long and short vowels, however, is not consistently observed in rhythmic values since syllables with long vowels might be sung to short notes and vice versa. The prefix, which in lum tang yao would be sung to two eighth notes, two quarter notes, or to a short-long pattern, and of course there is no downbeat on the next syllable to differentiate the prefix. Though there are numerous exceptions, most accented words receive a quarter note or interval requiring a dotted eighth, but because many unaccented words also may be sung to these values, the distinction is blurred. In transcriptions the eye can divide the beats by slightly changing note values here and there, and in a few passages measure lines could be drawn, but the ear cannot hear these accents unless able to understand the poetry technically. Transcriptions, in fact, reflect only relative note values because it is impractical to notate the exact values in conventional notation. The guiding principle is the natural rhythm of speech.

Because melodic considerations sometimes took precedence over word-tones in lum tang sun, coordination was rarely one hundred percent and might be as low as thirty-three percent. Lum tang yao, freed from rhythmic regularity and therefore the regularity of melodic motives, should embody the lum principle to its fullest extent; coordination should be one hundred percent. This ideal figure was rarely achieved, but in fact coordination was greater even to the point that specific pitch tones could be assigned to specific pitches in many cases.

The kaen accompaniment to lum tang yao is difficult to transcribe. Whereas kaen and singer had to keep to the same pulse in lum tang sun, in lum tang yao there is no regular pulse for the singer. The kaen player therefore plays a tempo giusto improvisation in either lai noi or lai yai depending on the singer's range throughout, regardless of the pitches or rhythms of the singer. It serves a background function, although the relative tempos are the same. The only time when the two must join is during cadential vocalizations when the accompanist must follow the singer, either sustaining sonorities, changing pitches as the singer descends or ascends, or attempting to follow the vocalizations themselves.

Lum döi

Contemporary mawlum glawn performances end not with the traditional lum tang yao, often also called lum lah (farewell), but with lum döi. There are three döi which may be used: tamadah (ordinary), kong (referring to the Maekong river), and pamah (referring to Burma). Although the elderly Mawlum Sui asserted that the word döi was interchangeable with dia meaning "short," it is more likely that it is a transmutation of dai meaning "south" referring to southern Laos. The styles of southern Laos most certainly influence döi hua non dan and possibly influenced the above three as well. The subject of lum döi is often love banter and allows the performance to end on a more cheerful note than if lum tang yao were the ending.

Döi tamadah uses glawn poetry sung according to lum principles, but the remaining two döi have texts written in the fashion of popular songs, that is, without a classical form, rhyme scheme, or tone pattern. All are sung to the yao scale but in tempo giusto; the meter, however, may be duple or compound duple depending on whether the kaen accompaniment consists of groups of three notes or dotted pairs. In performance the singers usually mix the three dŏi together without breaks between the poems, but dŏi tamadah usually predominates. Originally the language of dŏi kong and dŏi pamah was Siamese, but today the poems tend to mix Lao and Siamese, while dŏi tamadah was always entirely in Lao.

The three transcriptions together present several examples of dŏi tamadah, dŏi kong, and dŏi pamah. Example 18 was recorded jointly by Mawlum Boonpeng (female) and Mawlum Wichian (male), both of Oobon, and includes all three dŏi; Example 19 was recorded by Mawlum Kumboon also of Oobon and includes all three dŏi; Example 20 was recorded by Mawlum Ken and also includes all three. The complete performances, however, are many times longer than the transcriptions in which only selected poems were used to illustrate the techniques and problems of dŏi singing.

Dŏi tamadah. A single line of glawn poem requires at least seven syllables divided into two phrases, one having three syllables, the second four. Four of these seven are accented while the remaining three and the final rest are not. In dŏi tamadah lines having only seven syllables (or nine syllables including the prefix) are quite rare, but if only seven are used, each receives one accent in dŏi; thus each line has eight accents rather than four. (See Example 21)

In a line taken from Kumboon's dŏi tamadah (Example 22) there are eight syllables plus a prefix. The beats would be expected to follow rhythmic pattern (a) as indicated in Example 22, but in fact they follow pattern (b) which illustrates a distinguishing characteristic of dŏi tamadah rhythm. The result is that to the ear the breaks occur not at the ends of lines, since they are immediately joined with the following prefix, but within a line. Persons unacquainted with lum dŏi, such as Westerners or even Central Thai, are easily confused, especially if following a written text transcribed line by line.

In lum tang sun lines having as many as ten syllables exclusive of the prefix are rather uncommon, but in dŏi tamadah lines having up to fourteen or more syllables are common. The dŏi tamadah used in Northeastern nung bra-mo-tai (shadow puppet theatre) is distinguished from that of lum glawn because it regularly squeezes in as many syllables as possible and at a faster tempo than lum glawn. The line in Example 23, also by Kumboon, illustrates a line having fourteen syllables.

Because the kaen accompaniment figures with Kumboon's singing in Example 19 are obviously in duple meter, her singing too follows duple meter, but the other singers represented sing in a compound meter, notated as 6/8 because the kaen plays three notes per accent, six per two-accent measure, and thus 6/8 meter. Their poetry, moreover, lacks lines of fourteen syllables which complicate the rhythm, but lines with from ten to twelve syllables are common. The line in Example 24 by Mawlum Ken, having only eight syllables, illustrates a more usual rhythmic setting. Among singers using 6/8 meter, however, there is an occasional tendency to return to 2/4 for very brief periods creating complex rhythms with the kaen which continues to play in 6/8. The prefix to line 4 in Example 18 by Boonpeng together with the next two syllables illustrates this phenomenon (Example 25). It is especially characteristic that kaen introductions change meters at least once and often more (Example 26).

Each poem begins with at least two short introductory lines which are highly stereotyped and mean essentially "greeting." Each of these lines consists of either three accents or three accents preceded by an upbeat. The phrases in Example 27 typical of all singers open Boonpeng's first dŏi

(Example 18 continued on following page.)

(Example 18 continued on following page.)

Example 18. Lum ḍöi (tamadah, pamah, kong) sung by Boonpeng and Wichian.

(Example 19 continued on following page.)

Example 19. Lum dŏi (pamah, kong, tamadah) sung by Kumboon.

(Example 20 continued on following page.)

(Example 20 continued on following page.)

Example 20. Lum d̈ói (kong, tamadah, pamah) sung by Ken Dalao.

Example 21. The eight accents in a line of dōi poetry.

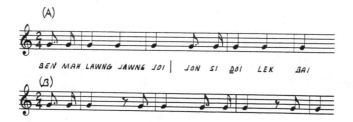

(A)

BEN MAH LAWNG JAWNG JOI | JON SI DOI LEK BAI

(B)

Example 22. Line 3 (dōi tamadah) of Example 19 sung by Kumboon illustrating doi rhythm.

BAWK HAI | KOI NEE MAEN HAH GIN CHEE | HEE GIN   BEE BEE KAWNG JAO NUM NAE

Example 23. Line 5 (dōi tamadah) of Example 19 sung by Kumboon illustrating a complex line having fourteen syllables.

UN NOI | NOI   YAO YAO | LAH KÜ MAENG YANG   SIN

Example 24. Line 21 (dōi tamadah) of Example 20 sung by Ken illustrating a typical setting of a line of dōi poetry.

... SAWN   DAI   DA   LIANG (4)   KIANG MIA LUNG NUN HAI   JAO   HANG   JUNG ...

Example 25. Parts of lines 3 and 4 of Example 18 (dŏi tamadah sung by Boonpeng illustrating a transient shift in meter from compound to duple.

DRONES
LAI YAI

Example 26. Mm. 1-8 of a kaen introduction illustrating two changes of meter from 6/8 to 2/4.

(1) OI   JA PEE   MAW LUM   (2)   KRUN PEE   NUN JAO   CHAI   LUM ...

Example 27. Lines 1 and 2 from Example 18 sung by Boonpeng illustrating typical opening phrases.

tamadah in Example 18. These may be extended to four or more lines by varying the words or using other typical phrases.

At the end of the body of the poem the singer must add two ending phrases, the first having a mai-ek (') tone mark on the last word, and the second ending with a mai-toh (✓) word. The vast majority of singers use phrases that speak of "cream-colored cheeks" (nah nuan), the most common being "nun lah nuan nah." The last three syllables of the second phrase will be repeated for the cadence. Mawlum Ken's ending phrases, like those of most singers, are extended through repetition and reordering of words:

first phrase	nun lah pee nah nah nuan nah
	wa nah nah nuan nah
second phrase	hawm glin mah yak dom jao de
	wom jao pe poo glang oi
	poo glang oi

Not indicated in this romanization is the fact that the seemingly repetitious syllable nah varies in tone and therefore in meaning. Further, the first oi in the second phrase has mai-ek, but the second has mai-toh as required for the cadence.

The vocal range used in dŏi tamadah rarely exceeds an octave and a fourth (from a to d" in lai yai) and in the case of Mawlum Ken is kept within a single octave. Given these limitations, it is not surprising that certain melodic patterns emerge. Because the melodic line is more active than in lum tang sun, it is able to realize the proper word-tones more consistently, but the result is a more jagged melodic contour. This fact plus the rapid tempos requires an agile voice lest the intervals become sloppy. An examination of sixteen dŏi tamadah including those transcribed here reveals an average tempo of ♩ = 139 in 2/4 meter or ♩. = 139 in 6/8 meter; the extremes varied from 120 to 154. In fact five of the sixteen exceeded 150. If the lines of poetry average only twelve syllables each, the rate of word delivery is at least 225 syllables per minute, truly an incredible pace.

The accompaniment for dŏi tamadah is nearly always continuous repetition of a simple pattern lasting little more than one measure. These may be seen in the introductions and at various places in the transcriptions. Kumboon's accompanist plays groups of four sixteenth notes in duple meter while the others play groups of three sixteenth notes in compound meter. Coordination of pitch is unnecessary except at cadences where the kaen tends to follow more closely, but coordination of the beats is extremely important. Singers who cannot sing in time with their kaen players are considered amateurish or beginners. Accompanists must further be able to change modes quickly when the vocal ranges of the various singers require such changes; as they alternate male and female the kaen usually changes from lai noi to lai yai or vice versa depending on whose voice range the kaen matches.

Dŏi kong. Dŏi kong differs from dŏi tamadah in several fundamental ways, but a listener unaware of the differences might not detect them for reasons to be discussed. The melody, rather than being generated according to the lum technique, follows fixed phrases, but not to the extent that those of "America the Beautiful" or even the Thai National Anthem do. Secondly, the poetry is neither glawn nor in Lao; when dŏi kong first appeared, it was entirely in Siamese. Its form is not traditional but of the type used in pleng look toong ("children of the fields") popular songs. There is neither patterned rhyme nor a tonal scheme, but the number of accents per line is usually seven. The transcriptions include examples of dŏi kong by Kumboon (Example 19), Boonpeng and Wichian (Example 18), and Ken (Example 20).

Ideally, a complete dŏi kong poem consists of four lines of poetry each having seven accents. The first two lines may or may not be identical and the last line may consist of syllables totalling only four accents which are then repeated to complete the line. Because the poems vary greatly, however, it is better to conceive of them as eight phrases rather than four lines, and each phrase having four accents (unless the final accent is omitted in a rest). It is necessary to think in terms of phrases because many poems have incomplete lines and total from five to seven phrases and in a few cases because of repetition even nine phrases. The following poem sung by Kumboon (from Example 19) consists of eight phrases grouped into four lines, the first and second of which are identical and the last being a phrase and its repetition. The third line begins with a three-syllable parenthetical phrases which receives two extra accents, then the proper line

is preceded by yet another upbeat syllable which, occupying the second
half of the measure, gets another accent for a total of ten:

Line 1   ngam gra / rai doo bai doo / bai suat song law / lao

Line 2   ngam gra / rai doo bai doo / bai suat song law / lao

Line 3   (dai ben / koo) krawng / rao gawt ao gawt / ao ja joop bao /

          bao müan pee / um

Line 4   paw ngam / kum chuk dai kah / mü paw ngam / kum chuk

          dai kah / mü

In contrast, the following lines sung by Wichian (Example 18) in his second
stanza total only five phrases since the first two are missing entirely as is
the second phrase of the last line:

mah / jü mah / jü hua awk la / mü pee taep mai / wai

ying / mawng ying jon / jai mawng glai mawng / glai sun ga mai /

büa sot sui lon / lüa da rah / tai

Both the first and second lines loan their final beats or accents to the
beginning of the following lines.

For rhythmic variety singers are inclined to alter the placement of
even-numbered accents (those falling in the second half of each measure)
by placing a rest after an odd-numbered accent and moving the next accented syllable to the upbeat position. This cannot be done if there are
any unaccented syllables between the main ones, however. The same kind
of displacement of accents was also observed in dōi tamadah but usually
restricted to the second and sixth accents.

Probably the most common version of the dōi kong is that taught in
the schools to the kaen wong (kaen ensemble) in which large groups must
play together. In 2/4 time there are four lines each having four measures
for a total of sixteen. (Example 28)   In terms of phrases, the melody
may be further broken down into groups of two measures each as shown in
the following outline:

Phrases 1-2	A	A'
Phrases 3-4	A	A'
Phrases 5-6	B	B'
Phrases 7-8	C	C'

There are thus three melodic lines in dōi kong, A (sung twice), B, and C,
but four lines of poetry.

A casual perusal of the dōi kong transcribed reveals that the melodies
are not quite that simple. The variations occur because of three factors:
(1) changes to accommodate word tones; (2) changes to accommodate
extra syllables; (3) changes made through the singer's individual initiative.
Example 29 is a comparative transcription which presents only the melodies
of four dōi kong in addition to the kaen version (Example 28).   Only the

Example 28. The melody of d̄oi kong played by the kaen ensembles.

(Example 29 continued on following page.)

(Example 29 continued on following page.)

Example 29. D̄ŏi kong performed by (a) Kumboon, (b) Ken, (c) kaen solo, (d) Wichian, and (e) Boonpeng.

first notes of each measure tend to be the same, the other parts of the phrase varying greatly. As in the case of d̄ŏi tamadah, Kumboon's meter was 2/4 while that of the others was 6/8. If these initial pitches are arranged continuously as a melody, the structure of d̄ŏi kong in its simplest form is thus:

Example 30. The fundamental melody created from the initial notes of the measures in each of the four phrases of d̄ŏi kong.

The accompaniment on the kaen may be continuous by repeated patterns as observed in d̄ŏi tamadah, but most often the player follows the outline of the melody. His playing, however, creates heterophony which only matches the singer on the first note of each measure. Examples of sole kaen d̄ŏi kong will be found in Chapter 6 which differ only slightly from the accompaniments played by skillful players.

D̄ŏi pamah. In structure d̄ŏi pamah differs little from d̄ŏi kong. Both are fixed melodies but only in their broad outlines; both use poems of the style of popular songs written primarily in Central Thai although both types now admit some Lao words. Melodically, d̄ŏi pamah consists of $5\frac{1}{2}$ lines, one of which is a repetition, or eleven phrases totaling twenty-two measures in either 2/4 or 6/8 meter. In terms of poetry, there are five full lines plus a sixth which includes a repeat the last half of the preceding line. As in d̄ŏi kong, each phrase receives four accents and a full line eight including the final rest or upbeat to the next line. The following poem sung by Kumboon (Example 19) is compelte:

ruk / pee mai sang mai / hai wan nawk kom / nai nawng mai dawng / gan

ruk / pee mai sang mai / hai wan nawk kom / nai nawng mai dawng / gan boon pa / la som / pan tee dai sang / wai yoo num / mah

kaw hai / pee met / dah ga roo / nah nawng / dui

maen chee / wit mawt / mui ja fak duang / jai wai kiang / tü

ja fak duang / jai wai kiang / tü

The structure of this poem is then A A B C D D'. In this particular poem there is rhyme similar to that of gap, i.e., the last word rhymes with the word on the fourth accent of the following line. This is not a required pattern, however, but only a characteristic of this particular poem.

The melodic structure of dŏi pamah as sung is less consistent than that of dŏi kong. Again, the kaen wong ensemble plays a tune by this name which has become highly stereotyped, as shown in Example 31. The structure of the melody, like the poetry, is A A B C D D':

Example 31. Dŏi pamah as played by kaen wong ensembles.

This version compared with the melodies of the three transcribed versions reveals a pitch pattern similar to that of dŏi kong though the pitches of the second half of phrases 1, 3, and 9 are somewhat uncertain. (See Example 32) These pitches converted into a continuous melody create another simple pattern similar to that of dŏi kong. (Example 33)

For someone not only well informed about the structures of both dŏi kong and dŏi pamah but experienced in hearing them, there are still difficulties in telling the two apart. One of the key differences is that when full lines are present, each line in dŏi kong ends on a while those of dŏi pamah end on e, c, d, and e respectively. The custom of shifting even-numbered accents to the upbeat position after a rest also prevails in dŏi pamah as does the practice of singing poems of different lengths. Kumboon's dŏi pamah (Example 19) is complete, but both Ken's (Example 20) and Boonpeng's (Example 18) total only nine phrases.

Dŏi hua non dan. While dŏi hua non dan is performed only in mawlum moo, all well-trained and experienced mawlum glawn can sing it, and in fact better than mawlum moo singers who generally have less training. As noted in Chapter 3, the name hua non dan is derived from the name of

(Example 32 continued on following page.)

Example 32. D̈öi pamah performed by (a) Kumboon, (b) kaen solo, (3) Ken,
and (d) Boonpeng.

Example 33. The fundamental melody created from the initial notes of the measures in dŏi pamah.

a village, Dawn-dan, thirty-four kilometers southwest of Mook-dahan in Nakwan-panom province near the Maekong River. In past years this dŏi was also called dŏi see poom dŭm, a term which has now become associated with dŏi tamadah. Dŏi hua non dan is similar to the singing styles heard across the Maekong River around Savannakhet, specifically lum kawn sawun, lum ban sawk, and lum mahasai.

The poetry which forms the body of dŏi hua non dan is ordinary glawn with an average of seven to nine syllables per line, not the fourteen or more of dŏi tamadah. Most writers restrict themselves to the third and fourth lines of the stanza, however, and use suffixes more liberally than found in lum glawn. Each poem must begin with two introductory phrases before the first full line of poetry appears. One of the most common first phrases is "oh jung wah jai pee chai oi" meaning roughly "greeting." These phrases typically begin with "oh" and end with "oi," syllables which have no more meaning than "oh" and "aw" in English. After the final line of poetry, there must be several ending phrases, the number depending upon the singer. These too follow a pattern, usually the word "gaem" (cheek) encountered in the introduction to lum tang sun, plus two rhyming words. Kumboon's ending line in Example 34 begins "jung wah gaem mai mai" followed by "jung wah gaem bŭn wŭn."

Each line of glawn has four accents with unaccented words between, unlike in dŏi tamadah where the latter also receive stress giving a full line seven accents plus a rest. It is uncertain which is the case in dŏi hua non dan, but because the number of syllables is rarely more than nine per line and often only seven, the four basic accents have greater weight. Although suffixes may have up to eight syllables, they receive only two accents, as in "pee yoo ban / dae rŭ yoo ban / doom" sung by Kumboon. Introductory phrases, like suffixes, get two accents, while most ending lines have four.

Taking Kumboon's poem (Example 34) as an example of a fairly complex structure, the lines classify as shown below:

Example 34 continued on following page.)

Example 34. D̈öi hua non dan sung by Kumboon.

lines	Explanation
1-2	Introductory lines
3	Third line of stanza
4	Suffix
5-9	In order, lines four, three, four, three, and four of glawn stanzas
10-11	Suffixes
12-13	Third and fourth lines
14-15	Ending lines

(kaen interlude before a new poem begins)

16	Introductory line
17	Third line
18	Suffix
19-23	Glawn see with two accents per line. Line 23 consists of two phrases of glawn see which together equal a fourth line of a glawn stanza
24-26	Ending lines; lines 24 and 25 together constitute a full line while line 26 is a repetition of line 25.

Dŏi hua non dan uses the sun scale in tempo giusto, virtually all sing-ers using 6/8 meter. The vocal range for most is from a to c", an octave and a third. Compared to dŏi tamadah, dŏi hua non dan is sung at a more leisurely pace, often less than half that of dŏi tamadah. Kumboon's tem-po is 32, comparable to other dŏi hua non dan recorded, whereas dŏi tam-adah was often sung at tempos of 150 or more. In mawlum moo a pair of lovers often join hands and sway back and forth while singing dŏi hua non dan to each other.

There is a tendency to end third lines with d and fourth lines with g, but this pattern is broken often, especially in Example 34 by Kumboon. She commonly ends the four lines with the intervals c - d or d - c well. Lines which are not part of the glawn, that is, introductory phrases, suf-fixes, and ending lines, nearly always end on c, less commonly on d. The final cadence is patterned as shown in Example 35.

Example 35. The most usual cadence heard is dŏi hua non dan.

Mawlum pŭn

Lum pŭn differs from lum glawn in many ways, the most important being that this genre is performed by one person, usually male, and that the poems are epic-length nitan (stories) written in glawn and based on jatakas, Lao tales, or Lao history. Whereas norms in lum glawn can be ascertained by comparing any number of practicing singers, generalizations regarding lum pŭn are risky because of the paucity of living singers. In-formants universally acknowledge that lum pŭn is older than lum glawn, and further, that only lum pee fah may be older. Lum glawn performances

divide neatly into three parts, tan sun, tang yao, and döi, and similarly
scales and rhythms are associated with their respective portions. Thus lum
glawn was discussed first because in lum pün the distinctions between tempo giusto and parlando-rubato and especially between scales are more difficult to isolate and explain. Two excerpts will be examined in transcription:
(1) Orapim sung by Tawng-yoon (Example 36); (2) Jumbah-seedon sung by
Tawin (Example 37).

Lai yai lum pün played by solo kaen is distinguished from ordinary lai
yai through different drones, the former using a' and a", the latter e" and
a". A more important distinction, however, is scale, for lum pün makes
use of six pitches, a, b, c, d, e, and g, b being the sixth. The following
kaen solo excerpt called lai yai lum pün played by fifty-year-old Pun Chonpairot has been reduced to a single melodic line to illustrate the use of the
b, a "sour note" (siang som). Similar examples were recorded by several
other kaen players. The most striking characteristic of the extra pitch, b,
is that it appears only at cadences while the five usual pitches of the yao
scale (a, c, d, e, g) predominate elsewhere. The cadences isolated from
the body use a reduced scale, a, b, d, e. Thus it is as if there were two
scales present, one having four pitches, the other five. (Example 38)

The singers whose styles most closely approximated that shown in kaen
solo were Tawng-yoon (Example 36) and Tawin (Example 37). Tawng-yoon's
accompanist, Tawng-koon, a blind kaen player who was not her usual
accompanist, played in lai yai lum pün mode in tempo giusto. The performance began with a kaen introduction, the routine "but nee" ("now")
which usually begins nitan, then the first two lines followed by a short
interlude. Tawng-yoon's use of the b appeared regularly but not exclusively at cadences, the three exceptions being in lines 1, 7, and 12. Lines 1
to 15 were sung in parlando-rubato, but line 16 changed without break to
giusto and continued in this manner until the end of the section. Her setting of the accents of the lines was entirely normal as discussed under
lum tang sun in lum glawn.

Tawin's performance was accompanied in lai noi mode using five
pitches, but the kaen player had never before accompanied lum pün. Tawin's scale in portions other than the cadences was pentatonic, but as he
approached a cadence he began using d, e, g, and a, the e being the parallel pitch to b seen in the lum pün kaen solo and Tawng-yoon's cadences.
Whereas Tawng-yoon changed from parlando-rubato to giusto and continued until the end of the section, Tawin remained in parlando-rubato
throughout except during the latter part of line 21 and all of line 22. His
tempo was 80 and Tawng-yoon's 96, both much slower than contemporary
lum glawn.

Theatrical Genres

Mawlum moo. When modern mawlum moo began in Kawn-gaen province in 1952, the singing style was said to be like that of lum pün or lum
rüang. Old Kawn-gaen style mawlum moo made use of both tempo giusto
and parlando-rubato, but both were sung to the same scale, yao. The free
rhythm sections were sung one line at a time with a pause following, and
sections in tempo giusto were sung to nature description poems called dün
glawn (walking poem) which are related to the dün dong in Kawn-gaen
style lum glawn today. One sometimes also encounters the term lum wiang
to denote mawlum moo, but the term only distinguishes lum moo from lum
plün.

(Example 36 continued on following page.)

(Example 36 continued on following page.)

Example 36. Lum pün (Orapim) sung by Tawng-yoon.

Example 37. Lum pün (Jumba seedon) sung by Tawin.

Example 38. A melodic reduction of mm. 6-25 of lai yai lum pün played by Pun Chonpairot on the kaen.

Mawlum moo's popularity and development centered in Kawn-gaen province while lum glawn was the traditional favorite in the Oobon area. When female mawlum Chawiwan Dumnün, an established Oobon lum glawn singer, joined the Rungsamun mawlum moo troupe about 1963 as leading lady, her transfer of Oobon style's smoothness to mawlum moo had an instant and far-reaching effect. Her style was more melodious, more connected and embellished than usual in older mawlum moo. The Rungsamun troupe became the leading troupe in the region and soon, as is necessary where popular demand determines trends, others quickly followed suit. As a result, more troupes today perform in the Oobon style, the older Kawn-gaen style with its dün glawn being extremely rare.

The transcription taken from the story Nyah gin bling (Grandmother eats leeches) performed by the Pet-boorapah troupe of Wabee-batoom district, Mahasarakam province, and sung by the leading male, illustrates modern lum moo at its best (Example 39). Because the glawn poetry is part of a story, there is no introductory "oh," but instead a phrase such as "but nee" ("now") opens the section. The rhythm is parlando-rubato throughout, the scale yao, and the mood serious. The extensive vocalizations which characterize this style are not meant to illustrate particular words but come at the end of especially meaningful phrases having great emotional content. These vocalizations are generally much longer than those found in lum glawn-tang yao. Some Northeasterners assert, however, that in spite of the melancholy mood and expressive delivery, mawlum moo is less effective emotionally than lum glawn. The reason is that in the latter genre lum tang yao comes early in the morning as the climax to a night of singing, is very short but poignant, and indicates the parting of two lovers; in lum moo it constitutes nearly the entire evening and thus wears thin through repetition.

Melodic relief is provided through the use of dün glawn in Kawn-gaen style, but more and more today by döi tamadah, kong, and pamah in all

(Example 39 continued on following page.)

Example 39. <u>Mawlum moo</u> (<u>Nyah gin bling</u>) sung by the Pet-boorapah troupe.

styles. Because shows begin with an hour or more of popular music played on Western instruments, these instruments are also available to "jazz up" the <u>dŏi</u>. A few troupes have also begun incorporating <u>pleng look-toong</u>, popular songs based on regional traditional forms, into the story, these also accompanied by the Westernized ensemble. A more traditional interpolation is provided by <u>dŏi hua non dan</u> as described earlier in this chapter. To perform this <u>dŏi</u>, a couple which is in love joins hands and swings slowly back and forth--like pods of kapok--while singing <u>dŏi hua non dan</u>. Lastly, many <u>lum moo</u> performances end with a <u>lum glawn</u> cycle-- <u>tang sun</u>, <u>tang yao</u>, and <u>dŏi</u>. While the latter have nothing to do with the story, few of the other interpolated melodies such as the <u>dŏi</u> do either;

they are added at the discretion of the troupe and for the pleasure of the audience.

Mawlum plün. Whereas the mood in lum moo is rather serious, at least during the singing, the mood in lum plün is light. Lum plün's rapid rise in popularity may be attributed to its appeal to young people, its lightheart-edness, liberal use of modern instruments, and popular beat. The poetry remains ordinary glawn, but its quality is rarely above that of hacks since writers tend to shy away from this genre. One convention observed in lum plün poetry is that each section must end on a second line of the stanza which has a mai-toh (√) accent thus producing either a low-falling or a low tone. If the section ends on the fourth line which has no tone mark, a short phrase such as "la nah" (ละนำ) having the mai-toh must be added.

Lum plün performances follow a simple pattern with little variation. From behind the curtain on stage right an actor, accompanied by kaen and pin (lute), sings the "but pah gung" ("open the curtain") in parlando-rubato using the yao scale, and normally accompanied in lai noi. After as few as two lines of poetry, normally the first and second lines, there is a cadence directly from which begins a tempo giusto section introduced by the entire ensemble, i.e., kaen, pin, drums, and other percussion instruments. The tempo is always fast, averaging close to 130, although in one case the tempo was only 104. During the interlude between the two rhythms, the performer dances (fawn). At the end of the poem as the music continues, he will often continue to dance, but the style in lum plün is rarely very graceful. And so the show continues from 9 p.m. until early dawn.

Although the excerpt cited here (Example 40) does not necessarily bear out the statement, there is a tendency in the slow section to vary the tessitura and volume, the first and third lines sung higher and louder than the second and fourth. The overall range is much greater than that en-countered in previously discussed genres, an octave and a fifth in Example 40. There is a certain quality about lum tang yao in lum plün that is difficult to describe in technical terms but easy to recognize and distin-guish from lum moo; it is a certain clipped quality, emotionless, and stereotyped which makes this portion sound less than spontaneous. The originators of lum plün, some of whom are still performing, were not trained singers unlike those who started mawlum moo, but had only imi-tated other styles as best they could. Because lum plün has been more the domain of amateur troupes than lum moo, which boasts highly trained professional organizations in some cases, there would be a tendency for one troupe to imitate another, even copying its cruder details to the point that the style became hardened. Today this is followed religiously with the result that lum plün's style has apparently evolved little over the years.

The faster portion begins with a short phrase followed, at least in the excerpt, by the stanza's third line, which is repeated before going on to the fourth line. The poetry is divided according to its proper accents and set in tempo giusto rhythm but using the pitches of the yao scale much as in Kawn-gaen style dün dong or dün glawn. One characteristic that dis-tinguishes the rhythm is syncopation, more commonly a factor in the pre-fix than in the rest of the line. In Example 40 syncopation is seen in lines 3, 4, 5, 9, 10, 12, and 13. In many of these cases the last syllable of the line, rather than being set to a quarter note, was set to an eighth note, shifting the prefix of the following line into a quarter-eighth rhythm.

Lum plün's monotony is rarely broken as in lum moo where döi of various kinds may be added. Occasionally, however, the story calls for

(Example 40 continued on following page.)

Example 40.   Mawlum plün (Saen Kawn Long) sung by the Kwunjai-Müang-lat troupe.

entertainment, for which a short mawlum glawn cycle may be used. Such is rather rare, and in fact most lum plün singers cannot perform lum glawn. Spoken dialogue and extended jokes told by the dua dalok (comedian), however, separate portions in both lum moo and lum plün. As pointed out earlier, the performers cannot act as they sing because they must stand under the microphone. This together with the overall domination of vocal sections leaves both lum moo and lum plün woefully under-developed dramatically. The acting tradition which made Siamese ligeh relatively exciting was not carried over into mawlum moo and plün, genres which amount to little more than singing and dancing with scenery.

NOTES

1.   James N. Mosel, "Sound and Rhythm in Thai and English Verse," in Pahsah lae nungsü [Languages and Books] (Bangkok, 1959), pp. 31-2.

2.   Bang-kum, Sung-Sin-sai, p. 148.

3.   Boon-peng, "lum plün" (Example 5), lines 10-15.

4.   See p. 13.

5.   Kerr, Lao-English Dictionary, 1: 442.

6.   Ibid., 2: 686.

7.   The concept of a secondary finalis or reciting pitch, explained briefly in Chapter 1, should be recalled at this time. Throughout those styles using the sun scale, the finalis or note of relaxation in the lowest; in terms of kaen modes, these are g in sootsanaen, c in bo-sai, and d in soi. With few exceptions, however, the finalis is avoided until the final cadence. The pitch a fourth above the finalis (c in sootsanaen, f in bo-sai, and g in soi) becomes an intermediary resting point or reciting pitch during these extended periods.

8.   Haas, Thai-English Student's Dictionary, p. 296.

9.   Kerr, Lao-English Dictionary, 2: 687.

10. Choom is see nah choom means literally "color-crowded rice field," but it is used only to produce rhyme.

11. Kerr, Lao-English Dictionary, 1: 505.

12. David Morton, The Traditional Music of Thailand (Los Angeles, California: Regents of the University of California, 1968), pp. 13-14.

13. See Bell Yung, "Creative Process in Cantonese Opera I: The Role of linguistic Tones," Ethnomusicology 27-1 (January, 1983): 29-47.

14. George List, "Speech Melody and Song Melody in Central Thailand," Ethnomusicology 5 (1961): 30.

15. Kerr, Lao-English Dictionary, 1: 535.

V.

The Kaen, Description and History

Introduction

Of the instruments used among the Lao, the kaen is by far the most significant. No other instrument has attained such refinement in tuning, playing techniques, and repertory, and no instrument better symbolizes the Lao people. The kaen, described briefly in Chapter 1, is a bamboo mouth organ in raft form whose tones come from tiny metal reeds fitted into the walls of the pipes inside the hardwood windchest. (See Figure 39 on page 190) These reeds, classified as free, sound only when the pipe's finger hole is covered.

The word kaen has several meanings in Lao. Firstly, kaen may mean "poor," "indigent," or "lacking." A second meaning denotes a species of hardwood trees called Hopea, e.g., kaen hia is the Hopea odorata (Roxburgh). The Lao kaen tree is called dakian in Central Thailand. Lastly, kaen denotes the Lao mouth organ whose windchest is sometimes made from the kaen tree. The name kaen probably did not, as some Northeastern Thai speculate, evolve from the onomatopoetic combination "kaen laen kaen laen" referring to the sound of playing this instrument. The classifier word for kaen is either dao, referring to the windchest, or duang, referring to long, narrow objects.[1] The latter word is preferred in the villages while dao is usual in cities.

Kaen are made in four sizes according to the number of pipes. The smallest, called kaen hok or less commonly kaen go, has six pipes--hok means "six"--arranged in three pairs. Kaen jet ("seven") and kaen baet ("eight") have fourteen pipes in seven pairs and sixteen pipes in eight pairs respectively. Lastly, kaen gao ("nine") have eighteen pipes in nine pairs. There is no standard length for each, however, though kaen hok are usually the shortest and kaen gao the longest. (See Figure 40) Since pipe length and pitch are directly related, the kaen maker pitches his instruments according to the range of the singers they accompany or the preference and convenience of the player. Kaen hok may be as short as fifty centimeters, shorter than this being impractical, and as long as ninety centimeters; the average is approximately sixty centimeters. Kaen jet and kaen baet average one meter in length, though some may be as short as

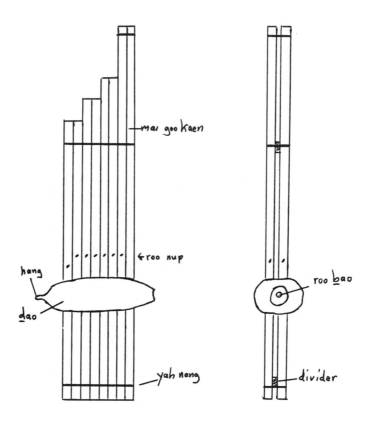

Figure 39. A kaen.

sixty centimeters or as long as 140. Kaen gao, now very rare, averaged at
least two meters in length and are said to have required powerful lungs.

In the past kaen tended to be much longer than they are today. Various travellers' reports from the nineteenth century include references to
such kaen. One of the earliest reports is that if Sir John Bowring who in
April, 1855, was entertained by Prince Chutamani, full brother of King
Mongkut (Rama IV) who in 1851 had been crowned the Second King and
called Pra Pinklao.[2] The Second King, as noted earlier in Chapter 2, was
an enthusiast for things Lao and naturally played the kaen. When Bowring
visited him, the Second King played upon a kaen eight feet long and presented it to Bowring as a souvenir of the occasion.

H. Warington Smyth, whose book Five Years in Siam contains the most
complete and accurate early account of the kaen, comments that kaen
were classified according to length using the Lao unit sawk which equals
fifty centimeters.[3] A two-sawk kaen was therefore one meter long, a
four-sawk kaen two meters, and so forth. He stated that the four-sawk
kaen was standard for his time. In a slightly earlier account, Smyth described a concert he witnessed in which a six-sawk kaen was used.[4]

Figure 40. The various sizes of kaen. From left to right, three kaen hok, kaen baet, and kaen gao.

Several times he commented on the lung power required by such a long instrument. Prince Henri d'Orleans, whose Around Tonkin and Siam appeared in 1894, described the difficulties attendant to using such a long instrument. "A man carrying a Laotian organ, which he has difficulty in setting up, follows them [the singers]. The pipes of the organ are so long-- nearly fourteen feet--that he is finally obliged to cut a hole in the roof, but the damage can be easily repaired."[5]

Similarly, Madelaine Colani mentions kaen at least three meters long.[6] Today such instruments may be seen in the National Museum in Bangkok which has three long kaen or unspecified age. Playing such an instrument was primarily difficult not because they were so heavy but because they required so much breath. Players tended to tire out quickly. Obviously, in earlier times when players seldom travelled beyond the next village, carrying such a kaen was not a major problem. Today the situation is different because kaen players travel far and wide in busses and small trucks, making such instruments inconvenient.

Except for the kaen hok, whose six pipes play only an anhemitonic pentatonic scale, the complete tuning system of the kaen includes seven pitches in an octave. (See Figure 41) As will be shown later, five penta- tonic modes have been derived from this series of pitches. Upon first encounter, the arrangement of pitches appears quite illogical, and indeed

Figure 41. The pitches of the <u>kaen</u> in ascending order with pipe numbers.

there is no consistent pattern. Figure 42 showing the pitch arrangements of the various <u>kaen</u> sizes does not take actual pitch into account. Instead the system advocated by Professor Jarunchai Chonpairot is followed. In this system the first pipe on the left is <u>c</u>', the octave of the second pipe on the right, <u>c</u>. This system thereby avoids the use of sharps and flats.

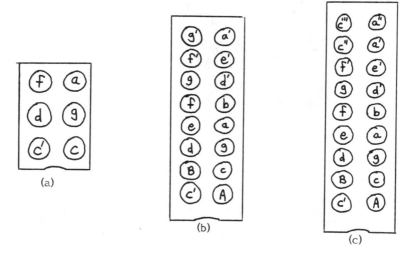

Figure 42. Pitch relationships of three <u>kaen</u> sizes: (a) <u>kaen</u> hok, (b) <u>kaen</u> <u>baet</u>, and (c) <u>kaen gao</u>. The lower end represents the mouthpiece.

The seemingly erratic placement of pitches will appear more rational when the theory and technique fo <u>kaen</u> playing are discussed in Chapter 6. For now it is sufficient to say that there are five pentatonic modes gener- ally used, three of which follow the <u>sun</u> scale and two the <u>yao</u> scale. Fol- lowing the pitch system shown in Figure 41 the scales are seen in Figure 43. One must further bear in mind that it is difficult to play more than three neighboring pipes in succession in a given mode since the fingers are wider than the pipes. <u>Kaen</u> makers and players over time create a system in which the pitches of the five modes came to be arranged in such a way that the playing of four consecutive pipes is avoided. A sixth mode, on the <u>yao</u> scale starting on <u>e</u>, is possible though rarely played because at this point the system breaks down and five consecutive pipes appear. The

Figure 43. The two scales and five modes available on the kaen baet.

kaen's pitch arrangement might be compared to a typewriter keyboard whose order of letters makes as much sense as the kaen's pitch arrangement but fits the fingers for a given language. Similarly, the pitch arrangement of the kaen fits the Lao musical language.

While the general name for the bamboo kaen tubes is mai goo kaen, individual tubes are called lok kaen or literally "children of the kaen." Further, each pipe has its own name, though it must be admitted that not every kaen player could recite them. The following list gives these names beginning from the mouthpiece moving towards the tail of the windchest.[7]

1. Kaen hok (six pipes)

   First pair
   R(ight) mae se. Mae means "mother" but when combined with another noun may mean "the great one," while se means "unsteady" or "leaning." The combination might be translated as "the unsteady one." It is also called bo kwah ("right thumb"). Pitch c.

   L(eft) bo sai. Bo sai means "left thumb." Pitch c'.

   Second pair
   R sanaen. Sanaen is a poetic word having to do with love, though it also refers to the bamboo platform on which women in labor lie, the platform of a pirogue, or a bench. Pitch d.

   L mae gae, literally the "old mother" or perhaps simply "the old one." Pitch g.

   Third pair
   R hup toong or rup toong, literally "to receive a field." Pitch f.

   L mae goi sai. Goi denotes the little finger. The three words together mean the "left little finger" although that finger does not play the pipe. Pitch a.

2. Kaen baet (sixteen tubes) N.B. By eliminating the eighth pair, the list also applies to the kaen jet (fourteen tubes).

   First pair
   R toong ("full"). Pitch A.
   L bo sai ("left thumb"). Pitch c'.

Second pair
   R mae se ("unsteady one"). Pitch c.
   L mae wiang. Wiang, meaning "city," together with mae
   implies the "urban one." Pitch B.

Third pair
   R sanaen (see kaen hok, second pair, right). Pitch g.
   L mae gae ("old one"). Pitch d.

Fourth pair
   R hup toong ("receive a field" or "accompany toong").
   Pitch a.
   L mae goi kwah ("right little finger"). Pitch e.

Fifth pair
   R look wiang ("city child"). Pitch b.
   L mae goi sai ("left little finger"). Pitch f.

Sixth pair
   R gae noi ("little old one"). Pitch d'.
   L sanaen (same as third pair, right). Pitch g.

Seventh pair
   R goi kwah[8] ("right little finger"). Pitch e'.
   L goi sai ("left little finger"). Pitch f'.

Eighth pair
   R sep kwah ("right accompaniment"). Pitch a'.
   L sep sai ("left accompaniment"). Pitch g.

The ninth pair on the kaen gao with eighteen tubes has the same names as
those of the eighth pair.
   An analysis of this system reveals that all pairs except c, g, and a
show the mother-child relationship. The octave g' has instead a technically descriptive name. Similarly, the middle a is called the accompaniment to the lower one while the upper c' is called "left thumb."
   The free reed found in the kaen consists of a small piece of metal into
which a tongue of various possible shapes is cut (See Figure 53). The
tongue is flat and even with the slot because it must produce the same
sound whether the player inhales or exhales. While reed tongues are themselves not tuned exactly, those of the lower pitches are shaved thinner at
the fixed end and those of the higher pitches at the tips. Following this
general principle, the maker matches the reed to a tuned column of air in
the bamboo tube whose limits are set by two pitch holes cut into the tube.
Were the tubes cut to the exact length required, pitch holes would be
unnecessary, but for aesthetic reasons kaen makers cut equal pairs which
graduate from short to long, necessitating the hidden pitch holes.
   If the kaen lacked finger holes, all reeds would sound at once when the
player blew. The addition of finger holes, however small, destroys the
acoustical coupling of reed and air column by altering the wind pressure
causing the reeds to remain silent. Sachs explains that without a finger
hole the pressures from the inside and outside are equalized causing the
reed to sound, but the finger hole causes an imbalance of pressures forcing
the reed tongue out slightly.[9] Even if the finger hole is partially clogged

by bits of kisoot, the black sticky substance which seals the pipes in place and inevitably works its way into finger holes when used to stop drones, the pipe will not sound. A good kaen, moreover, responds immediately when the hole is completely covered, even when the player taps his finger as fast as possible.

Kaen Making

Kaen are made in village homes where makers build the instruments from start to finish, often selling it directly to the buyer as well. Kaen makers are always male by tradition. Most kaen makers farm their own rice fields too. During the planting season, from May to July, and the harvest, in November and December, few makers have time to build kaen.

Before learning to build kaen, the student must learn to honor his teacher in a wai kroo or yok kroo ceremony. The ceremonial objects are similar to those of the mawlum's wai kroo ritual. There is no absolute rule governing these, but Mr. Tui of Ban Lao-kam in Roi-et province mentioned the following as being basic: five pairs of candles and flowers, four of them placed inside small containers made of banana leaves, the fifth in a metal bowl; a piece of cloth worn by women called sin; a piece of white cloth one wah long (two meters); and four one-baht coins ($.20), two of which will be returned to the student.[10] The student also learns to repeat magic words whose meaning is mostly unknown to him. These are of two varieties though both involve Pali words or imitations thereof. The first is kata which are words to invoke magical powers, and the se-cond is uw, words to protect the maker, strengthen his art, and fend off unfair competition. As a student, the maker must repeat these words three times to the teacher. After an apprenticeship of perhaps five or six years depending on his native skills, the student may begin making kaen in his own home. But each year at the beginning of the kaen-making season, normally January, he is expected to repeat the wai kroo ceremony as a gesture of respect to his teacher.

Kaen are composed of four basic materials, bamboo pipes, a hardwood windchest, metal for the reeds, and a black sticky substance to seal the pipes in place. Makers rarely secure the materials themselves, but rather buy them from itinerant salesmen coming from the producing areas. The bamboo used to make the tubes is a special type called mai hia (Lao) or mai sang (Siamese), a variety which grows as long as four meters and has a consistently small diameter (Figure 44). Makers also use a variety called aw of the Arundo or Phragmites species. For makers in Northeast Thailand, the most important producing area is Laen-chang Mountain in Goochin-narai district, Galasin province. Makers, who call the tubes mai goo kaen ("kaen tube wood"), prefer bamboo which is not more than one year old because as it gets older the nodes become very hard and difficult to penetrate. Naturally there is little bamboo of this type over a year old since the producers cut it once a year. They then deliver the tubes bundled into groups of sixteen called lap in caravans of buffalo carts or small trucks during February and March in the midst of the dry season. The tubes must then dry in the sun for at least a month.

The windchest (Example 45) is carved from one of several hardwoods including bradoo-mai (also called mai bradoo), kayoong or payoong, kaen (also called dakian), nam taeng (also called nam daeng or rawiang), dabaeng (also called sabaeng, garat, or in Cambodia darat), or gratom (also called gratoom). The root is used in every case except nam taeng and gratom

Figure 44. Village children beneath <u>kaen</u>-pipe bamboo drying in the sun.

Figure 45. Comparison of block of wood as bought by <u>kaen</u> maker and finished windchest.

from which the trunk is used.[11]   Mai bradoo (Pterocarpus macrocarpus, Kurz.) is probably the most popular since it is soft and easy to carve. Upon receiving the wood, which is dug during the rainy season and cut into small blocks the size of the windchest, the maker again buries them in the ground to keep them soft and moist until needed.   The ivory windchests mentioned by Smyth must be considered unusual.[12]

Kaen reeds consist of an alloy of silver and copper since either of these alone produces poor quality reeds. Makers of low quality kaen, however, will resort to using old scraps of brass. Mr. Tui derives his metal from old Siamese coins which he melts into an alloy and cools in water. His source of silver is the one baht coins from around 1917 when the baht was worth a great deal and made of relatively pure silver. Copper comes from sadung coins (one hundred sadung equal one baht) from around 1935 during the reign of Rama VII. Some makers near Roi-et buy the metal already prepared from men in Ban Baw-pran in the same district. These small sheets of metal, called loha in units called lap, measure approximately thirty centimeters long, four centimeters wide, and one millimeter thick, and cost fifteen baht ($.75) each.

The black substance which seals the pipes in place is called kisoot, a waste product similar to beeswax from the maeng kisoot insect. This six-legged, winged insect lives in tree trunks in hilly country, but another variety called kisoot din piang lives in earthen nests in flat fields. The latter variety is also believed to have magic charms. Middlemen dig out the kisoot in large lumps to sell to kaen makers. Although one writer[13] says that kisoot must be mixed with charcoal from a soft wood or banana leaves to keep it from becoming sticky, Mr. Tui stated and demonstrated that kisoot is simply pounded on a wood block with a wetted wooden beater until it becomes pliant (Figure 46). Kisoot will neither become hard nor melt under ordinary circumstances, though storing kaen in intense heat will cause the kisoot to melt and run onto the reeds, thereby silencing them. Players commonly pinch off small pieces of kisoot to stop the drone pipes.

Making the individual parts of the kaen and assembling them into a finished product require a number of relatively simple tools. Since most of these are special for kaen making and made of metal, the makers buy their tools from craftsmen who specialize in this sort of work. While kaen makers build instruments from start to finish, they do not necessarily do one instrument at a time. Mr. Tui usually had anywhere from a few to a dozen or more partially finished kaen in his home which could be completed in a few hours if necessary. This system gives prospective buyers a choice of size and pitch.

The first and most demanding part to prepare is the reeds, which ultimately determine the quality of the instrument and the reputation of its maker. The initial preparation of the reeds involve five tools. First, the loha sheet of alloy must be pounded flat to a thickness of approximately one millimeter on a crude anvil called a tung (Figure 47). The tung consists of a large block of wood approximately thirty centimeters long and twenty centimeters square with a piece of metal shaped like a small railroad spike driven into one side. The exposed end of this spike is flat. Using a hammer called a kawn-lek or kawn-saw whose head is metal and handle wood, the maker pounds the loha to its proper thickness (Figure 48).

The maker then turns to his traditional cutting surface, a section of an elephant's leg bone (Figure 49). These bones, whose length varies but rarely exceeds one meter, are purchased in Soo-rin province near the

Figure 46. A <u>kaen</u> maker in Roi-et province pounds the <u>kisoot</u> until it becomes pliable.

Figure 47. The anvil (<u>tung</u>) on which reeds are pounded.

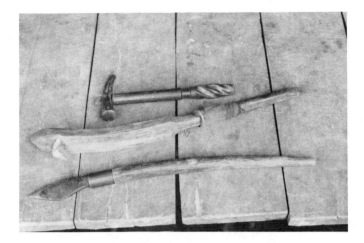

Figure 48. Three kaen-making tools: (top to bottom) hammer, "monkey-hand stick," and large knife.

Figure 49. Kaen-maker, Mr. Tui Rüang-siarun of Lao-kam village (Roi-et province), uses hammer and chisel to cut reeds in a strip of metal; his cutting surface is an elephant's leg bone.

Cambodian border where elephants are still domesticated for work. One side of the bone is filed down to make a flat cutting surface. Using a chisel called sio-yai ("large chisel"), the maker cuts off a stripe of loha metal four millimeters wide. Then, using another chisel called sio-lek ("small chisel"), he proceeds to cut out the three sides of the reed tongues (Figure 50). Each reed in the continuous and uncut strip is identical in size and shape (Figure 51). Then taking a section of a variety of bamboo called mai sah or piu mai sang whose skin is quite rough, the maker files the tips and edges of the reed tongues until they move easily through the aperture (Figure 52).

These tiny reed tongues may be cut in any of at least three shapes. Smyth[14] shows clearly a reed tongue whose one side is straight and the other with an angle. (Figure 53a) I have disassembled an inexpensive kaen purchased near the Mahasarakam market whose reeds measured four millimeters by thirteen millimeters. The tongue was very slightly wider at the base (1.5 millimeters) than at the tip (one millimeter [Figure 53b]) Mr. Tui's reeds also have tapered tongues, but they are wider at the base. Two nineteenth-century kaen from Laos in the Stearns Collection (University of Michigan) have reeds whose length varies from 2.0 centimeters to 1.0 centimeters respectively from the deepest to highest pitches, a characteristic now rarely observed.

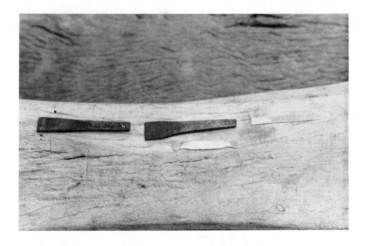

Figure 50. (Left to right) Two chisels for cutting reeds, a thin piece of metal for slipping the reed in place, and a reed (below).

The maker must then prepare the pipes of the kaen. While the bamboo is remarkably straight when delivered, some tubes must be straightened before use. After sufficient time to dry in the sun, the maker takes the curved tubes and heats them over a fire until they become pliable. Using a tool unique to kaen making called mai mü ling (literally "monkey hand stick"), proceeds to straighten the tubes (Figure 54). The mai mü ling is made from a curved piece of wood about four centimeters wide,

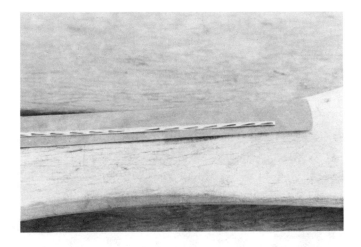

Figure 51. A finished strip of reeds for the kaen.

Figure 52. Using a rough piece of bamboo, Mr. Tui files the kaen reeds
smooth.

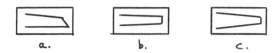

Figure 53. Three possible reed shapes, as described in the text.

Figure 54. Mr. Tui straightens a bamboo pipe with the "monkey-hand stick" (mai mü ling).

two centimeters thick, and twenty-five centimeters long with a narrow handle extending its length to forty-eight centimeters. Near the end opposite the handle is a small elbow-shaped piece of wood, the end of which is bored through the main piece. Placing one end of the curved tube under the elbow restrainer, the maker pulls the tube over the convex side until it becomes straight. After being cut to proper length, the bamboo tubes still have nodes (kaw) which must be pierced before the pipes can be used. Using a metal stick about fifty centimeters long called a lek-see which has been placed in a fire until red hot, the maker forces its enlarged conical tip through the nodes. If the tube is long, he extends the lek-see with bamboo sections.

It is usual among conscientious makers that in a finished kaen the nodes should form a straight line just below the windchest. The sixteen tubes are therefore cut with this in mind. Further, the four longest tubes are equal while the remainder are cut in successively shorter pairs. Using a knife called meet-dawk (See Figure 48), the maker cuts reed holes called roo lin (hoo lin in Lao) in the tubes two finger widths above the nodes (Figure 55). The meet-dawk, whose metal blade is ten centimeters long and curved wooden handle about thirty-five centimeters, is not exclusive to kaen making, for it is also used in Central Thailand to make the klui,

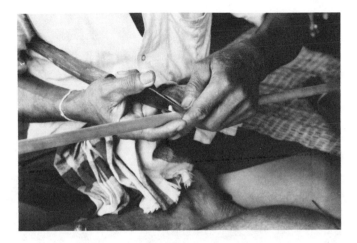

Figure 55. Using the knife, Mr. Tui cuts a hole in the pipe for the reed.

a bamboo fipple flute.
    Using the meet-dawk, the maker cuts a slot in the side of the tube
six millimeters wide and eleven millimeters long. The size of this aperture has been determined through experience, for he uses no measuring
devices. He then makes slits at each end of the aperture each about one
millimeter deep. Now he places a small brass tongue called mai saen
(ironically "wooden skimmer") under one slit and inserts one end of a reed,
now cut from the strip. Again using the meet-dawk, he shaves the reed
tongue thinner depending on the pitch it is to sound (Figure 56). If the
pitch is deep, the tip of the tongue must be thicker than the base. If the
pitch is high, the tip must be thinner than the base. This is a general
rule, and no great pains are taken at this time to shave the tongues to a
fine tolerance or graduate the thicknesses. The maker then inserts the
other end of the reed again using the mai saen as a kind of shoehorn
(Figure 57). The reed is then sealed airtight into place with calcium
hydroxide mixed with a little water. This fine powder, called boon, is
made from the shells of field oysters which are burned to an ash and
mixed with the water to form a white paste. It is often mixed with kamin,
a dark yellow ginger-like root known elsewhere as tumeric, which causes
the boon to become bright red. In recent times makers have sometimes
used ordinary face powder.
    After all the reeds have been fitted into the tubes, it is time to cut
out the pitch holes (roo pae or hoo pae in Lao) which determine the speaking length of the pipes. Each of the seven pitches on a kaen baet (sixteen
tubes) have upper octaves as well. The lower pitch is called mae ("mother") while the upper is called look ("child"). The "mother" must be prepared first. Taking the first pipe on the right (low A), the maker sets its
pitch according to the range of the singer the kaen will accompany (in
which case the singer must be present) or the convenience and taste of a
soloist. If the kaen will accompany a troupe, he must use standardized
pitches. In the case of mawlum moo, the first pitch hole will be 8½ finger

Figure 56. With the reed partially inserted, Mr. Tui shaves the reed to its proper thickness.

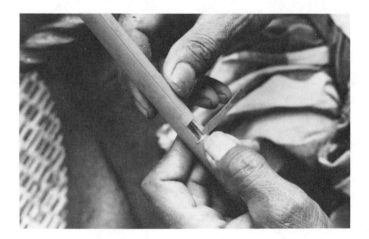

Figure 57. Sliding the reed over the hole and into place.

widths below the reed while for mawlum plun it will be eight widths.
These pitch holes, measuring 1.5 centimeters by 1.0 centimeters, must be
cut on the side opposite the reed so that they may be hidden from view
since the reeds face outwards within the windchest.

Taking a piece of palm leaf, he then measures the distance from the
bottom of the reed to the top of the pitch hole (Figure 58). To find the
upper pitch hole, the maker measures off three lengths above the reed
with the original strip of palm leaf and cuts another pitch hole. This will
be the foundation pitch for the kaen. The principle is that three quarters
to the speaking length is above the reed and one quarter below it. The
octave, the fourth pipe on the right, is then set by folding the original
strip in half and proceeding according to the rule. For various reasons,
such as nongraduated reed lengths, the pitch will be slightly flat but is
corrected by enlarging the upper pitch hole until the octave is pure. The
kaen maker, placing his mouth over both reeds, blows them together to
compare pitches (Figure 59).

Figure 58. Using a strip of palm leaf, Mr. Tui measures the distance to
the pitch hole.

Secondly, the maker sets pitches for the d pair (L-3 and R-6). Taking
his original strip of palm leaf, the maker folds half of it in half resulting
in a strip three quarters the original length. Then, measuring one length
below the reed and three above, he again cuts two pitch holes. The maker
will then compare the a' with the d' as he compared the octaves, listening
to the fourths and fifths which should be roughly in tune.

At this point the system of folding the strip of palm leaf breaks down.
The next pitches set are the two g pipes (R-3 and L-6) which are in unison
and therefore identical. To accomplish this, he places the octave a pipe
next to the g pipe and cuts a pitch hole even with the center of the lower
pitch hole of the a pipe. (Figures 60 and 61) Making a scratch at this
point, he cuts the pitch hole towards the end of the tube. Then comparing

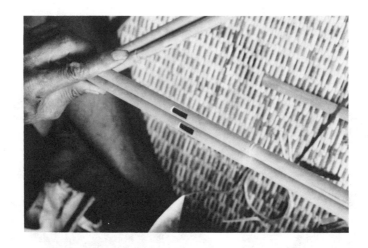

Figure 60.   The pitch holes for certain pairs of pipes are compared visually.

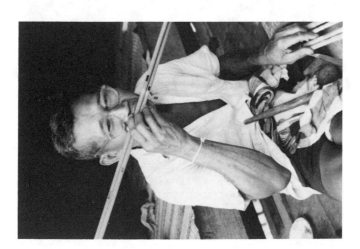

Figure 59.   Mr. Tui checks the tuning of two pipes by blowing them together.

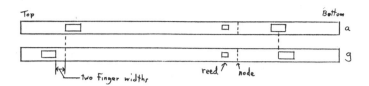

Figure 61. A visual comparison of the g and a pipes.

the two pipes again, always keeping the nodes in a stright line, he makes
another scratch about two finger widths above the upper pitch hole of the
a' pipe. He then cuts the pitch hole, but it must be tuned in comparison
with the two d pipes. Obviously, the second g pipe will be cut like the
first.

The next pair to be set, c and its octave (R-2 and L-1) is accomplished
by comparing the finished lower d pipe with the unfinished lower c pipe.
(Figure 62) Placing the nodes in a straight line, the maker cuts pitch holes
in the c pipe beginning one finger width above the lower pitch hole of the
d pipe and 1½ to 2 fingers below the upper pitch hole. The holes are
therefore cut toward the center rather than the ends. The holes are shaved as needed when the maker compares the c pitch with g or a. To find
the octave of c he measures with a new piece of palm leaf from the reed
to the top of the lower pitch hole. As in the case of the a and d pairs,
the strip is folded, marked off once below the reed and three times above
it, and the pitches compared aurally.

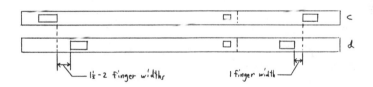

Figure 62. A visual comparison of the c and d pipes.

The e pair (L-4 and R-7) is derived from the g pipe. Again placing the
lower pipe in relation to the g pipe, he cuts a lower pitch hole whose top
is even with the bottom of that of the g pipe. (Figure 63) Then he cuts a
top pitch hole whose bottom is one thumb width above the top of the g
pitch hole. The pitch can be compared aurally with the a pipes. The octave e will be determined as described above using a piece of palm leaf.

The next to last pair is the f and its octave (L-5 and L-7). In this
case the maker compares the lower f pipe with the lower e pipe in the
usual manner. (Figure 64) He cuts the upper pitch hole so that its bottom
is even with the top of the e pitch hole. For the lower hole, he makes a
scratch five millimeters below the top of the pitch hole for the e pipe.

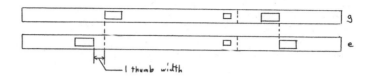

Figure 63. A visual comparison of the g and e pipes.

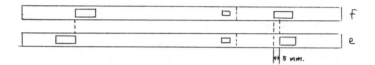

Figure 64. A visual comparison of the f and e pipes.

Then checking aurally with the c pipes, he enlarges the hole until the pairs are in tune. Again the f octave is set as described in earlier cases.

The last pair is the b and its octave (L-2 and R-5). Comparing the lower pitches with the lower c pipe, the maker cuts the upper pitch hole so that its bottom is even with the top of the c pitch hole. (Figure 65). Then he makes a scratch about one third below the bottom of the lower pitch hole and cuts upwards until the pipe is in tune with the e pair.

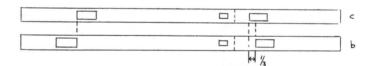

Figure 65. A visual comparison of the c and b pipes.

Finally the superoctave, a' (R-8), two octaves above the fundamental, and the g' octave (L-8), both of which are used as drones and do not appear on the kaen jet (fourteen tubes), are set from the lower pipes using the palm leaf method described earlier.

Throughout this process the maker will improve the voicing of the reeds whenever necessary by further scraping or shaving them until the timbre is correct and remains so during inhalation and exhalation. While the system of folding palm leaf into various lengths breaks down, the ratio principle quite unknown to the maker is nevertheless involved. When the maker folds the strip in half, he uses the ratio 2/1 or halving the pipe's length to produce the octave. When he folds the strip to 3/4 its original length to produce the fourth above, he is using the ratio 4/3. The

fifth, whose ratio is 3/2 or 2/3 the length of the fundamental pipe, pre-
sumedly could have been found by folding the strip into thirds. Makers
have learned this system of pitch setting by rote from their teachers and
understand little of the rationale behind it. In the case of comparing two
pipes, this is little more than the result of having found the proper lengths
by trial and error at some time. The relationships were then simply memorized and passed down from teacher to pupil.

Next the maker must carve the windchest of daokaen from whatever
wood he has chosen. To do this he may use the meet-dawk with which he
cut both reed and pitch holes or somewhat larger versions, one similar to
a machete and called simply meet, the other similar to the meet-dawk
but having a blade about thirty centimeters long. The dao, which is about
fourteen centimeters long, must be smooth on the outside, but the unseen
inside may be left rather rough (Figure 66). At one end, a blowing hole
called the roo bao is cut into the slightly concave mouthpiece. At the
other end, which remains closed, there is a narrow tail called the hang-
daokaen which is sometimes decorated with simple ring carvings. (Figure
67)

Figure 66. Using a large knife, a kaen maker carves the windchest.

The word dao has several meanings in Lao. One meaning is "to collect"
or "assemble," and while it is true that the dao collects the tubes together

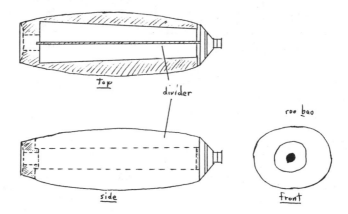

Figure 67. Side, top, and front views of a <u>daokaen</u> (windchest).

and supports them, this meaning is probably not the source of the term. The most widely known meaning is "breast" or "breast-shaped object." Indeed, the <u>dao</u> is sometimes called <u>dao nom</u> or literally "woman's breast." Moreover, the <u>hang</u> ("tail") clearly resembles a teat. As will be elaborated later, the <u>kaen</u> player's <u>wai kroo</u> ceremony, like the <u>kaen</u> maker's, uses an unusually large number of objects associated with women. One <u>kaen</u> player, in fact, told me that the <u>kaen</u> is a "female instrument." The meaning of <u>dao</u> which is of most interest, however, is "gourd" or "waterjar with a long neck." The ramifications of this meaning considering the fact that many mouth organs found elsewhere in Southeast Asia usually have gourd windchests are significant.

With the completion of the <u>dao</u>, the maker may then proceed to finish the instrument or put it aside until a prospective buyer comes along. To complete the instrument, the maker must first finish the <u>dao</u> and then prepare the <u>kisoot</u>. Before the tubes can be inserted into the <u>dao</u>, flat bamboo dividers must be installed along both the top and bottom of the <u>dao</u> to separate the pipes and keep them straight. These dividers, measuring about one centimeter wide, five millimeters thick, and ten or more centimeters long, are fitted into small notches in the <u>dao</u> without the aid of glue. Since they are flat on top while the <u>dao</u> is curved, the top corners of the dividers protrude and must be shaved flush with the surface of the <u>dao</u>. As a result, the dividers parallel the shape of the <u>dao</u>.

As noted earlier, <u>kisoot</u> is prepared by pounding it on a wood block with a wooden beater dipped in water. The water prevents the <u>kisoot</u> from sticking to the beater. It should also be noted that <u>kaen</u> makers and players normally moisten their fingers with spittle before working with the <u>kisoot</u> to prevent its sticking to the skin. After the <u>kisoot</u> has become solid black in color and pliable, the maker breaks off small pieces and rolls them into round strands resembling licorice sticks about thirty centimeters long. These he lays on the floor beside him (Figure 68). Then he begins inserting the tubes into the <u>dao</u> with the reeds facing outwards

Figure 68. With kisoot rolled into strips, the kaen maker wraps some around each pipe.

(inside the dao). He starts with the first tube on the right and proceeds toward the rear of the kaen, then on the left side from the rear to the front. After placing each tube inside the dao, he wraps a piece of kisoot around it both above and below the dao without smoothing it or sealing the openings completely (Figure 69). When all the pipes are inserted, he uses his moistened fingers to smooth the kisoot, force it into all the cracks, and places more between the rows which is forced into the cracks with a piece of bamboo.

Then the maker places a bamboo divider between the two rows of pipes about two centimeters from the bottom end of the kaen. The end of a long strip of locally grown grass called yahnang ("female grass" or "young grass medicine"), krah, or krua mai has been placed into a slit in the end of the divider before placing it between the rows. This grass must be soaked in water first, then have its brown outer skin shaved with the meet-dawk. The method of wrapping and tying varies slightly from maker to maker but follows a general pattern. The maker encircles the tubes once or twice, and on the third round at the halfway point he pushes the grass between the tubes, around the strands on the opposite side, then through again and laces it around the strands a couple of times. Lastly he knocks the kaen soundly on the floor to make certain all pipes are even at the bottom.

Figure 69. The cross section of a half-completed kaen.

Blowing into this kaen will cause all pitches to sound simultaneously. It is the missing fingerholes that would prevent the reeds from sounding. Using a strip of thin bamboo, the maker places it around three sides of the tubes about five or six centimeters above the dao and secures it on the fourth side with a leftover piece of yah nang grass. By now he will have placed a number of iron sticks, lek-see, into a fire so that the tips have become red hot. Using the bamboo strip as a guide, he then burns finger holes called roo nup two or three millimeters in diameter into the pipes (Figure 70). The finger holes of the front two pipes, because they are played by the thumbs, face the player and are about two to three centimeters above the dao. The last pipe on each side, because they are placed by the little fingers, will also be lower than the rest, usually three to four centimeters above the dao. The placement and diameter of the finger holes are not constant from one maker to another, some placing them much closer to the dao. The dao mouthpiece may extend up to two centimeters in front of the pipes, though some makers will shorten it considerably. Because Westerners have longer noses and thicker fingers than Lao, they often experience difficulty in playing the kaen.

Now that individual pitches may be played, the maker begins checking each note to make certain the pitch and timbre are correct and matched, that octaves, fourths, and fifths sound in tune, and that pitch and timbre remain constant whether he inhales or exhales. When a reed appears to

Figure 70. Using a red-hot poker, Mr. Tui burns a finger hole into each pipe.

need finishing, the maker pushes the pipe downwards from the dao until the reed is exposed. The kisoot remains in place though he must be careful not to let any catch on the reed as it passes. He will then shave the reed if necessary, file it with rough bamboo, or poke it with the mai saen. He can test it by placing his mouth over the reed, covering the finger hole, and blowing. When he is satisfied that the instrument is playable, he binds the tubes with yah nang grass about two thirds way up before the pairs of tubes begin their stepwise reduction in length. He also binds the four longest pipes, though without a divider.

As noted earlier there is no standard pitch for kaen. Kaen are normally used individually or with a single singer whose range it must match. There are no known records of any government influence over music such as was known in old China where the Imperial Music Office set a basic pitch for each dynasty. Nevertheless, all kaen that I have observed have the same intervallic relationships whether produced in Oobon, Roi-et, Kawn-gaen, or Laos. On first encounter it is difficult to detect any practical differences between the tempered Western diatonic scale and the tuning system of the kaen. The intervals beginning with the c pair (L-1 and R-2) are tone, tone, semi-tone, tone, tone, tone, semi-tone, just as the Western diatonic major scale. While leading tones are obviously missing in the Lao pentatonic scales, there are clear differences between major and minor thirds and sixths.

In July, 1974, I used a Strobeconn to determine in cents the intervals of two kaen baet and one kaen hok. In testing the instruments, I had to blow the pitches and thus the wind pressures were unstable and slightly different from one test to another. Figure 71 provides a statistical summary of the intervals in cents on the three kaen tested.

The semitones of the first instrument varied from 86 cents to 101 cents during the first trial and from 83 to 100 in the second, while the whole tones varied from 181 cents to 217 cents during the first trial and from 185 cents to 219 cents in the second. The other instrument showed similar results. Figure 72 provides a summary of the averages. Thus it is seen that indeed the pitches of the kaen played in sequence match very closely the pitches of the Western equal-tempered diatonic scale. It should be added that the traditional method of setting the kaen's pitches as described earlier precludes any Western influence.

In this respect the Lao tuning system is quite different from that of Siamese (Central Thai) instruments where there are seven equi-distant intervals in an octave. Whereas a Western whole step is 200 cents and a semitone 100 cents, the Siamese interval is a theoretical 171.4 cents.[15]

Mr. Tui reported that new kaen often do not sound as well as players would like, but after a break-in period of several weeks or months, the instrument's tones will improve. If the instrument continues to be used regularly, it will retain its qualities while irregular use will allow the reed tongues to become hard or corrode. A good kaen, if cared for, will last ten years or more. The lifespan, however, depends more on the tubes than the reeds since improper handling will result in cracked or broken tubes. Kaen should be stored vertically in a cloth bag to prevent the reeds from warping which would alter the timbre and volume. If stored in the open, a kaen may be attached by two forces. The first is dirt and sand, these being airborne much of the time in the extremely dry Northeast region. The second is insects, especially red ants, which build nests inside the dao, ruining the kaen. Extremely dry, cold weather, which is common during December and January in the Northeast, causes the kaen to sound somewhat out of tune, while extremely humid weather during the rainy season causes the kaen to sound sluggish and subdued. If a kaen is left in direct sunlight or left in a closed car during the heat of the day, the kisoot will melt and run into the dao, ruining the reeds. During the winter kisoot may become brittle and crack.

Professional and other serious kaen players purchase their kaen directly from the maker in his home. They may order in advance, choose from several unfinished kaen, or if the maker has any on hand, choose from several finished instruments. Dilettantes and youthful students buy their kaen in the provincial and district town markets, usually from itinerant salesmen who may or may not have made the kaen. These salesmen are often seen under the trees around the post office or other public buildings surrounded by tricycle-taxi drivers, people coming from the market, and general idlers.

Today kaen are made in at least eight of the sixteen provinces of Northeast Thailand as well as several in the Central region. The latter provinces include Soopan-booree (Suphanburi), Rat-booree (Ratburi), Sara-booree (Saraburi), Pet-booree (Petburi), Brajin-booree (Prachinburi), Na-kawn-sawan (Nakhornsawan), Pitsanoolok (Phitsanulok), and Petchaboon (Phetchbun). Little is known of the kaen from these provinces except that the dao of kaen from Sara-booree and Brajin-booree provinces are

Pitches	Kaen _baet_ (1)		Kaen _baet_ (2)		Kaen hok	
	Trial 1	Trial 2	Trial 1	Trial 2	Trial 1	Trial 2
A-B	189	191	200	198		
B-c	93	100	93	96		
c-d	217	208	209	207	202	204
d-e	198	202	198	201	(d-f) 313	(d-f) 310
e-f	86	87	102	103		
f-g	212	213	200	197	179	180
g-a	208	202	199	204	213	217
a-b	181	185	192	185	(a-c) 298	(a-c) 292
b-c'	101	98	107	110		
c'-d'	215	219	202	205		
d'-e'	205	206	207	205		
e'-f'	87	83	101	101		
f'-g'	191	192	194	194		
g'-a'	217	216	216	212		

Figure 71. Summary of intervals in cents on three kaen.

	Kaen baet (1)		Kaen baet (2)			Kaen hok	
	Trial 1	Trial 2	Trial 1	Trial 2		Trial 1	Trial 2
semi-tone	91.7	92.0	100.7	102.5	whole tone	198.0	200.3
whole tone	203.3	203.4	201.7	200.8	minor third	305.5	301.0

Figure 72. Statistical summary of average intervals in cents on three kaen.

said to be made on lathes. Kaen making outside the Northeast can be explained by the fact that the Siamese armies carried thousands of Lao from Wiangjun in the early nineteenth century into Central Thailand, and some of them maintained traditional arts such as kaen making. There are only a few makers in each of these provinces who make kaen for their friends or sometimes sell them to souvenir shops and exporters in Bangkok. Low quality specimens, probably from Central Thailand, have begun turning up in American gift and import shops, but these are rarely playable.

In the Northeast region the most important province by far is Roi-et where kaen making is concentrated in the district surrounding the provincial capital. Of the seventeen villages in See-gaeo subdistrict, twelve are known to have kaen makers. In 1964 it was estimated that eighty percent of the families in See-gaeo subdistrict town, whose population was then about 240 families, included kaen makers.[16] In Lao-kam village where Mr. Tui is the best known maker, an estimated thirty men were making kaen in 1973. In addition to See-gaeo, five villages in Müang-lat subdistrict have kaen makers as well as seven villages in Baw-pran district. This list is doubtless incomplete, but there is no central organization of kaen makers.

In Kawn-gaen province to the east kaen makers are known to live in villages in three districts, Poo-kio, Nawng-rüa, and Ban-pai. In Galasin province two districts are known to have makers, Gamalasai and Kao-wong. The former district is near the Roi-et border close to See-gaeo while the latter is in a mountainous area and includes a village where Pootai people make kaen. Goompa-wabee district in Oodawn-tanee province has at least one village where kaen are made. Nakawn-panom province along the Maekong River is known to have one kaen-making district, Nagae. Mr. Tui said that most kaen made in Nakawn-panom are sold across the river in Laos.

In Oobon province kaen are made in at least two districts, one surrounding the provincial capital and the other to the east in Piboon-bungsahan district. Makers in Roi-et, however, consider kaen from Oobon inferior. Formerly, kaen making flourished in Mahasarakam province bordering Roi-et, but today it is known in only two villages, one in Na-chuk district and one in Kosum-pisai district. Lastly kaen are made in Lung-noktah district of Yasoton province, but the kaen observed from this area in a shop were of poor quality.

Kaen making in Laos is not so widespread as in Northeast Thailand. Kaen were known to be made in Wiangjun province including at the School of Fine Arts in Wiangjun where kaen are highly finished. The Lao prefer kaen to which a zebra-stripe design has been added. When the kaen is otherwise finished, the maker places strips of banana leaf around the tubes and holds the instrument over a fire for a few minutes. Upon removing the banana leaf, a brownish design appears. Kaen with this sort of design appear in Central Thailand as well, but in the Northeast makers and players prefer plain instruments. Mawlum Sootee-sompong of Roi-et, who travelled with USIS propaganda teams in Laos for fourteen years, reported that most of the kaen played in Laos either came from Thailand or their makers had migrated from there. No informant could name specific Lao provinces where kaen making flourished though kaen makers no doubt live here and there in isolated villages.

In short, Northeast Thailand is the center of kaen making. Furthermore, Roi-et province probably produces as many kaen as the rest of Thailand combined. When Mr. Tui was asked why there are so many kaen makers around See-gaeo subdistrict, he replied that some of the villages in this district were very old, older than Roi-et city whose history goes back to Khmer times before the Lao came. He believes that the kaen was invented in this area and only gradually spread to other provinces explaining why so few makers live elsewhere. As explained earlier, mawlum singing flourishes in the provinces along the Chi River from Oobon to Kawn-gaen. Roi-et, being the center of this area, is a natural place for kaen making. It is also close to the areas where the bamboo grows. Villages which specialize in one craft, such as silk weaving, umbrella making, silver making, and pottery making are common throughout Thailand. That the craft originated in that particular village does not necessarily follow, though.

Myths and History

The Lao, like many other peoples, use myths to explain the origin of certain aspects of their cultures. Not unexpectedly, the Lao have myths concerning the origin of the kaen. Perhaps the most prominent is that told in the kaen-making villages around Roi-et.

Once upon a time there was a hunter who while seeking deer in the forest heard the rapturous sounds of the garawek bird. When he returned to his village, he began telling everyone about its wonderful song. A certain widow, upon hearing his tales, desired to hear the bird for herself and asked the hunter to take her with him on his next trip. Agreeing, the hunter led the widow deep into the forest where the garawek began singing as usual. "Listen to the bird's song. Is it not charming?" asked the hunter. As the widow fell more and more in love with the bird's song, she said, "How can I enjoy the song whenever I want to hear it? If I stay here there is no food or shelter and wild beasts may harm me. If I want to come often, it is a long and difficult journey." Then she had an idea. "I must invent an instrument which will imitate the singing of the garawek."

Upon returning to her village, the widow experimented with several types of instruments, some plucked, some bowed, some struck, and some blown. None could reproduce the sound of the garawek to her satisfaction. At last she cut a small piece of bamboo resembling a flute and found that it made an exquisitely

beautiful sound, very much like the garawek. Gradually she
improved the sound until she was pleased and considered it a
success.

Then, desiring to present her instrument to the king,
Basenti-goson, she began seeking someone to sponsor an audience for her. By the time she found someone, she had made
several more instruments, improved the body and sound, and
gained more experience. When all was ready, she and her
sponsor went to the palace. Upon arrival they asked and received permission to enter. Both entered the great hall
crawling on their knees as is the custom, stopped at a proper
distance from the king, paid their respects and sat quietly.
Then the king asked, "Why have you come here?" The widow's
escort replied, "Your majesty, the king, I brought this woman
so that she might show you a new musical instrument that she
has invented. She desires to give you the instrument with
deep respect and gratitude as you are the owner of her life."

Pleased after hearing the widow's story, the king instructed
her to play her instrument. Paying respect to the king, she
sat politely and properly and began playing her song. When
she finished, she asked if it was not beautiful. The king replied
that it was fair and asked her to continue playing. She played
until after her last song when she asked, "Are you pleased now?"
The king said, "Tia nee kaen dae." ["This time it was better."]
She said, "What shall the instrument be called?" The king
replied, "You may call it according to my words, kaen."[17]

Considering how the Southeast Asian climate tends to destroy written
documents and that various armies from time to time have destroyed
whole cities and their treasures, it is no wonder that few early documents
on the kaen remain. The Lao lack elaborate tombs such as the Chinese
built in which they preserved not only the bodies of famous people but
everyday articles, written records, and sometimes musical instruments.
Consequently, the early history of the kaen remains essentially a blank.
Some speculate that the kaen was derived from other instruments
still familiar to the Lao such as from the panpipes, unaware that the step
from a bundle of flutes to an indirectly blown free reed is a large one.
Indeed, both Westerners and Thai are inclined to translate kaen into "panpipes." According to S.E. Tiao Somsanit,[18] the kaen derived from the
wot, a circular panpipes about twenty to thirty centimeters long with a
large round tip of beeswax at one end which guides the air into the tubes.
Ordinarily the wot is a children's toy attached to a string and flung through
the air. A few have attempted to play the wot as a musical instrument
though without much success. It is highly unlikely that the kaen and wot
have more in common than bamboo tubes. (See Figure 6, p. 16)
Since Siamese historical documents relating to music before 1767 are
virtually nonexistent, one is forced to turn to European sources for information. References to the kaen before the second half of the nineteenth
century are few. The earliest and most problematic is the instrument
illustrated in Marin Mersenne's Harmonie universelle of 1637 where "Proposition XXXV" shows an "Indian" instrument consisting of twelve narrow
tubes in a disassembled state.[19] The free reed is clearly illustrated, but

the pipes, while in graduated lengths above the reeds, are also graduated below the reeds. The windchest is missing, but Mersenne states, "Now this instrument is rather similar to our organs, and can produce an excellent concert of flutes, which a single person will be able to play by means of a skin similar to that of the musette."[20] We must assume that Mersenne's description includes errors since a multi-tubed free-reed instrument is not likely to have been played as a bagpipe, but we cannot be sure that this instrument is the Lao kaen either.

The earliest known illustration of the kaen among the Lao is found on the exquisite gilded base relief front wall under the portico of Wut Mai (Vat Mai) in Luang-prabang, Laos. Finot gives the date of this building as 1796,[21] but Clarac and Smithies give 1820.[22] Near the left door there is a classical Siamese ensemble and above it a kaen player. The instrument, however, is unclear in its details. While the tubes appear to be very short, the windchest cannot be seen well enough to determine its shape.

Of the dozen-plus descriptions of the kaen in the later nineteenth and early twentieth centuries, all but one are based on the observations of Europeans in Central Thailand or contact with Siamese musicians visiting Europe. A number of writers describe the kaen in other terms. Frederick A. Neal's 1852 account of Siam, which includes the earliest written reference to the kaen after Mersenne, calls it a luptuma.[23] Anna Harriette Leonowens similarly calls it luptima in her 1870 The English Governess at the Siamese Court.[24] Slightly later both Hermann Smith[25] and A. J. Hipkins[26] refer to the kaen as phan, a term commonly used even today in Central Thailand. The well-known Central Thai melody "Lao phaen" is intended as an imitation of the kaen.

That the kaen baet with sixteen tubes has not always been the standard instrument is easily seen in pre-twentieth-century sources. Mersenne's illustration has twelve tubes while chronologically the next description, by Neale in 1852, asserts that kaen had from ten to twelve tubes. "A Traveller," writing in an 1857 Southern Literary Messenger issue, also stated that ten was the usual number of tubes and that length varied from about a six-foot average to some fifteen feet.[27] Leonowens, possibly copying details from earlier writers, also mentions twelve as the normal number.[28] Smyth, however, writing in 1898 reports:

> That the present form [fourteen tubes] of the instrument is now stereotyped is evident from the difficulty I had in getting any one to make me one with sixteen reeds (and two octaves). The answer was always mai dai, it is impossible; mai koe, it has not been customary. But I got one at length from an unusually enterprising Wieng Chan man who makes large numbers of kens for sale; but it is a four-sawk (6 ft. 8 in.) instrument, and demands powerful lungs. A smaller size he maintained it was impossible to make such compass.[29]

P. A. Thompson's 1910 account also describes the kaen as having fourteen tubes,[30] as does Graham's of 1912.[31]

Whereas the kaen with sixteen tubes is universal today in Northeast Thailand, kaen players who have travelled in Laos report that the kaen jet with fourteen tubes is still very common though the kaen baet is becoming more so since Lao often buy their instruments from across the river in Northeast Thailand. According to Mr. Tui, the kaen baet only became popular in Northeast Thailand during the period 1910 to 1930.

Kaen appear to have been well-known in Central Thailand in the nine-teenth century. Neale lists the instrument among classical Siamese instru-ments as if played with them and adds that the "luptuma" is an instrument of Siamese invention.[32] As noted earlier, the Second King was an enthu-siast for things Lao when Sir John Bowring visited Siam in 1855.

> Once, calling on the Second King, I found him playing on a singularly harmonious instrument, composed of reeds of the bamboo, an instrument nearly eight feet in length: it was, he said, a gift from the Prince of Laos, and he gratified me by presenting it for my acceptance.[33]

A further mention of the Second King's kaen playing activities appears in the Chronicles of the Fourth Reign for the year 1865.

> During his lifetime, the Second King had constructed at baan sii thaa district a small place for pleasure and open air enjoyment where he had a Laos-style pavillion erected for his personal convenience. He enjoyed playing the Laotian reed mouth organ known as khaan, and he often journeyed to the town of phanadnikhom, to the Laos district of sam prathuan, within the city limits of nakhoonchajsii, and to baansiithaa district, within the limits of saraburii, where he would pass the time playing the Laotian musical instrument.[34]

A most interesting tale about the kaen and its use in Bangkok is told by A. W. Graham in his 1912 description of the country.

> The ken has long ago made its way to the south and is very much admired by the Siamese. A well-trained band of fifteen performers is maintained in Bangkok by one of the Royal Princes who, being himself an accomplished musician, has provided it with an extensive repertoire, the orchestra for which he has arranged himself. The band plays Scottish airs and European dance-music most effectively.[35]

Finally, it is interesting to note several appearances of the kaen in Europe. M. A. Grehan illustrates a large case containing Siamese instru-ments at a mid-nineteenth-century "Exposition de S.M. le Roi de Siam" in Paris which includes two kaen.[36] Among the instruments which Hermann Helmholtz evidently observed from Siam at the London Inventions Exhibi-tion in 1885 was a kaen,[37] but while he measured the tuning of the Sia-mese instruments, did not mention that of the kaen. A. J. Hipkins also mentioned the "phan" from this exhibition in his 1921 study of instru-ments.[38] Lastly, E. M. von Hornbostel's landmark study on form in Siamese classical music based on a visiting ensemble in Germany and pub-lished in 1920 includes a photograph showing among other musicians two kaen players.[39] No mention is made of them in the text, however.

The Function of the kaen

There are two traditional functions for the kaen. The first is to accompany mawlum singers and mawlum moo and mawlum plŭn troupes. For this they use kaen baet today though the kaen jet was more usual in

earlier days. Kaen gao with eighteen tubes, which normally measured two
meters or more, usually accompanied mawlum pün though today the few
surviving mawlum pün use kaen baet. The kaen gao is rarely seen today,
and few players have had any experience with it. Mr. Tui reported when
he made one for me that he now builds only two or three a year. I must
confess that I have never encountered one in a village and found only one
player, Mr. Soot-tee, age sixty-eight in 1973, who could play it with con-
fidence.

The kaen hok is an anomaly because it is widely made and sold but has
no apparent function. Most players, when asked if they play kaen hok,
smile and protest that it is merely a child's instrument. Some informants
told me that children are given a kaen hok on which to learn when young
and later graduate to a kaen baet. Still I have observed relatively few
children playing the kaen hok. Some makers produce large numbers of
poor quality kaen hok which eventually do become gifts to children much
as we give our children plastic whistles. The kaen hok, however, is capable of relatively serious playing though few good performers will admit
an ability on this instrument. The kaen hok is also capable of accompanying mawlum though no self-respecting mawlum would use one today except
as a joke. A more likely explanation is that it may be the predecessor or
original form of the larger kaen used today. In this sense it is an anach-
ronism, a vestigal organ as it were, which still remains but has lost its
function.

Secondly, kaen may be played solo. But while some players have
become accomplished virtuosos capable of playing the entire repertory in
several distinct styles, they have virtually no forum for their playing.
There are no solo kaen concerts, no time set aside in a mawlum performance for virtuoso displays by the accompanists, and few recordings of solo
kaen. While the government television station at Kawn-gaen (TV 5) sponsored contests in 1971 and 1972 for the best mawlum glawn singers and
mawlum moo troupes, it rejected the suggestion for a similar contest for
kaen players claiming that this would bore audiences. The kaen player's
low status is reflected in the amount of money he collects in a mawlum
performance. Even though he will have worked as hard as the singer, he
will collect only ten to twenty percent of the amount the singer receives.
He is merely a functionary who provides support and background for the
singers who dominate.

A generation or more ago, however, solo kaen playing had a distinct
function in village society which has largely disappeared today. It was
formerly the custom in Northeast Thailand and may still be in Laos that
in the evening after the work was done the parents would retire for the
night leaving their children to their own devices. Arranged marriages
were not characteristic among ordinary Lao. The girls, therefore, would
sit in the public portion of the open homes, the hüan noi or literally
"small house," and wait for their boyfriends. The men, meanwhile, singly
or in groups, would begin walking to the villages and homes where their
girlfriends lived. To maintain courage and announce their arrival, the men
played the kaen as they walked through the fields and village streets.
Women would come to recognize the playing of their favorite suitors.
Upon arrival at the home where the women had assembled, the kaen playing ceased while men and women engaged in a literary joust called
pa-nyah.[40] After the courting was finished, the boys would return home
again playing their kaen. An eyewitness account written in 1886 took
note of this custom.

The Lao are very fond of music and love to sing and dance.
Many of the young men have curious reed organs which they
play skillfully. They are light and sweet-toned, and are very
well adapted to their wild and wierd melodies. You can hear
them answering each other through the night as they come
from far away to visit the pretty, blade-eyed girls in the distant
villages, and you can imagine those same girls listening intently
for the familiar notes they love best in all the band.[41]

Kaen playing of this type, like pa-nyah, has become extremely rare
today since those who formerly practiced it are now captivated by the
popular music heard incessantly on the radio and from wong dondree
("music ensembles") which now perform rock and roll at temple fairs. The
lure of the modern, exemplified by electric guitars and organs, saxophones,
and girls in mini-skirts, has replaced traditional customs such as pa-nyah.
Still, the kaen remains a popular instrument for all sorts of celebrations.
One often sees young men, usually inebriated, playing the kaen in parades,
or more soberly in groups going from house to house collecting money for
a tumboon at a nearby wut. Some enterprising Northeasterners have been
known to go to Bangkok to sell cheap kaen on New Year's Eve to be used
for general noise making among the many Lao workers there.
    A well-known function for solo kaen is as a beggar's instrument. It is
common to see blind beggars playing the kaen in provincial and district
towns. Led by a boy or a wife, the beggar squats in front of a shop,
places a cup on the ground, and begins playing. If someone places a coin
in the cup, he moves on to the next shop. While most of these beggar
musicians are merely competent to play a few basic pieces, a few turn
out to be accomplished musicians. One such player, Mr. Wichian from
Oobon, went to Chiangmai in North Thailand because he thought he could
make more money there. Mr. Gerald Dyck, who was studying Northern
Thai music in Chiangmai, recorded Wichian and found him to be extremely
talented, having an extensive repertory.[42] Beggar players also appear at
temple fairs, evening markets, and other celebrations such as Red Cross
fairs where on a good night they may earn more than an ordinary laborer
does in a day.
    A more recent use of kaen is in the kaen wong or "kaen ensemble."
While in the villages kaen are only played by men and rarely in groups of
two or more, secondary schools and colleges began developing kaen ensembles after World War II. Ironically, girls usually dominate kaen wong.
Since all instruments must be matched in pitch, one kaen maker must
build all the instruments in a set. Because kaen wong normally perform
classical Thai melodies without the use of drones, kaen jet are adequate.
In this sense kaen wong is hardly a Lao custom since it is obviously an
imitation of the Central Thai ensembles, though the latter perform hetero-
phonically according to the characteristics of each instrument and the
kaen wong performs more or less in unison. Kaen wong are rarely found
in villages except in special dance troupes which perform in parades and
contests.
    Jarünchai Chonpairot describes three possible ensembles, a small one
with three to five kaen, a medium group with seven to ten kaen, and a
large group having twelve to twenty-four kaen.[43] He also notes that fifty
to one hundred kaen in a parade are effective. The kaen may be all of
the same size or different sizes an octave apart. In 1974 the College of
Education in Mahasarakam, Thailand, purchased from Mr. Tui a large

ensemble consisting of both kaen baet and kaen hok tuned an octave higher. Prof. Jarünchai, the leader, chose kaen baet so that they could be used for other purposes as well. The Mahasarakam Teacher Training College had earlier purchased a kaen wong having three sizes, kaen hok, medium length kaen jet and long kaen jet an octave deeper. Another writer describes three sizes, the small ensemble consisting of two large, two medium, and two small kaen, a medium ensemble having two large, three medium, and three small, and a large ensemble with two (or four) large, four medium, and four (or two) small kaen.[44] He notes that ching (finger cymbals), flutes, fiddles, and drums may be added as well.

Kaen are sometimes combined with other instruments in traditional performances. Smyth described an orchestra he observed in the 1890's in Luang-prabang. "We had a full orchestra of a couple of kens, a couple of two-stringed violins, and a high-pitched flageolet."[45] Danielou[46] and Souvanna Phouma[47] note that in Lao court music, which is similar to Siamese court music, the mahori or sep noi ensemble is composed of ranat (xylophone), kawng wong (bronze gongs mounted on a circular wood frame), saw (fiddles), drums, ching, and several kaen. It is similar to the mahoree ensemble in Bangkok except that kaen are not used in Central Thailand. Though the kaen is tuned quite differently from these other instruments, it seems to disturb no one.

NOTES

1.   Classifiers are words used for "how many objects" in plurals, such as "shoes, three pairs." Thus, three kaen would be "kaen sam dao" or "kaen sam duang."

2.   Bowring, The Kingdom and People of Siam, 2: 324.

3.   Herbert Warington Smyth, Five Years in Siam, from 1891-1896 2 vols. (London: John Murray, 1898) 1: 199.

4.   Herbert Warington Smyth, Notes of a Journey on the Upper Maekong, Siam (London: John Murray, 1895), p. 82.

5.   Prince Henri d'Orléans, Around Tonkin and Siam (London: Chapman and Hall, Ltd., 1894), p. 371.

6.   Madeleine Colani, "Essai d'ethnographie comparée," Bulletin de l'Ecole Francaise d'Extrême-Orient 36 (1936): 214.

7.   Pra Oobalee-koonoo-bamajan, Rüang kaen [The Story of the Kaen] (Bangkok: 1964), pp. 14-16.

8.   These are the octaves of pipes whose names were the same but preceded by mae.

9.   Curt Sachs, The History of Musical Instruments (New York: W. W. Norton, 1940), p. 182.

10. Pra Oobalee-koonoo-bamajan in his Story of the Kaen (Bangkok, 1964, p. 20) lists the following as necessary for a kaen maker's wai kroo ceremony: four baht, a piece of cloth called sin, a piece of white cloth, a bottle of rice whiskey, a hen's egg, five pairs of flowers and candles, a comb, a mirror, and a small clump of hair.

11. Ibid., p. 6.

12. Smyth, Five Years in Siam 2: 292.

13. Pra Oobalee-koonoo-bamajan, Story of the Kaen, p. 6.

14. Smyth, Five Years in Siam, 2: 294.

15. Morton, The Traditional Music of Thailand, p. 12.

16. Pra Oobalee-koonoo-bamajan, Story of the kaen, p. 24.

17. Ibid., pp. 2-4. See also, Anne Marie Gagneaux, "Le khene et la musique Lao," Bulletin des Amis du Royaume Lao 6 (1971), 176-7; Som Patrsandorn, "The Story of the kaen, klui, saw, and bia" written down by A. Bush-pages, Wittaya-sarn, January 8, 1958, pp. 13-14.

18. Gagneaux, "Le khene," p. 177.

19. Marin Mersenne, Harmonie universelle, 3 vols. (Paris, 1636; reprint ed. Paris: Editions du Centre National de la Recherche Scientifique, 1965), 3: 308; trans. Roger E. Chapman in 1 vol. (The Hague: M. Nijhoff, 1957), Proposition XXXV.

20. Ibid.

21. Louis Finot, "Recherches sur la litterature Laotienne," Bulletin de l'Ecole Francaise d'Extrême-Orient 17 (1917): 8.

22. Achille Clarac and Michael Smithies, Discovering Thailand, 2nd ed. (Bangkok: Siam Publications, 1972), p. 261.

23. Frederick Arthur Neale, Narrative of a Residence in Siam (London: Offices of the National Illustrated Library, 1852), p. 236.

24. Anna Harriette Leonowens, The English Governess at the Siamese Court (Boston: Fields, Osgood, and Co., 1870), p. 170.

25. Hermann Smith, The World's Earliest Music (London: Wm. Reeves, 1904), p. 210.

26. A. J. Hipkins, Music Instruments Historic, Rare, and Unique (London: A. and C. Black, 1921), p. xviii.

27. "A Traveller," "Siamese Amusements," Southern Literary Messenger 23 (May, 1857): 367.

28. Leonowens, English Governess, p. 170.

29. Smyth, Five Years in Siam, 2: 293-4.

30. Peter Anthony Thompson, Siam: An Account of the Country and the People, Oriental Series, vol. XVI (Boston: J. B. Millet Co., 1910), p. 175.

31. A. W. Graham, Siam: A Handbook of Practical, Commercial, and Political Information (London: Alexander Moring Ltd., 1912), p. 161.

32. Neale, Narrative of a Residence, p. 236.

33. Bowring, The Kingdom and People of Siam, 2: 88.

34. Jao-pra-yah Ti-pah-gor-ra-wong, The Dynastic Chronicles, Bangkok Era, the Fourth Reign (B.E. 2394-2411) (A.D. 1851-1868), 2: 354-5.

35. Graham, Siam: A Handbook, p. 162.

36. M. A. Gréhan, Le Royaume de Siam, 3rd ed. (Paris: Challamel Aime, Libraire-Editeur, 1869), unnumbered illustration.

37. Hermann, L. F. Helmholtz, On the Sensations of Tone, 2nd English ed., revised, based on 4th German ed. of 1877 by Alexander Ellis (London: 1885; reprint ed., New York: Dover, 1954), p. 556.

38. Hipkins, Musical Instruments Historic, p. xviii.

39. Erich M. von Hornbostel, "Formanalysen an siamesischen Orchester-stücken," Archiv fur Musikwissenschaft 2 (1919/1920): 307.

40. See Chapter 1, pp.

41. Mary Lovina Cort, Siam: Or, The Heart of Farther India (New York: A. D. Randolph and Company, 1886), p. 359.

42. Gerald P. Dyck, "They also serve," in Selected Reports in Ethnomusi-cology, vol. 2, no. 3 ed. David Morton (Los Angeles: University of Calif-ornia, 1975), p. 207.

43. Jarǔnchai Chonpairot, Kaen wong [Kaen Ensemble] (Mahasarakam Thailand: The College of Education, 1972), p. 24.

44. Pra Oobalee-koonoo-bamajan, Story of the Kaen, p. 13.

45. Smyth, Five Years in Siam, 1: 197.

46. Alain Daniélou, La musique du Cambodge et du Laos (Pondichéry [India], 1957), p. 14.

47. Prince Souvanna Phouma, "Music," in Kingdom of Laos, p. 88.

VI.

Kaen Playing in
Northeast Thailand

Introduction

Because the kaen baet with sixteen pipes is standard throughout North-east Thailand, it may be assumed that all discussions of kaen playing involve this instrument unless otherwise noted. Kaen players normally stand erect or sit in the cross-legged position, although squatting may sometimes be observed among blind kaen players going from shop to shop in the towns playing and begging. The kaen is held with the palm of each hand placed around the dao (windchest) with the finger tips covering the roo nup (finger holes). With the mouthpiece placed firmly against his lips, the player tilts the kaen to his left with the portion below the dao parallel to and resting against his right arm. The left wrist is flexed with the arm away from the kaen. If this position becomes tiring, he may tilt to the right, reversing his arms. Westerners find the kaen rather uncomfortable to play primarily because our noses are too long--Thai noses are flat and broad--and prevent the thumbs from playing the front pipes properly. Westerners, therefore, must hold the instrument vertically or even tilted slightly forward.

The two thumbs play the front pair of pipes, whose finger holes face the player. Though the rear pair (L-8 and R-8) may be played by the little fingers--and in fact the roo nup are lower to accommodate them--only expert players do so. For most players either of these two pipes will be sealed with small lumps of kisoot causing them to sound as drones. The remaining three fingers each control two consecutive pipes, the index fingers playing pairs two and three, the middle finger controlling four and five, and the ring finger six and seven. This pattern may be broken, however, when two neighboring pipes normally stopped by the same finger must be alternated several times in succession. Most players touch the roo nup with their finger tips, but some use the fleshy part of their fingers while others play flat-fingered. Curved fingers, however, tend to reduce the inequality of length and give the player greater dexterity and speed.

Because the reeds of the kaen are built to sound the same pitch on both inhalation and exhalation, the player must sustain the tone indefinitely with a minimum of interruption. It should be noted that kaen players do not practice circular breathing, i.e., breathing through their noses while maintaining a constant pressure from their cheeks, a technique used elsewhere in Thailand and Asia. The rate of breathing varies according to the quality of the <u>kaen</u> (fine instruments requiring less air), the length of the instrument (a long tube requiring more air), and the health of the player. Players, however, tend to draw the new breath on the regular accents. While players rarely discuss breathing, they do emphasize that blowing in short spurts is unwise because it is hard on the reeds and causes the player to become slightly dizzy from hyperventilation.

The use of tonguing and the resulting articulation may be exploited by skilled players for a variety of effects which will be noted later in specific instances. Players usually articulate each note with the tongue touching the roof of the mouth as if saying "la-la-la-la . . . ." Passages may also be played without tonguing to give it a more legato style. Lack of tonguing, however, makes the transition from inhalation to exhalation more noticeable and also emphasizes any unevenness in the player's finger technique. The drones, far from sounding continuously as in bagpipe music, respond to tonguing. A few players, usually for comic effect, have been known to flutter-tongue, but such a technique is quite exceptional.

As shown in Chapter 5, the tuning system of the <u>kaen</u> has seven pitches in the octave, some being whole steps and others half steps. Played in succession starting on R-2 or L-1, they form what is for practical purposes a diatonic major scale. Starting on either R-1 or R-4, they form a natural minor scale. Since the <u>kaen</u> has no standard pitch level, all transcriptions will equate the lowest pitch (R-1) with the pitch <u>A</u>, and thus there is no need for sharps or flats.

Figure 73. The pitches of the <u>kaen baet</u> with corresponding pipe numbers.

These seven pitches, however, do not constitute a scale, for Lao <u>kaen</u> playing follows the two pentatonic scales noted earlier, called <u>sun</u> and <u>yao</u>. Exceptions are found in accompanying <u>lum pün</u> when a sixth pitch is added as well as when players use either of the remaining two tones for special effect. The Lao tuning system is thus radically different from the Siamese tuning system where there are seven intervals theoretically an equal 171.4 cents apart.[1] Lao music, sounding more like Western music in its tuning, is thus easier for the Western ear to interpret and does not sound "out of tune" to us like Siamese music does.

Although Lao <u>kaen</u> players recognize five and possibly six modes, each a pentatonic scale, there are no theorists to impose logic on or extend these rudimentary theories. Unlike Indian and Chinese musicians, Lao players have no known written theoretical treatises to consult. The only writers who have attempted any sort of theoretical discussions were Western trained and interpreted the material according to Western musical thinking. The following discussion is a Westerner's attempt to interpret this material according to Lao practice, taking into consideration the music of neighboring cultures.

Each of the five modes has a name, sootsanaen, bo sai, soi, yai and
noi. They may be grouped in two ways. If we assume that the final tones
of pieces in these modes constitute a tonic or finalis, and as will be shown
later the melodic and harmonic characteristics of each piece justify such
an interpretation, we may consider sootsanaen, bo sai, and soi as a group
because each follows the same interval pattern, that of the sun scale:

Figure 74. The three kaen modes which follow the sun scale.

The pitch f appears only in bo sai and the pitch b only in soi. Yai and noi
together with an unnamed and little-used mode beginning on e constitute
a second grouping; these modes follow the yao scale.

Figure 75. The three kaen modes which follow the yao scale.

In each mode the two unused pitches are called siang som, literally "sour
notes" according to Tawng-koon, a highly-skilled blind kaen player from
Roi-et.
   The second grouping involves pairing modes which use the same pitches
but have different finals. Sootsanaen and yao both use the pitches g, a,
c, d, and e, but the former begins on g and the latter on a. The prominence of the minor third (a to c) in yai gives this mode a "minor" feeling
while the prominence of the major third (c to e) in sootsanaen gives this
mode a "major" feeling. The same relationship may be found between bo
sai and noi on the one hand and between soi and its unnamed cousin on e
on the other. The association of such foreign concepts as "major" and
"minor" are not inappropriate since sootsanaen, bo sai, and soi are meant
for a positive, happy mood, and yai, noi, and the e mode for a sad mood.
   Players conceptually group the modes in both ways since when performing solos they will tend to play sootsanaen, bo sai, and soi as a group
followed by yai and noi. When accompanying singing, however, if lum
tang sun is in sootsanaen, lum tang yao and lum döi will be in yai, or if
the first is in bo sai, the second will be in noi. The relationship between
soi and its little-used relative is not a problem because players rarely
accompany in soi. Although a few players use the e mode effectively, it
has certain limitations especially with regard to ambitus and the fact
that it would present the player with five consecutive pipes, the technical
problem which the seemingly illogical pitch arrangement of the kaen seeks
to eliminate.

Each of the six modes has at least one drone, these being produced either by placing a small wad of kisoot over the finger hole of the drone pipe or closing it with a finger. In five cases the drones consist of finalis and fifth and in one the final only, with few exceptions they are the highest pitches available. The only exception to the final-fifth rule is sootsanaen which uses only the final drone though the fifty is usually added manually in the final sonority. When playing in sootsanaen mode, the fourth finger of the left hand stops g (L-6), and a bit of kisoot stops the upper g (L-8); the drones are never released unless a special effect is desired. In bo sai the left thumb closes the upper c (L-1), while kisoot stops the upper g (L-8). Both soi and noi, because their tonics are d, close d and a (R-6 and R-8) with kisoot, while in yai kisoot closes e and a (R-7 and R-8).

Pitches may be played singly or in octaves. As a general rule, however, the lower octaves are rarely played alone because they tend to be overpowered by the drones. The ear follows the lowest sounding pitches as the melody line whether the upper octaves are played or not. If the separation from the lowest pitch to the highest is two octaves rather than one, as is the case with low a and high a (R-1 and R-8), the dominance of the lower pitch may be eliminated if there is a normal octave pair sounding between these extremes. For example, the e octave pair (L-4 and R-7) may be sounded in conjunction with the high a drone (R-8) and the low a (R-1), but the ear hears e as the melody pitch rather than a though it is lower.

Sootsanaen and yai require only simple octaves, but bo sai, soi, and to a lesser extent noi, require intermediate pitches as well. These stereotyped sonorities are fixed as part of the modal pattern and give these modes their distinctive sound. Until the individual improvisations in each mode are discussed, we shall not mention these or optional sonorities which increase the harmonic complexity of kaen music. Playing the kaen jet (fourteen tubes) or kaen gao (eighteen tubes) differs in no way from playing in kaen baet except that kaen jet lack the eighth pair of pipes thereby eliminating one of the drones in several modes and the kaen gao may add extra drones. Because L-8 on kaen gao is c" instead of g', in playing sootsanaen the player holds only one drone, L 6 (g), with his finger. In bo sai, however, he closes L-8 and L-9 (c" and c''') with kisoot, and for soi, noi, and yai adds R-9 (a"). Kaen hok (six tubes) is capable of playing only two modes, bo sai and noi, but in neither case are pipes stopped with kisoot. When playing noi, the player stops L-2 (d) with his second finger and in bo sai holds L-1 (c) with his thumb.

The meaning of the terms for the modes may be explained as follows: Sootsanaen is the most complex because of its emotional connotations. Soot means the "end," the "highest," or the "most." A naen is a person's original spouse from an earlier, i.e., a previous life, the belief being that one may only marry in this life a person who had been the spouse in a previous life. Sa is a shortened form of sai meaning "thread," though it could also relate to sao meaning "distance" or "measuring stick." Sanaen or sai-naen, then, would be the tie that binds the couple together, an abstraction combining current love with a kind of eternal union. It is also possible that originally the term was sootsanaen ("the end of the mountain") or that soot derives from sutra in Sanskrit. If soot does derive from sutra, the term may have been sutra soomeroo ("mountain sutra"). The current term, sootsanaen, does not require literal translation, however, for it is merely a beautiful, poetic word; perhaps it is the title of a kaen piece intended to be heard by the remote naen; some say it is a "melody of love."

Bo sai, on the other hand, simply means "left thumb," the finger producing one of the drones. Soi is a verb meaning "to tear into fragments" and refers to the short phrases that characterize soi. Yai, meaning "large," "great," or "bass," is the lower pitched mode related to noi meaning "small," "dimunitive," or "soprano."

Kaen players prefix each mode name with the word lai, e.g., lai soot-sanaen. While this word means "piece" in musical practice, in fact there is no way to distinguish the scalar mode from the improvisation. Whether asked to play sootsanaen or lai sootsanaen, the player always responds with an improvisation. The exact meaning and origin of the word are obscure, however, for no known dictionary defines the term in other than nonmusical meanings. Jarunchai Chonpairot believes the word lai [ลาย] relates to music through its definition of "side" in that the word refers to a limited area. In Lao (Wiangjun) this term is spelled lai [ລາຍ], but the dictionary definitions include several meanings for words spelled lai in Lao but rai in Thai, e.g., menu (rai-gan-ahan in Thai, lai-gan-ahan in Lao). Kerr's definition of the term lai [ไล] as a Sanskrit-derived word meaning "rhythm, cadence" must be discounted, for the vowel is shorter than the term for "piece" and the word has no musical meaning to Northeasterners.[2]

It is with Indian musical theory that Lao music has more obvious relationships. The early influence on the Lao court of Khmer civilization which was heavily Indianized is well-known. The Tai peoples encountered Indianized civilizations throughout the south including besides the Khmer, the Mon, Burmese, and Malay. Because pieces played in each of the five basic modes are improvisations and because the modes do not exist as isolated series of notes in the minds of Lao performers, it appears justifiable to classify these five modes as modes akin to the Indian raga, Javanese patet, and Arabian maqam. The word lai by which players refer to the pieces (e.g., lai bo sai) refers to improvisations in which characteristic melodic patterns, rhythms, and sonorities are constantly varied. A player cannot define sootsanaen in the same way he can describe the Thai National Anthem, a fixed melody. He can only improvise using stereotyped patterns which together constitute the piece.

Though female students in schools now play kaen in ensembles (wong), they do not do so in a traditional village setting. Male players are typically farmers living in villages; educated men tend to consider the instrument too rustic for their status in life. Non-Lao men such as Chinese or Indians know little of the instrument, for they are city dwellers and businessmen. Kaen players are generally less well educated than singers, for literacy is not required of an accompanist. Whereas village boys and men play the kaen without social stigma, those who attend secondary school or college leave such entertainments behind when they assume the dignity and refinement of higher education. The kaen is thought to be an idler's instrument, an entertainment for old-fashioned men resisting modernization and Western popular music.

Considering the relatively formal training given singers, it is ironic that kaen players are largely self-taught. Because the kaen hok is called a children's toy, it would be expected that players begin on this tiny instrument and later graduate to the standard kaen baet, but in fact no player-informant reported such a progression. Mr. Soot-tee Chai-dilut (born 1907) of Ban Kawn-gaen southwest of Roi-et, reported that his father taught him and his brother for a period of three years, but the training was informal. By the age of eight, Soot-tee was already accompanying mawlum pee fah and by thirteen began accompanying solo singers, both mawlum pün and glawn. Soot-tee reported that either kaen jet or kaen baet was usual for lum glawn, but kaen gao was used to accompany mawlum pün as well as for solo playing. Although Soot-tee, who had seven years of education--exceptional for kaen players--spent five years as a monk and worked for some years variously as a teacher and clerk for the highway department, he continued to play the kaen for money until age sixty-six. His style is based on that of the players whom he heard, liked, and therefore imitated. He felt that he had reached a professional level many years ago when he stopped learning new styles and techniques. Today he remains largely unaffected by the generally faster tempos and recent additions to the repertory.

In Ban Nawng-waeng-kuang seventeen kilometers southwest of Roi-et three more elderly kaen players told similar stories. Loon Sila-toolee, born in 1913, reported that he began playing the kaen baet at age fifteen but quit in 1936 when he got married. Loon stated that lum glawn used kaen baet and lum pün the kaen gao, but the kaen baet was then much longer than today. Loon, because he had not played for nearly thirty years, was able to perform only the five basic lai and these badly, but reported that he had played other pieces formerly. A nearby neighbor, Sootah Sawut-pon, born in 1916, stated that he too began kaen at age fifteen without a teacher. Sootah also reported the use of kaen gao with mawlum pün and the extended lengths, up to two meters, of kaen baet during his youth. Mr. Pun Chonpairot, born in 1923, the most skilled of the three, began playing when he was twelve or thirteen, his father, a professional kaen player, giving him informal training. He also reported training two or three students, but again only informally.

Mr. Tawng-koon Si-aroon (1937-1979) of Ban Nawng-koo-kok twenty kilometers southwest of Roi-et, blind since contracting a serious childhood disease at age three, was by far the most gifted and technically polished kaen player known in Northeast Thailand until his untimely death in 1979. Tawng-koon's abilities, however, were barely known outside his immediate area for as stated earlier there is no forum in which a kaen player may display his talents. Tawng-koon supported himself by raising chickens and fighting cocks as well as buying kaen from the makers and reselling them at a profit to distant players. When he was twelve, his father, a middling kaen player, bought him a kaen baet and taught him to play lai noi and sootsanaen. By age sixteen he was travelling with professional mawlum and received many suggestions from them which improved his playing.

When he was twenty, Tawng-koon spent two days in Ban Nawng-dat in Bua-yai district, Korat province, studying kaen formally with Ajan Tai-awn Gaeo-jun. He was in fact the only kaen player-informant who had studied formally. As part of his training he learned a wai kroo and made an offering consisting of the following: he placed a white cloth, face powder, hair cream, a comb, a mirror, as well as the usual five pairs of candles and flowers with twenty-five baht ($1.25) in a bowl and covered that with a pasin (colorful cloth worn by women). He also learned magic words (kum aw) to protect himself. Tawng-koon explained that the kaen is a female instrument, and for that reason the wai kroo offering includes many items associated with women. The kaen itself suggests the female anatomy in its windchest, dao, meaning among other things "breast." The hang-dao or tail suggests a teat while the grass which binds the pipes at three points is yah-nang or literally "female grass." After his two days of training, Tawng-koon had no further training but continued to copy those aspects of other players' techniques which interest him. Tawng-koon was exceptional for being able to play in many distinct styles showing a keen understanding for kaen playing of his own generation as well as the preceding one. His technique and repertory will be discussed in greater detail below.

On several occasions Tawng-koon attempted to teach me the fundamentals of kaen playing by the traditional method. The first piece to be learned according to him is lai yai because it is least complicated technically. Sootsanaen is said to be the most difficult. Tawng-koon played short motives and patterns which I had to imitate. When he heard an incorrect sound, he stopped to place my fingers over the correct pitches telling me to play octaves, singles, or pairs of pitches. At the end of one session I asked him to play a very simple version of lai yai using these fundamental patterns. This is shown in Example 41.

Example 41. An easy version of lai yai for beginners played by Tawng-koon.

The position of the kaen player in relation to that of the mawlum singer is humble. No player could claim to be completely professional since he could not earn any money except by accompanying, and there is of course no singing during pansah, the Buddhist lent. During this season both players and singers return to farming. In terms of income, a kaen player receives only a small percentage of the amount paid to singers. The amount would rarely exceed one hundred baht ($5.00) for a night when singers would expect from eight hundred to fifteen hundred baht each. He is not an equal partner with the singer and is not called upon to entertain the audience with solos or surpass the singers in any way. If a kaen player wishes to show off his technique or perform witty pieces, he would do so only for a private, nonpaying audience. Kaen player-informants never demanded a fee before recording for me, though all gratefully accepted the ten to fifty baht offered when the session was finished.

Whereas mawlum singing styles are differentiated according to regions-- i.e., Oodawn-Kawn-gaen style and Oobon style--solo kaen playing does not per se follow this division though a few players such as Tawng-koon attempted to differentiate the two. Instead a more important distinction is that of age since players modify but little their styles after achieving a satisfactory level of competence. In other words, players of, for example, the generation born around 1913-23 have not attempted to keep up with current trends and continue to play in the styles popular during their earlier years. While Tawng-koon distinguished three ages, men from fifty to sixty, men around forty, and men younger than forty (in 1973), the evolution has been gradual and only obvious when the extremes are compared.

The major differences between old and new styles are those of tempo, form, and repertory. As with the pace of life in general, musical tempos hav accelerated in recent years. Older players claim they cannot accompany today's mawlum because of the tempo factor. Secondly, younger players are more inventive in some respects, giving their improvisations more variety of texture and design than those of older men. The older styles tend to be more static, more like the accompaniment than a solo and show little differentiation from man to man. Lastly, older players tend to play only the five basic modes plus two or three more pieces which are all but universally known among kaen players. Younger players, especially men such as Tawng-koon, have invented new pieces or imitated various singing styles unknown forty years ago. Many of these new pieces will never become widely known, for they are idiosyncratic to a few players, but the attitude is far more eclectic than the relative conservatism of older players.

Solo improvisations may take one of two major forms, the direct imitation of a mawlum performance complete with introduction and the melodic style of the singer, or a virtuoso display of technique which ignores the vocal aspects and instead develops accompanimental figures into an independent composition. The pieces may be referred to by their technical names, e.g., lai sootsanaen, lai bo sai, and so forth, or by various poetic words or phrases which call up associations with mawlum singing, e.g., lai yai hua dok mawn ("lai yai, the head falls off the pillow"). Even if the lai is not given, as in the title mae mai glawm look ("the widow sings a lullaby to her child"), all players know this is played in lai noi.

In addition to these five improvisations which are prerequisite for every player, there are certain other pieces which are so widely known as to be basic as well. The most important is maeng poo dawm dawk ("bees around the flowers") which is played in bo sai. Another important piece which is played in either lai yai or more commonly lai noi is known under a variety of names including lom put chai kao ("wind blowing through the hills"), lom put pai ("wind blowing the bamboos"), lom put prao ("wind blowing the palm trees"), or poo tai in reference to upland Lao living in the mountains of Sagon-nakawn and Nakawn-panom provinces. A third group includes all those pieces which are less widely known, from lai rot fai ("song of the train") familiar to most younger players to goolah hab noon ("the goolah people carry kapok bales") known only to Tawng-koon and a few friends.

The repertory of individual players varies widely. Only the most ama-teurish can play less than the basic five modes, but many skilled players restrict themselves to these and perhaps two other pieces. A blind but highly skilled player named Joi from a village near Barabü in Mahasarakam province claimed his entire repertory consisted of five pieces, but while not including sootsanaen added an improvisation called galüng in the rarely used e mode. Soot-tee was able to perform at least eleven pieces includ-ing one of his own invention. Tawng-koon had by far the largest repertory of over thirty pieces plus numerous variations of some, while Wichian, an Oobon player who went to Chiang-mai, played twenty-nine pieces.[3] Tawng-koon, unlike most, continued to invent new pieces drawing up both Thai classical and popular songs as well as native styles. There is also a small class of kaen players who have gone to Bangkok as movie stars and re-cording artists and have adopted the kaen to popular music in pleng look toong, the popular songs which plunder regional styles. Most prominent among them is Samai An-wong who plays popularized versions of the tradi-tional improvisations in the movies.

Improvisations in the Five Basic Lai

Sootsanaen. Because sootsanaen is a extemporization, it is only par-tially predictable. No single definition can possibly cover all the possible melodic and rhythmic patterns or harmonic combinations. It is easier to describe the twenty-seven individual sootsanaen recorded than to describe what is common to all of them. Many factors may influence the sound and form of sootsanaen including the player's generation, his geographical background, manipulation of sonorities, and his overall skill and musician-ship. The latter will determine such aspects as tempo, a smooth or choppy flow, manipulation of texture for variety and form, and ability to rise above mere melodic formulas towards a whole musical composition.

Ears unaccustomed to the kaen are easily confused when unable to recognize the landmarks which distinguish sootsanaen from the other lai. Few players have more than one basic sootsanaen, but now and then appears a man like Tawng-koon who has absorbed the styles of several generations, geographical regions, and plays them with a variety of tech-niques. Some may argue that because Tawng-koon is only one young man from Roi-et, not several men of different ages from different regions, he cannot possibly understand other styles as well as the actual men who play them. But because no kaen player's style remains absolutely static, through unconscious absorption of later trends, there is no pure "old style" or "con-temporary style." Instead, the change from the two extremes has been a gradual one in which some mixing of old and new characteristics may be expected.

The sixteen informants involved with kaen playing[4] were of two groups, those with whom I had a casual acquaintance through but one recording session and those with whom I had a continuing and musically intensive relationship. To the latter group belongs Soot-tee representing the older playing style as well as Tawng-koon representing the contemporary. In order to understand the repertory and technique of these men, intensive interviews were held in which I watched them play and attempted to note all finger combinations in each mode. In the case of Soot-tee, there was but one such session lasting approximately two hours in addition to recording sessions. In the case of Tawng-koon, whose repertory is nearly three times as extensive as Soot-tee's, four sessions each lasting two hours were held. Tawng-koon's blindness and inability initially to understand my purpose made progress slow and painful, but in the end much was learned.

The remaining fourteen players included six who responded to a radio announcement of a recording session in Mahasarakam, three old men sought out in a village near Roi-et, and five others encountered from time to time. In each case the player was asked to perform what he knew best, but when finished was often asked about other pieces which he sometimes recorded if he knew them. In a few instances the players had not performed for up to thirty years and were obviously out of practice. Unless recordings were made inside a studio or in my home, audiences gathered whose presence helped players perform their best.

In describing kaen music and its theory, certain Western theoretical terms shall be used including finalis for the first or strongest note of a lai, dominant for the fifth degree above the finalis, modality relative to the lai or mode, and modulation when players change lai within an improvisation. Sootsanaen, whose five pitches are g, a, c, d, e, is especially confusing to the ear because it alone among the five lai omits the dominant drone. Instead, the prominence of the c-d-e pattern misleads the ear into believing that the g drones are in fact dominants rather than finalis. Normally both g's (L-6 and L-8) are closed throughout the piece, the former with the left ring finger, the latter either with the left small finger or a bit of kisoot. Some players, especially those of the older generation which grew up with the kaen jet, omit the upper g. A few players also stop high a (R-8) with kisoot creating a sound that is strikingly dissonant.

In its most basic form sootsanaen consists of the two drones on g (L-6 and L-8) plus a, c, d, and e played in octaves. The ear tends to follow the lowest sounding notes meaning that when octaves are played the melody is relatively low sounding; if only the upper notes are used, the melody follows the upper octave. This gives the player an apparent melodic range of one and a half octaves, from A to e'. With the higher g' used as a drone, the ear willingly accepts the two lower (unison) g's together as either G, g, or g' depending upon its melodic context, giving the player in a sense two full octaves. The simulation of the lowest G is enhanced when the lower d (L-3) is added.

There are few formulas rigidly followed in performing sootsanaen, but some occur often enough to warrant mention. Older players especially like to begin with several rhythmic repetitions of the pitch g followed by a gradual expansion of the range, such as in Example 42, played by Soot-tee.

Figure 76. Melodic pitches and range of sootsanaen.

Example 42. <u>Sootsanaen</u>, mm. 1-10, played by Soot-tee.

Another common beginning is that performed in "old style" <u>sootsanaen</u> by Tawng-koon but encountered among older players themselves. It is especially sonorous to Western ears because of the full triad in the second and third measures and the complex cluster in measure 3. Clusters in <u>kaen</u> playing are quite common and will be encountered throughout the literature. Clusters are not random, though, for certain combinations are acceptable while others are not; they almost always consist of notes within the basic pentatonic scale rather than the "sour notes." Typical clusters are shown in Example 43.

Example 43. <u>Sootsanaen</u>, "old style," mm. 1-10, played by Tawng-koon.

Other typical sonorities include the middle <u>a</u> (R-4) added to the <u>e</u> pair, the addition of pitches <u>a</u> and <u>e</u> (R-4 and L-4) to the g and <u>d</u> combination (L-3, L-6, and R-3 with or without R-7) as illustrated in Example 43 above, or the addition of the lower <u>e</u> (L-4) to the <u>a</u> pair, especially in cadential formulas. The latter is especially apparent in the slower playing of older men where formula patterns tend to dominate more than in modern pieces.

Example 44. Excerpt from <u>sootsanaen</u> played by Pun Chonpairot.

A kind of harmonic tension is created when players temporarily use the lower f (L-5) while omitting the e pair. The result might be viewed as a transitory modulation to the scale c, d, f, g, a which in Lao terminology is bo sai. The drone g' acts as a temporary dominant. Although the lower f is only played alternately with the d pair, g and c pair, at high speeds the ear tends to hear the f as a continuous tone which produces to Western ears the sensation of an inverted seventh chord requiring resolution to a c chord. I say sensation because the combination f, g, and c does not in fact create a seventh chord. While it must be admitted that Western harmonic analysis is obviously foreign to Lao music, players nevertheless manipulate these sonorities for a tension-relaxation pattern. The following examples illustrate three such uses of f, the first by Brasüt (a continuation of an earlier example) showing the f used for melodic purposes as if modulating to bo sai (Example 45), the second by Tawng-koon showing the use of f combined with c (Example 46), and lastly one by the elderly Soot-tee in which the f is always played with the unison g (R-3) as well as the drone (L-6) but in a rapid pattern that exploits the elements of harmonic tension and rhythm rather than melody (Example 47).

Example 45. Sootsanaen, mm. 21-29, played by Brasüt.

Example 46. Sootsanaen, mm. 10-15, played by Tawng-koon.

Example 47. Sootsanaen, mm. 52-62, played by Soot-tee.

When accompanying mawlum, the kaen must change mode to lai noi when the singer begins a passage in see tun dawn, however fleeting. The singer may signal the player with the words "yao kaen yao" referring to lum tang yao or the player will instantly recognize the shift and follow. On occasion players may fail to do so and a dissonant clash results. In solo playing some players instinctively create an ABA form by modulating to lai noi, then returning to sootsanaen. The change cannot be made if the upper g' is closed with kisoot rather than the finger, but few skilled players use kisoot. When changing lai, the right hand stops high a' (R-8) and high d' (R-6) as the left hand releases the g pair. A specimen of this change may be seen in Example 52.

The tempo of sootsanaen varies greatly, from as low as quarter equals 84 (four sixteenth notes to a quarter) to 148. Soot-lee said that for older players there were three speeds, slow, medium, and fast. All slow sootsanaen except two purposely played in this fashion for ease of transcription were by players aged from forty-seven to sixty-nine, though these players also performed at quarter equals 120 and in one case 136. Players in their forties played in the 110-120 range, but only two such men were recorded. Younger players varied from 115 to 148 in all known cases. Many players both old and young had a tendency to speed up from five to twenty beats a minute when approaching the end to give their pieces added excitement.

Since there is no fixed form involved, these improvisations vary greatly in duration. When asked to record, most performed from one to two minutes, but most could have extended their improvisations to an hour had it been required. When accompanying mawlum kaen players must continue until their singer yields to the other. In the case of mawlum pün, there is no alternation or break from evening until morning, requiring incredible stamina and invention.

The meter of Northeastern Thai music is not as obvious as that of Siamese classical music where the ching (finger cymbals) beats time relentlessly. As David Morton has pointed out,[5] Siamese music is always duple and tends to a pattern of four sixteenth notes to a beat customarily notated in 2/4 time. Northeastern Thai music lacks both theoretical writings as well as guiding features such as the ching to shed light on the matter. When percussion does accompany Northeastern singing, however, its beats stress the notes that would have been transcribed as downbeats in any case. Bar lines in transcriptions of ordinary kaen improvisations sometimes create problems though. In some passages there is an obvious accent recurring every two or four quarter notes, but in others the pattern appears to shift.

In examples written in 2/4 meter it is often necessary to extend isolated measures by one half or one full beat because the accent shifts. The following passage, played almost as a formula by Tawng-koon, illustrates such an instance(Example 48). In Example 49, a passage played by Brasüt, the accented beat shifts causing the addition of a measure in 3/8 among ordinary 2/4 measures. These shifting accents may result from two factors. One is the extreme speed of the piece during which the player simply gets mixed up, and probably this accounts for many such shifts. The other is by design, especially as shown in the example from Tawng-koon in which the strong beat shifts several times within a short passage (Example 50).

In rapid playing the sixteenth notes appear to be even, but in slower tempos a dotted pattern usually emerges. This pattern, however, varies considerably within a given piece from being sharply accented to nearly

Example 48. <u>Sootsanaen</u>, "Oobon style," mm. 1-6, played by Tawng-koon.

Example 49. <u>Sootsanaen</u>, mm. 18-22, played by Bräsut.

Example 50. <u>Sootsanaen</u>, mm. 41-46, played by Tawng-koon.

even and with all degrees between. Furthermore, if the piece is very slow, the dotted pattern sometimes begins to sound more like compound duple meter rather than duple. Such a passage could be transcribed as ♫ ♫ in 2/4 meter or ♩ ♪♩ ♪ in 6/8. Players seldom speak of rhythm beyond the general term <u>jungwah</u> and could not verbally define the correct from the incorrect.

Whereas some players tend to improvise using continuous sixteenth notes, others break up such apparent monotony with eighth notes or much less commonly dooted eighth notes. One such pattern that emerges is ♫♩ ♫♩ , but the pattern ♫♫♩ ♫♫♩ repeated several times has a pleasing effect on the rhythmic flow. Soot-tee's playing, which is characteristic of the older style, exploits the combination of continuous sixteenth notes alternating with the weaker sound of the lower g drone played alone to generate an almost hypnotic rhythmic drive, as shown in Example 51 following.

Example 51. Sootsanaen, mm. 26-34, played by Soot-tee.

Many factors contribute to defining form, among them texture, modulation, tessitura, and rhythm. If these factors are not exploited, the piece
takes on a sameness that reduces it to mere repetitions of formulas.
There are no fixed forms known in Lao music comparable to the three
rhythmic levels of Siamese classical music (chun) which generate a trisec-
tional arrangement of changing tempos in a pleng tao. Instead players try
to give pieces variety by using octaves for one passage, lower or upper
notes alone for another, temporary modulations involving either the subtle
use of f or the more obvious shift to lai noi, as well as polyphonic effects
that border on rudimentary counterpoint. It would seem that nothing is
specifically prohibited. Some players begin using normal octaves, others
single notes, some with an introductory passage, some without, some
alternating passages with and without the f, some never using it. The
following improvisation reproduced in full is that of an audacious virtuoso
showing off by opening in lai noi. Note the simultaneous use of both the
a and g drones when he shifts from noi to sootsanaen the second time in
mm. 57-58. (Example 52)

Sootsaenaen, then, is a lai or mode whose potential is far from limited.
In asking a random player to perform sootsanaen, you may get a plain
version or complex one, a slow one or a fast one, one with variety or one
full of repetitious formulas, and in fact most players are capable of both
possibilities.   Unless their personal imagination is limited through poor
technique or satisfaction with stereotyped formulas, the compositions are
constantly different. Much of what applies to sootsanaen applies equally
to bo sai, soi, yai, and noi. It is sootsanaen, however, that offers the
greatest variety of harmonic combinations and styles, and that is no doubt
why players consistently rate it as the most difficult of the five lai.

Bo sai. Bo sai sounds unlike sootsanaen, particularly in its sonorities.
The high g' (L-8) is stopped with kisoot or little finger while the thumb
holds the upper c' (L-1); it is this latter drone which gives the lai its
name, for bo sai means "left thumb." Of the five pitches, c, d, f, g, a,
only f and g are played alone, the former with its octave, the latter in
unison. The c pair must be played with g, the d pair with middle a (R-4),
and the middle a with the upper d' (R-6). The melodic range of bo sai
extends from low A below the finalis to high a, though the upper two
pitches are less commonly used. (Figure 77)

To the Western ear bo sai is less consonant than sootsanaen, for the
g drone (dominant) conflicts with the pitches f and a, whereas the lack of

(Example 52 continued on following page)

Example 52. Sootsanaen (beginning with lai noi) played by Tawng-koon.

Figure 77. Melodic pitches and range of bo sai.

a dominant drone in sootsanaen (d) allows related pitches c and e to sound
without conflict. Because of the added notes and drones, it is more difficult to hear the melodic line of bo sai than sootsanaen. Especially at
lower tape speeds the ear tends to follow the intermediary pitches rather
than the lower ones. The low A (R-1), when added to the combination a
and d' (R-4 and R-6)--the usual combination for melodic A--may be perceived melodically as low A or merely a sonorous addition, depending upon
melodic context. In short, the ear must become accustomed to hearing
this lai before the melodic element becomes clear.

As in the case of sootsanaen, tempos show a clear increase from older
to younger players. Based on sixteen recordings of bo sai, the tempos
averaged from quarter equals 80 to 138; both average and median were
116. Older players, however, averaged 105 while younger players averaged
127. A few players increased their tempos during the improvisation, some
as much as 28 beats, a phenomenon encountered in sootsanaen as well. As

in the case of all lai, duration depends on the occasion, but the recordings varied from one half minute to nearly three minutes.

A formula opening to lai bo sai consists of the c-g diad (L-6 and R-2) combined with rapid repetitions of the upper d' (R-6). This is often followed by a short passage whose rhythm may be somewhat free ending with further repetitions of the opening sonority. Then the main body of the improvisation begins. Such a beginning follows the convention of a lum tang sun performance. Observe the cluster in measure 7 of the following example where the d and f "chords" are combined:

Example 53. Bo sai, mm. 1-11, played by Soot-tee.

While bo sai is often played using only the standard sonorities, a few others may be heard from time to time. The final chord may be identical to the opening chord or with the lower e (L-4) added forming an apparent major triad with added ninth:

Example 54. An alternate final sonority for bo sai.

Tawng-koon and Soot-tee both combine the lower g with the usual middle a combination, but Tawng-koon not only tends to use it more but adds the lower A and d to it as well. The following passage, because of its relative dissonance, is more notable for its rhythmic than melodic effect:

Example 55. Bo sai, mm. 23-26, played by Tawng-koon.

Tawng-koon not only availas himself of all possible harmonic combinations but exploits the fact of texture to a greater extent than other players. The upper c pitch, which is held by the thumb but articulated by the tongue, may be used alternately with other pitches of its tessitura for effective contrast. Example 56 illustrates such a passage used in a virtuoso manner.

Example 56. Bo sai, mm. 29-35, played by Tawng-koon.

Tawng-koon similarly achieves considerable contrast of texture by boldly releasing the c drone and replacing it with the lower g (R-3) for a limited time. Moreover, just preceding the drone change are two measures in which he uses only plain pitches instead of the usual combinations. Ordinary players lack such a refined technique and rely on basic patterns only. (Example 57)

Example 57. Bo sai, mm. 56-66, played by Tawng-koon.

While modulation to sootsanaen would seem to be an obvious possibility since the drone g is already functioning, only one player recorded, Soot-tee actually did so. Although in this passage he uses only the lower octaves of sootsanaen, Soot-tee stated that he sometimes uses pitches in octave pairs or only the upper notes too:

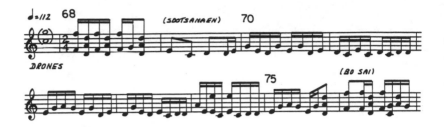

Example 58. Bo sai, mm. 68-76, played by Soot-tee.

Regarding rhythm, the patterns for the vast majority of performances are simple and tend toward continuous sixteenth notes with some contrast provided by occasional eighth notes. One such pattern is ♩ ♪♪ ♪♪♪♪. In very slow playing, Soot-tee often alters the four sixteenth-note pattern to ♪·♪♪♪, the first two notes always being d's. While extra beats occur from time to time, especially in rapid playing, Soot-tee sometimes uses syncopations to good effect when his downbeats otherwise occur regularly:

Example 59. Bo sai, mm. 38-43, played by Soot-tee.

The following transcription (Example 60) of a complete bo sai performance by Tawng-koon will illustrate how the various elements fuse into a characteristic piece.

(Example 60 continued on following page)

(Example 60 continued on following page)

Example 60. Bo sai, complete, played by Tawng-koon.

Bo sai may also be played on the kaen hok, but as noted earlier few competent players do so. The finger combinations for bo sai on such a small instrument must obviously be simpler. Furthermore, the performance as a whole will be necessarily limited in range and texture. Figure 78 shows the range and finger positions for bo sai on the kaen hok.

Figure 78. Melodic pitches and range of bo sai on the kaen hok.

Although the kaen accompaniment in both performances of mawlum pee fah observed was lai yai, nearly every informant reported that bo sai was the traditional lai for this ceremony. Because of its connections with mawlum pee fah and the oft stated belief that this ceremony is the oldest form of mawlum, bo sai is widely believed to be the oldest lai for kaen and therefore the first solo piece. Tawng-koon, Soot-tee, and Sui, the latter also a mawlum, all recorded bo sai solos in pee fah style. The tempos varied slightly, from Soot-tee's 80 to Sui's 98, all well below the 116 average for ordinary bo sai solos. Doi duan hah is a little understood vocal piece associated with an annual ceremony to feed the spirits. Two kaen players, Tawng-koon and Pun, recorded examples of doi duan hah which were essentially slow versions of bo sai similar to bo sai lum pee fah. Tawng-koon, however, differentiated bo sai lum pee fah from doi duan hah. In the former, the rhythm was slow and steady creating a relatively lyrical melodic line of sixteenth notes broken occasionally by a falling fifth pattern of eighth notes:

Example 61. Bo sai lum pee fah, mm. 1-9, played by Tawng-koon.

Doi duan hah, on the other hand, was characterized by two patterns, ♪♫ ♫♪ and ♪♫♫ ♪ ♫♫ . The latter, because of the liberal use of low A, had greater resonance than lum pee fah. Note that consequently the melodic pitches are often between the extremes. Tawng-koon later opined that solo doi duan hah is sometimes played in mawlum moo for fawn dancing when a couple goes to the garden, but this has not been substantiated by other informants. (Example 62)

Example 62. Döi duan hah (bo sai), mm. 1-13 and 52-54, played by Tawng-koon.

Soot-tee's performance of bo sai pee fah, like Tawng-koon's ďoi duan hah, is slow and resonant. The cluster in measure 10, while peculiar to Soot-tee, si stunning in its tension and fullness. The stately tempo and full sonority of this improvisation illustrate how different in nature bo sai may be from the opposite extreme of virtuoso display normally encountered. (Example 63)

Example 63. Bo sai (old style), mm. 1-10, played by Soot-tee.

Soi. Similar to bo sai in its harmonic combinations, lai soi nevertheless sounds distinctively different; but like bo sai, the melodic line is easily confused with added pitches. Perhaps because the ear becomes accustomed to the sounds of the kaen and knows habitually that the third between the two drones, d' and a' (R-6, R-8), is f, a minor third (rather than a major third e as between bo sai's drones c' and g'), even though neither is part of the scale, they each sound distinctive. Though the most usual modulation from both sootsanaen and soi is to lai noi, the change is a major one from sootsanaen but only a small one from the latter because the drones are identical for both soi and noi.

Lai soi's range, like that of bo sai, is nearly two octaves, although again the top note is rarely used. Extending from low A to high g', soi exploits sonorities whose extremes are somewhat greater than those of bo sai and sootsanaen, as shown in Figure 79.

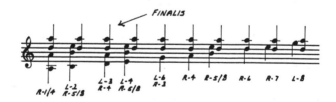

Figure 79. Melodic pitches and range of soi.

The tempos encountered during the fourteen recorded performances in my collection varied as much as those of bo sai but at a slightly higher over-all rate. The slowest was 90 beats a minute while the fastest was 144, six beats more than the fastest bo sai recorded. The average was there-fore 123, though for older players it was 117 while younger ones maintain an astonishing average of 134.

Soot-tee's opening phrase in <u>soi</u> was similar to that of <u>bo sai</u>, beginning with the tonic "chord" plus ninth, a short passage of rhythmically free figures followed by another tonic "chord":

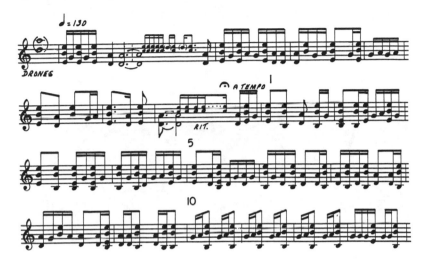

Example 64. <u>Soi</u>, mm. 1-9, played by Soot-tee.

Tawng-koon, however, begins this example with increasingly dense combinations which after achieving momentum merge with the usual patterns:

Example 65. <u>Soi</u>, mm. 1-9, played by Tawng-koon.

Whereas <u>bo sai</u>, especially at slower tempos, tended to melodic, <u>soi</u> more often consisted of rhythmic and harmonic patterns to give it drive but they diminish the prominence of the melodic element. After the most common rhythmic pattern--continuous sixteenth notes--one encounters both a ♩ ♫ ♫ pattern and a ♫ ♩ ♫ ♩ pattern, these generating great momentum when used continuously. This rhythmic motive may take several harmonic forms as shown in Example 66, including the following two:

Example 66. Soi, mm. 9-13, played by Soot-tee.

Example 67. Soi, mm. 17-19, played by Tawng-koon.

The following three figures (Example 68) also occur from time to time in lai soi.

Example 68. Three harmonic figures common to lai soi.

Five of the fourteen lai soi recorded modulate temporarily to lai noi creating an ABA form. As shown in Example 69 by Soot-tee, the transient lai noi may be somewhat extended and in a few other recorded samples became a full-fledged lai noi improvisation. Note the syncopations preceding the change to lai noi, sycopations that another player, fifty-year-old Pun, also played but without the modulation; also note the use of lower notes in lai noi, similar to the sootsanaen section in Soot-tee's bo sai (Example 58). Other players, however, usually play octaves. A complete transcription of Tawng-koon's lai soi appears in Example 70.

Sootsanaen, bo sai, and soi all have much in common, and yet a listener familiar with kaen music can immediately distinguish them. To discover why, it is necessary to compare several factors, among them the relative frequency of the ptiches of the scale, ranges, and sonorities. To examine the pitch frequency question the table in Figure 80 has been compiled from two randomly chosen performances of sootsanaen, and one each of boi sai and soi. The pitch numbers correspond to the basic five pitches of the mode read ascendingly. Thus pitch one of sootsanaen is g, pitch two is a, and so forth.

The most frequent pitch in all three lai is the third one, c in sootsanaen, f in bo sai, and g in soi. While the fifth pitch is relatively infrequent

Example 69. Soi, mm. 31-48, played by Soot-tee.

(Example 70 continued on following page)

Example 70. Soi, complete, played by Tawng-koon.

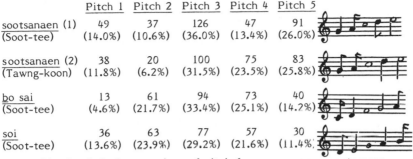

	Pitch 1	Pitch 2	Pitch 3	Pitch 4	Pitch 5	
sootsanaen (1) (Soot-tee)	49 (14.0%)	37 (10.6%)	126 (36.0%)	47 (13.4%)	91 (26.0%)	
sootsanaen (2) (Tawng-koon)	38 (11.8%)	20 (6.2%)	100 (31.5%)	75 (23.5%)	83 (25.8%)	
bo sai (Soot-tee)	13 (4.6%)	61 (21.7%)	94 (33.4%)	73 (25.1%)	40 (14.2%)	
soi (Soot-tee)	36 (13.6%)	63 (23.9%)	77 (29.2%)	57 (21.6%)	30 (11.4%)	

Figure 80. Statistical comparison of pitch frequency among sootsanaen, bo sai, and soi.

in bo sai and soi, it is much more frequent in sootsanaen, but the second pitch is far less frequent in sootsanaen than in the other two lai. It is not surprising, then, to find that in sootsanaen patterns alternating three and five (d and f, e and g, respectively) dominate.

In range, all three modes span the entire gamut of the kaen, from low A to high a' two octaves above. Only expert players ascend to the last two or three pitches, however. A major difference among the modes is that sootsanaen's finalis, the simulated G (below A, the lowest actual pitch) is the mode's lowest pitch while bo sai may descend to A below its finalis (c) and soi may descend two pitches, A and c, below its finalis (d).

To aid in comparing the sonorities of each pitch of each mode, the following figure shows each of the five basic pitches of sootsanaen, bo sai, and soi respectively. Sootsanaen's pitches have been transposed up a fourth and soi's pitches have been transposed down a second to facilitate comparison. Thus, sootsanaen's drones are c' and c", bo sai's c' and g', and soi's c' and g' also.

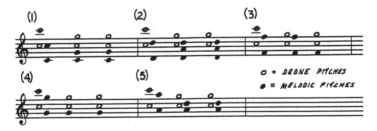

Figure 81. A comparison of the sonorities for each of the five pitches of sootsanaen, bo sai, and soi respectively, transposed to bo sai pitches.

An immediate difference is that sootsanaen's drones are octaves of the finalis while both bo sai and soi have the octave and fifth (actually twelfth). In sootsanaen the single pitch drone creates a second with the second pitch, a fifth with the third pitch, a fourth with the fourth pitch, and a third with the last pitch. In bo sai and soi, at least one second occurs in the second, third, and fifth sonorities. These clashes make bo

sai and soi sound distinctively different from sootsanaen. Indeed, bo sai
and soi are so close in interval relationships that sometimes the only way
to tell the difference is to listen for the use of one or two pitches below
the finalis. A seeming paradox is also created by the fact that the third
pitch in each mode occurs most often and would seem to be a tonic, but
in bo sai and soi this sonority is unstable because of the second (f/g).
Functionally, however, the third pitch of each mode acts as a kind of
reciting pitch or "tenor."

Yai. Lai yai, which follows the yao scale and means "greater mode"
or literally "big song," unlike the preceding three lai, is also known under
a profusion of terms. Some of these relate directly to mawlum singing
such as lai an nungsu yai (referring to lum tang yao), lum lawng kong
referring to the characteristic poems describing a trip down the Maekong
River sung in lum tang yao, and lum lah ("farewell") referring to the
mawlum's saying goodbye to the audience in lum tang yao. The terms
lai but satanee ("song for opening the station") and lai bit satanee ("song
for closing the station") refer to the fact that short excerpts of lai yai
are played to open and close mawlum radio shows. Pleng en en is a rarely
heard title which refers to a layman's imitation of lum tang yao or lai yai
with the sound

$$\text{♩♪ ♪♪}$$

"en en en en . . . . "

Some players also distinguish lai yai by region, Oobon style being slower
than Oodawn-Kawn-gaen style. Lai yai poo kio poo wiang, referring to
a mountainous district in southern Kawn-gaen province, is in Kawn-gaen-
Oodawn style, but the tessitura is very high and the upper drone, a' (R-8),
is played with the little finger. Lai se (literally "unsteady one") is the
same as lai yai poo kio poo wiang.

Three other titles require further explanation. Lai yai poo tao ngoi
kaw ("the old people raise their heads"), lai yai hua dok mawn ("the head
falls off the pillow"), and lai yai sao yik mae ("the girl pinches her mother") call up memories of old-time village life in which evenings were
filled with the sounds of kaen playing as the young men went forth to
court their favorite girls. The custom of len sao whereby boys competed
with girls in a witty exchange of proverbs and quotations from Lao literature called pa-nyah was proceeded by a walk, perhaps even from a neighboring village, during which the boy played his kaen to steel his courage
and announces his coming. Sometimes the parents would refuse the boy
permission to see their daughter telling him she was sick and had gone to
bed early. The disappointed suitor would then play his kaen, usually lai
yai, to say goodbye. As he left, the girl would pinch her mother, not in
anger but from lovesickness; thus lai yai sao yik mae. If the boy were
successful in gaining admittance, he would later leave the village playing
lai yai. As the sound became more and more distant, dissolving into the
darkness, the old people already in bed would lift their heads from their
pillows to catch the last strains of the kaen, thus lai yai poo tao ngoi kaw.
Sometimes they would strain so hard to hear the final notes that their
heads would slip from the pillow onto the floor; thus lai yai hua dok mawn.

All of these titles in themselves indicate little about how the piece
might be played except that those connected with mawlum tend to be in
a freer style directly imitating a singer and his accompanist. Lai yai hua
dok mawn today is often in the style of older players, while lai yai poo

wiang might indicate the brisk tempos of contemporary playing. Some players claim that certain percussive sounding patterns realistically imitate pinching in sao yik mae.

Lai yai makes use of the lowest pitch of the kaen, A (R-1), which acts as the finalis. The pitches in total span a practical range of nearly two octaves, A to g', all of which are commonly used. The drones, e' and a' (R-7 and R-8), reinforce the first and fifth pitches. Lai yai is appropriate for emotional expression, for grief, for longing, for disapointment, or for calling up recollections of better but long past days. Its use of the deepest pitch of the kaen gives it a somber atmosphere while its resonance is increased through the use of nearly the entire range of the instrument.

Besides the distinction of regional styles and generations, there is a more obvious difference between lai yai imitating a singer in parlando-rubato and lai yai in tempo giusto. Both styles might be found within a single performance, but listeners expect to hear the second style more than the first. Oobon-style playing tends to be slow, more like old-style playing, while Kawn-gaen style is much faster and tends to be less steady as to regularity of pulse. The oldest styles of lai yai are known under different titles such as mawlum pün, poo tai, or the group of titles imitating the sounds of the wind through the palms, hills, or bamboo. These will be considered separately.

The tempos of lai yai based on twenty-four performances by fifteen players vary widely, from 60 to 150, with an average tempo of 115, comparable to the three previously discussed lai. The average tempo for older players, however, is only 97 while that of younger players is considerably higher, 123. Only three players recorded speeded up and these moderately from 8 to 18 beats. The tempos of lum imitations, however, cannot be given precisely.

Though mawlum accompanists close only R-8 (a') with kisoot and hold R-7 (e') with a finger to facilitate modulation to lai noi, soloists usually cover both drones with kisoot to permit the playing of d' (R-6) with the fourth finger. The four lowest pitches must be played with their upper octaves while the middle a and pitches above it are played singly. The g may be played alone or with the other (unison) pipe.

Figure 82. Melodic pitches and range of lai yai.

The plainness of these pitches gives the melodic element in lai yai greater clarity than the other four lai. Improvisations generally open, close, and distinguish sections through the alternating of a cluster of all pitches except the highest g' (L-8), with the open fifth sonority consisting of e's and a's (Example 71). Three other clusters, reduced versions of the full cluster, produce melody pitches c, d, and e (Example 72).

Other occasional combinations are possible. If low e (L-4) is sounded with low A (R-1), the ear still perceives the pitch e, but with the sonorous

Example 71. Opening cluster and open fifth sonority (lai yai).

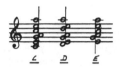

Example 72. The cluster for pitches c, d, and e.

A added. If, however, the middle a (R-4) is added to this combination, melodically the ear perceives it as low A. The c pair is often augmented with the pitch g (L-6), and similarly the upper c' may sometimes be played with the low A. Less commonly, players such as Kumbun from near Barabu in Mahasarakam province, use a percussive cluster consisting of the pitches a and b (R-4 and R-5).

A surprising characteristic of lai yai is the propensity of players towards using the "sour notes" (non-scale tones), particularly the b pair (L 2, R-5). Of the fifteen players recorded, twelve use b to greater or lesser degrees. This pitch is particularly prominent in Tawng-koon's lai yai sao yik mae when he executes a favorite passage which is widely used by other players too (Example 73, mm. 9-15).

The form of lai yai, as with sootsanaen, bo sai, and soi, is open to the imagination of the player. Older players such as Soot-tee, Pun, Sootah, and Loon, however, tended to follow an overall plan which must have been typical of playing fifty or more years ago. In this style the player begins with clusters, followed by improvisation in tempo giusto which tend to rise and fall alternately to allow variety through change of tessitura and texture. The section is then closed with more clusters, followed by another section similar to the first. Players may continue in this pattern simply following the sectional pattern of lum tang yao. Older players are much less inclined to the parlando-rubato style than younger players, who must be considered more inventive in this respect. Old style lai yai, nevertheless, has a certain charm which captivates its listeners though rarely impresses them with technical display or great speed.

Younger players are less predictable, less uniform in style, attempt to exploit variety for its own sake, and display technical skill if they possess it. Two players, Joi and Somjit, interrupted lai yai with either dŏi tamadah or dŏi kong. Although modulation to other lai is not usual in lai yai, accompanists must be able to change rapidly back and forth between lai yai and lai noi as male and female singers alternate, especially in lum dŏi.

The rhythm of lai yai generally follows the patterns found in the other lai, mostly simple patterns. Faster playing often takes the form of continuous sixteenth notes while slower playing may depend on continuous

Example 73. <u>Lai yai sao yik mae</u>, mm. 1-25, played by Tawng-koon.

dotted patterns. Good players, however, achieve variety without resorting to syncopations. Rhythmic variety is further enhanced by alternating passages in tempo giusto with passages in parlando-rubato, the latter an imitation of singing based on the tones and accents of imaginary poetry.

Example 74, an extended transcription of <u>lai yai</u> in old style by Tawng-koon, illustrates many of the aspects discussed. Note the formula cadences at measures 45 and 75, patterns common to most players.

<u>Noi</u>. Much that applies to <u>lai yai</u> applies equally to <u>lai noi</u>. Casual listeners unfamiliar with the <u>kaen</u> cannot readily distinguish <u>lai yai</u> from <u>lai noi</u>, for the scales and sonorities are nearly identical though at different relative pitches. In accompanying a <u>mawlum</u> in <u>lum tang yao</u>, it makes no difference whether the accompanist uses <u>lai yai</u> or <u>lai noi</u> provided the range is comfortable for the singer. The alternate titles for <u>lai noi</u> are considerably less varied than for <u>lai yai</u>. After <u>an nungsü noi</u>, referring to <u>lum tang yao</u>, the most common title is <u>mae mai glawm look</u> or <u>mae hang glawm look</u>, both meaning essentially "the widow sings a lullaby to her child."

The range of <u>lai noi</u> differs from <u>lai yai</u> in that its lowest pitch is a fourth below the <u>finalis</u>, opening up a melodic area not found in <u>lai yai</u>. The pitches therefore range from <u>A</u> to g' with <u>d</u> as the finalis, but the highest is rarely used. The drones are <u>d'</u> and <u>a'</u> (R-6, R-8), most players holding the d' with the finger rather than using <u>kisoot</u> (Figure 83). When playing <u>lai noi</u> in <u>mawlum moo</u>, players sometimes hold the middle <u>a</u> (R-4) instead of d'. The "sour notes," particularly <u>e</u>, are used somewhat but less so than in <u>lai yai</u>. The tempos of <u>lai noi</u> are among the fastest of the five

(Example 74 continued on following page)

Example 74. Lai yai, old style, complete, played by Tawng-koon.

Figure 83.   Melodic pitches and range of lai noi.

lai, averaging 118 with older players included. The range, however,
stetches from 70 to a remarkable 152 in which the player produces over
six hundred notes per minute if playing continuous sixteenth notes. Older
players, however, averaged only 95 while younger players averaged 133.
Three players increased their tempos during performance from 22 to 30
beats.

Older performers play lai noi as they do lai yai, framing sections of
tempo giusto improvisation between alternating clusters and open fifth
sonorities. The full lai noi cluster involves fewer notes than that of lai
yai but again encompasses all five pitches of the scale:

Example 75.   A full cluster and open fifth sonority in lai noi.

Younger players again are less predictable, preferring instead a greater
variety of textures and the use of nonmetrical lum imitation. In the
following example, Tawng-koon achieves considerable variety of sonority
by changing drones, first replacing the d' drone with the middle a, then
releasing that too, leaving only the high a' (Example 76). Players may add
another drone, the lower d (L-3) from time to time, then release it at
will. Only one player changed lai, a middling player named Koon, who
modulated briefly to lai soi before finishing his improvisation in lai noi.
Modulations to lai noi from lai soi, however, are very common.

In lai noi there is less opportunity for playing pitches other than f in
octaves since the octaves of both d and a are drones and the two lowest
pitches, A and c, are not commonly played. This leaves a practical range
of only one octave and a third, from d to f' above the finalis. The lower
d is nearly always combined with middle a, though, causing a certain
ambivalence with regard to melodic pitch. Similarly, depending upon melodic context, the ear may detect the combination of upper c' with the f
pair as either c or f. One also hears d and a combined with g, as well as
the lower and middle a's combined with the "sour note" e.

In Example 77 by Soot-tee it will be noted that the slow, dotted rhythm of the first twenty-four measures changes abruptly to continuous sixteenth notes at measure 25, which seems to double the tempo of the piece.
Moreover, Soot-tee in other performances sometimes played passages in
which he gave a strong accent to the fourth beat of each measure.

Example 76. Lai noi, mm. 71-94, played by Tawng-koon.

(Example 77 continued on following page)

Example 77. Lai noi, complete, played by Soot-tee.

In addition to boi sai, lai noi is also played on the kaen hok. Five of the instrument's six pitches are used, and two of them may be held by the fingers as drones, d (L-2) and a (R-3). A cluster consists of all five notes played at once. Tawng-koon, the only player who recorded kaen hok, nevertheless exploited this tiny instrument to the fullest of its capabilities (Example 78).

For the untrained ear, lai yai and lai noi are more difficult to distinguish from each other than sootsanaen, bo sai, or soi. The primary reason is that the two lai are in fact very similar in range, harmonic structure, and melodic patterns. Noi, however, may descend below the finalis to low c and A whereas yai descends only to its finalis, low A. The practical range of lai yai extends from low A to high g', an octave and seventh, but in lai noi, since the two pitches below the tonic are less commonly used, the range actually extends from low d to high f", an octave and a third. Both may use the "sour note" one step above the finalis, b in lai yai, e in lai noi. The frequency of pitches, shown in the following chart, reveals that in lai yai all pitches occur with roughly equal frequency while in lai noi the finalis pitch is significantly less common than the others. The finalis pitch of lai noi is normally combined with middle a creating a combination of d-a-d'-a'. If the melodic context leads to and from middle a rather than lower d, the ear will hear the combination as pitch a. Consequently the percentages given for the tonic of lai noi might change with another auditor. (Figure 84)

The drones in lai yai are normally plugged with kisoot and do not change, but in lai noi the fourth finger holds high d' making it possible to release this pitch. Furthermore, low d may be held as a drone, whereas low A in lai yai would almost never be held. The span between the finalis of lai yai and its drones, two octaves, is greater than in lai noi where the span is only an octave and a fifth. This difference, though, is not easily detected by the ear nor can it readily distinguish that the upper

Example 78. Lai noi played on kaen hok by Tawng-koon.

	Pitch 1	Pitch 2	Pitch 3	Pitch 4	Pitch 5	
lai yai (1) (Soot-tee)	30 (13.2%)	39 (17.2%)	52 (23.0%)	55 (24.3%)	50 (22.1%)	
lai yai (2) (Tawng-koon)	38 (26.2%)	19 (13.1%)	33 (22.7%)	29 (20.0%)	23 (15.9%)	
lai noi (1) (Soot-tee)	13 (5.2%)	49 (19.1%)	80 (31.8%)	52 (20.7%)	57 (17.9%)	
lai noi (2) (Tawng-koon)	5 (2.8%)	35 (19.6%)	49 (27.5%)	57 (32.0%)	32 (17.9%)	

Figure 84. Statistical comparison of pitch frequency between lai yai and lai noi.

drone in lai yai is the octave while the upper drone in lai noi is the fifth. Lastly, the sonorities, when compared at the same pitch level (lai noi), reveal identical pitches but in different octave transpositions. In the following figure the first sonority of each pitch is for lai noi, the second for lai yai transposed up a fourth:

Figure 85. A pitch by pitch comparison of the sonorities of lai noi and lai yai respectively.

The E Mode (Lai bong-lang)

As noted earlier, a few players perform in an unnamed mode following the yao scale beginning on e whose range extends from low A (R-1) to upper d' (R-6) following the scale pitches e, g, a, b, d, e. Except for the low A, pitches are not normally played in octaves since the e and b are duplicated with kisoot-held drones. Players questioned concerning this mode generally did not recognize it as anything other than a transposed lai yai or lai noi, but in fact it is the modal relative of lai soi, this mode, unlike sootsanaen and bo sai, lacking a recognized relative lai one step above the finalis. The pitch arrangement of the kaen which prevents more than three consecutive pipes from occurring breaks down in the e mode where pipes R-3 through R-7 occur consecutively as well as pipes L-2 through L-4.

Figure 86. Melodic pitches and range of the e mode.

Of the many kaen pieces recorded by me in Northeast Thailand, only two used the e mode. A blind player from Barabü named Joi performed such an improvisation which he called galüng which resembled lai yai to some extent, but was still more like the other recorded piece, bong lang or wua kün poo played by Tawng-koon and sometimes prefixed with lai. Galüng according to the Isan-Thai dictionary[6] are a branch of Pootai people, but Kerr[7] calls them Lao Song or Lao Kaleung (Galüng), i.e., upland Lao. A more correct definition is found in Lebar[8] where the Kaleung are included among the northern Kha groups which have recently migrated across the Maekong into Nakawn-panom and nearby provinces from Mammouane and Savannakhet provinces, Laos. The Kha are Mon-Khmer speakers whom some consider to be the oldest surviving inhabitants of the region. The relationship between Joi's kaen piece and the Galüng people cannot be explained.

Wua kün poo ("The cow climbs the hill") or bong lang (a bronze bell mounted on a cow) imitates the swaying of cattle from side to side as they saunter up a hill and the resultant clunking of the heavy bell. Bong lang is also a well-known title for improvisations on the kaw law, the vertical xylophone found in Galasin province, Thailand. This instrument, in fact, is popularly though incorrectly known as bong-lang. For Tawng-koon, wua kün poo is merely music, but for Wichian, the blind player from Oobon who went to Chaingmai to beg for a living, it became a vividly descriptive vignette involving intermittent mooing and humorous explanations not unlike Marin Marais' "The Gall-Bladder Operation." Wichian, unlike Tawng-koon, had to attract and hold an audience which more willingly donated money when properly entertained.

Joi's galüng, played at a tempo of 152, consisted primarily of formula motives, but variety was achieved through a change from dotted eighth notes to continuous sixteenths. Tawng-koon, who did not record a piece he called galung, nevertheless knew of it as appropriate in mawlum moo when either lai yai or lai noi were uncomfortable for singers. Tawng-koon's bong lang, on the other hand, was played at a much slower tempo, 92, to imitate the slow gait of the cattle. Besides the upper b and e drones, the lower e may be held with the left middle finger for short periods. Furthermore, Tawng-koon commonly plays lower B and e (L-2, L-4) in combination as well as upper d' and middle a (R-4, R-6). Excerpts from Tawng-koon's bong lang appear in Example 79.

The lom put group

Of far greater importance is an improvisation known under at least four titles but collectively for the purposes of this paper as the lom put ("wind blows") group. They are individually called lom put pai ("the wind blows through the bamboo"), lom put prao ("coconut palms"), or lom put chai kao ("through the hills"); it is also called pootai after the highland Tai living in the hills of Galasin, Sagon-nakawn, and Nakawn-panom provinces. Besides the identification with the hills, the Pootai are known for their plaintive, repetitious, nonvirtuoso musical style.

Lom put improvisations may be played in either lai yai or lai noi, but in both cases the drones are the same, middle a and high a' (R-4, R-8). The range parallels lai yai from low A to high e', an octave and fifth, and in lai noi from low A to high d', an octave and fourth. In lai yai, the more common of the two, a, c, d, and e are played in octave pairs while g is played in unison. A certain ambiguity alluded to earlier regarding

Example 79. Bong lang, mm. 1-8 and 15-30, played by Tawng-koon.

melodic pitch occurs again with the pitches a and e. Assuming the drones are constant, if the e pair is played alone, the melodic pitch is e, but if only low A and low e are sounded, the pitch is A. If the e is combined with low A giving a combination of three a's and two e's, the pitch, however, is e with a "bass note." The a pair is usually combined with e. As in lai yai, clusters may be played on the pitches a, c, or d.

The form of lom put is nearly always that of old style lai yai, periods of patterned improvisation framed by resting points of clusters alternating with open fifth sonorities. The tempo, like that of old style playing generally, is slow, between fifty-six and seventy or in rare cases up to ninety. With few exceptions the rhythm is either continuous sixteen notes or an eighth followed by six sixteenth notes. Example 80, an excerpt by Soottee, illustrates the seeming monotony which however is alleviated by the mournful, sonorous atmosphere. Players sometimes alter their articulation from legato to nearly staccato to imitate the sounds of blowing wind. The ever-inventive Wichian in Chiangmai blew some air out the side of his mouth to give his playing added realism.

A player named Somjai Milabarin of the Rungsamun mawlum moo troupe from Oobon has, in spite of the general lack of interest in solo kaen playing, recorded a number of improvisations on small forty-five

Example 80. <u>Lom put chai kao</u> or <u>pootai</u>, mm. 1-31, played by Soot-tee.

r.p.m. discs sold only in Northeast Thailand. Among them is his version of <u>lom put prao</u> in which after two periods of manipulating the pitches of <u>lai yai</u>, he modulates to <u>lai noi</u>. The first section of <u>lai yai</u> is melodically distinctive through its emphasis on triadic phrases using <u>c</u>, <u>e</u>, and <u>g</u>, a characteristic found rarely in the playing of other performers known to me who tend to insert <u>d</u> between <u>c</u> and <u>e</u>. The section in <u>lai noi</u> features a cascading motive (<u>f</u>, <u>d</u>, <u>c</u>, <u>a</u>) which also appears in a <u>lai noi lom put pai</u> by Brasut and is probably a widespread mannerism. The asterisks under certain beats in Example 81 indicate a short percussive attack on the notes <u>d</u>, <u>f</u>, and <u>f'</u> (L-3, 5, and 7) <u>in addition</u> to the notated pitches.

Maeng poo dawm dawk

Perhaps the most charming of all <u>kaen</u> pieces and that best known out-side the five <u>lai</u> in <u>maeng poo dawm dawk</u> ("bees around the flowers"). Although the scale pitches are identical to <u>lai bo sai</u>, the drones differ in that the upper <u>c'</u> is replaced by the lower <u>c</u> closed with <u>kisoot</u>. The high <u>g'</u> (L-8) is normally closed as well, but several performances heard either

Example 81. Lom put prao, mm. 1-5 in lai yai, mm. 1-17 in lai noi, played by Somjai Nilabarin of the Rungsamun mawlum moo troupe, recorded
on Hang paen-siang, siang yan S 121 Si 61, side 1.

omitted it partially or entirely. The pitch combinations characteristic of
bo sai are simplified to plain octaves or single notes, especially those of
the upper octave. The pitch b, a "sour note" in bo sai, is often admitted
in maeng poo dawm dawk for the slightly dissonant effect it makes in
rapid patterns. The tempo must be fast in order to simulate the sounds
of the bumblebee. The slowest recorded were 96 and 104, but the former
was on the breathy kaen gao and the latter by a performer of little skill.
The average among other players was an astounding 133 with older players
averaging around 122 and younger about 144 beats per minute.
    Older players tended to be less inventive or realistic than younger
ones, supporting again the contention that kaen playing has become more
individualistic and complex during the past thirty years. Pun, age fifty
(1973), from Ban Nawng-waeng-kuang, played the high c drone usual in
bo sai as well as the maeng poo drones in his performance. His playing
made no more than ordinary use of the upper register nor was it particularly gentle or bee-like. A listener unaware of the title would likely con-

clude he was hearing lai bo sai. Soot-tee, whose skill was greater than
that of Pun, played maeng poo consistently repeating the same motives,
and while the effect was still quite charming, his playing nevertheless
lacked the delicacy and invention characteristic of Tawng-koon. One
major reason is his lack of exploitation of either the highest or lowest
pitches; both Soot-tee and Pun restricted themselves to the midrange from
d to e', a ninth, while Tawng-koon ranged from A to f' an octave and a
sixth. Soot-tee's fleeting modulations to sootsanaen in mm. 43-47 of
Example 82 are typical of maeng poo, though Tawng-koon chooses to
close with this sudden modulation rather than insert it in the midst of the
performance, as seen in Example 83.

Example 82. Maeng poo dawm dawk, mm. 1-8, 39-51, 64-76, 133-137,
played by Soot-tee.

Example 83. Maeng poo dawm dawk, complete, played by Tawng-koon.

Tawng-koon, unlike Soot-tee, tongues sixteenth notes throughout the playing for a bee-like effect, although the ear still perceives notes of different values when pitches are held closed with the finger. Although it is probably unconscious on his part, Tawng-koon creates short passages of counterpoint by overlapping melodic fragments at differing tessituras. Examples may be seen in mm. 5-6, 14, 22, 25, 29, 36, 38, 42-43, 45, and 47-48.

Upon closer examination it will be seen that maeng poo achieves much of its effect through the motoric repetition of four-note motives. These may be combined with a transient drone as in mm. 16-20 of Example 83 or played alone. A similar charming effect was created in another performance by Tawng-koon by the addition of high f' combined with a motoric pattern:

Example 84. Maeng poo dawn dawk, mm. 8-12, played by Tawng-koon.

While maeng poo is a major piece with which every competent player is familiar, not everyone can play it because of its demands in technical skill and imagination. None but the best players volunteered to record it, and those of less than brilliant technique who were asked to do so played without charm or lightness. Tawng-koon's improvisations stood far above those of all other players for their logical manipulation of both traditional and idiosyncratic patterns in both form and descriptiveness. Whereas Soot-tee's playing could continue indefinitely, Tawng-koon's had a beginning and ending separated by a logical series of patterns which varied in tessitura, rhythm, and texture.

Lai rot fai

Lai rot fai ("the song of the train") attracts Westerners more than Thai or Lao. The younger players were just growing up when the steam locomotive first came to the Northeast from Korat to Kawn-gaen and finally through Oodawn to Nawng-kai. Players found that by alternating clusters and open fifth combinations in lai yai or lai noi, they could, with appropriate tonguing and articulation, imitate the sounds and rhythms of a train beginning its trip, blowing its whistle, and slowing down; the concept is not unlike that of Honegger's tone poem Pacific 231. Older players, however, find this sort of realism frivolous and refused to play lai rot fat. The piece naturally has nothing to do with mawlum, nothing to do with Lao tradition; it is merely a novelty piece.

In lai yai four combinations are likely to be heard: (1) a sonority of open fifths; (2) a complete cluster; (3) a cluster with low A included but without d's; (4) a cluster as in three but with the d's and without c's (Example 85). The form, tempos, and rhythms are left to the imagination of the player. Naturally the piece begins slowly, increases speed, then decreases. In lai yai the whistle note is basically g (in lai noi, b), but

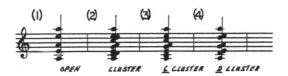

Example 85. The four most commonly used combinations in lai rot fai.

skilled players will go to great lengths to imitate a mournful whistle in the
night or the Doppler effect usually using the "sour notes." In the following
example in lai noi, Tawng-koon releases his drones while initially sounding
the whistle, then restores them into a combination complex both harmonically and rhythmically:

Example 86. Lai rot fai (lai noi) whistle played by Tawng-koon.

Wichian, the blind player in Chiangmai, again must be given the honor
for superior realism, since in order to play a supremely moving whistle on
a "sour note" half a step above the dominant, (c'), he resorted to the e
mode; he also forced air out of the side of his mouth and tapped his feet
to produce the clickety-clack of the rails. The following excerpt derived
from one of Tawng-koon's lai rot fai will serve to illustrate some of the
patterns used although it is difficult to convey accurately the tempo
fluctuations (Example 87).

Lai saw

Lai saw appears to be peculiar to Mr. Soot-tee. Using the same scale,
drones, and finger combinations as maeng poo dawm dawk, lai saw seeks to
imitate the playing of a fiddle. While both Central Thai fiddles, the saw-
duang with cylindrical body and saw-oo with coconut body, are known,
there are also two local fiddles, the saw-mai-pai and saw-bip. The former
is actually a bowed tube zither since the body is a section of bamboo while
the latter is a two-stringed fiddle having a discarded kerosene can or Hall's
Mentho-lyptus lozenge box as its body. Most likely, the kaen piece lai saw
imitates either the saw-duang or law-mai-pai. Tawng-koon often played
the saw bip imitating the lai of the kaen; he could also perform saw and
kaen together by stopping certain pitches of the latter with kisoot and
clutching both instruments so as to blow and bow together. Soot-tee's lai
saw differs from maeng poo only in its rhythms and lack of modulation to
sootsanaen (Example 88).

Goolah hab noon

Although Tawng-koon claims that others play the piece entitled goolah

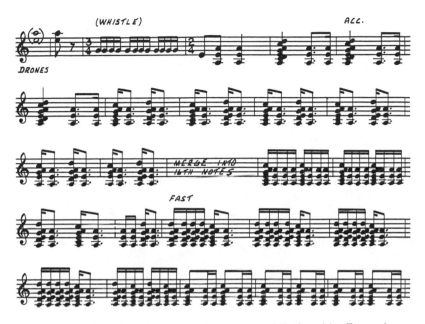

Example 87. A series of patterns from lai rot fai played by Tawng-koon.

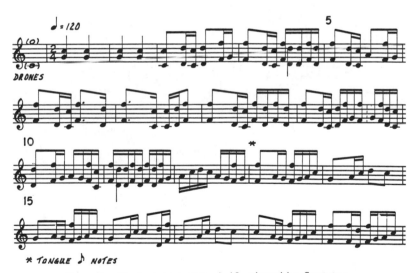

* TONGUE ♪ NOTES

Example 88. Lai saw, mm. 1-19, played by Soot-tee.

<u>hab noon</u>, he was the only player interviewed who could do so. <u>Noon</u> re-
fers to white, fluffy material which means in this case kapok, a product
which grows on certain tall trees in Northeastern Thai villages. <u>Hab</u>
means "to carry on the shoulders." <u>Goolah</u>, according to Dr. Charles F.
Keyes of the University of Washington,[9] is the Lao/Isan word for Burmese
but is sometimes applied to Taungthu or less commonly Shan. These people
travelled around the Northeast in the nineteenth century trading among
other things Burmese bronze gongs, cattle, and kapok. The term <u>goolah</u>
itself appears to be a cognate of the Burmese word <u>kola</u> referring to Westerners and Indians. South of Roi-et city near Suwanna-poom district
town there is a broad expanse of rice fields called <u>goolah hawng hai</u> ("the
goolah cry"). According to legend, the <u>goolah</u>, heavily burdened with
goods, became so tired trying to cross this vast treeless plain that they
cried out in pain and abandoned their merchandise. Tawng-koon says
players perform <u>goolah hab noon</u> to illustrate the rhythm of carrying bales
of kapok on the shoulders.

   <u>Goolah hab noon</u> is based on <u>lai soi</u> although the finalis <u>d</u> and the <u>B</u>
below it are omitted, leaving only <u>e</u>, <u>g</u>, <u>a</u>, <u>d'</u>, and <u>e'</u>. The lower <u>e</u> pitch
is always in combination with the lower <u>B</u>, and the middle <u>a</u> may be
played with or without the lower <u>A</u> and the upper <u>d'</u>. The drones are the
lower <u>d</u> (L-3) and the upper <u>a'</u> (R-8), the same as in <u>lai soi</u> except with <u>d'</u>
transposed downward an octave. An acoustical peculiarity of this piece
is that even though the upper <u>b</u> (R-5) is never sounded, the ear sometimes
clearly hears this pitch when the lower <u>e</u>-<u>B</u> combination is played. Whereas the following melodic contour is actually played, the ear hears that
shown below.

Example 89. <u>Goolah hab noon</u>, mm. 3-5, played by Tawng-koon, illustrating the pitches actually played and the perceived melody below.

The most characteristic rhythms are ♪♪♫ ♪♪ or ♪♫ ♪♫ ,
and to imitate a man's gait the tempo increases gradually, then decreases
at the end. Excerpts from Tawng-koon's <u>goolah hab noon</u> are shown in
Example 90.

   The foregoing <u>kaen</u> pieces may be classified as instrumental music, for
except when a basic <u>lai</u> is played in imitation of a singer, all represent
abstract music, imitations of nature, other instruments, or daily activities.
This list may be expanded when more pieces peculiar to one or two players are discovered. For example, neither Tawng-koon's <u>mahori</u>, an imitation of a Siamese string and percussion ensemble, nor <u>wai pra</u> ("paying
respect to the Buddha") were recorded. The title <u>mah yio sai dawng</u> ("a
dog pees on dry leaves") is sometimes mentioned, but it is merely a joke
and refers to no piece in particular. When players seek to invent new

Example 90. Goolah hab noon, mm. 1-14, 21-25, and 45 to the end, played by Tawng-koon.

pieces, they nearly always use one of the five lai, though drones may be transposed or finger combinations simplified or amplified. The second major group of kaen pieces includes those imitating vocal styles. A few are direct imitations of singing while others are solo elaborations of accompaniments.

Lum pün

The accompaniment for lum pün is played in lai yai, but the drones, like those of the lom put group, are middle a and its octave (R-4, R-8) rather than e' and a'. The scale differs from that of lom put, however, since the pitch b is integral, especially at cadences, a characteristic also observed in lum pün singing. As in the lom put pieces, all pitches except g are played in octaves while the A usually combined with e. The e pair may also be combined with the low A. Soot-tee's cadences in Example 92 are usually complicated through the combination of B, d, and low A followed by a cadential pattern alternating b and g within a cluster of A, B, e, and e'. Pun, however, uses in Example 91 the normal combinations noted above, though he may combine g with lower e. The average tempo for the six recorded examples was half equals 108, mostly in eighth-note movements.

Example 91. <u>Lai yai lum pün</u>, mm. 1-24, played by Pun Chonpairot.

(Example 92 continued on following page)

Example 92. Lai yai lum pǔn, mm. 1-36 and 70-100, played by Soot-tee.

What sets lum pün apart from lom put pieces besides the pitch b is
rhythm. While the characteristic pattern in lom put is ♪♫ ♫♫ ,
the pattern in lum pün is ♩♫ ♩♩ , although both also rely heavily on
even or dotted eighth-note movement. In form lum pün consists of sections
enclosed within cadences representing poems or stanzas while lom put consists of sections between clusters, the usual pattern in old-style lai yai
solos. Soot-tee, in both recordings, modulated to lai noi, then returned to
lai yai, but no other performers did so. Sui, a sixty-nine-year-old singer
from Kawn-gaen province, played lum pün under the title lum pee fah
indicating an earlier practice of accompanying the spirit ceremony in lum
pün style; the usual accompaniment, bo sai, he called lum song.

Lum dŏi

The differences between the accompaniment of lum dŏi and solo dŏi
are minimal since the accompaniment normally follows the vocal line.
Because playing dŏi is substantially easier than the basic lai, beginning
students in school kaen ensembles (kaen wong) begin with them. The dŏi
which do not normally follow a fixed pattern, dŏi tamadah, dŏi nung
daloong, and dŏi hua non dan, vary according to the rules of lum, but for
beginning kaen players, at least in ensembles observed, even these may
become fixed melodies. Obviously, five or ten students could not perform
differing melodic lines unless a kind of chaotic heterophony were desired.
Unison playing is the rule in kaen wong and the restriction of a fixed
melody a necessity.

Dŏi tamadah is normally played in lai yai with the usual drones but
may also be played in lai noi. As noted earlier, male and female singers
answering alternately sing to lai noi and lai yai respectively to match the
kaen's pitch. Solo players, however, rarely use lai noi. The following
version is that played by the kaen wong at the University of See-nakarin
(formerly the College of Education), Mahasarakam, led by Jarünchai Chonpairot:

Example 93. Dŏi tamadah played by the kaen wong in Mahasarakam.

In most solos and accompaniments, however, there is more rapid finger movement and greater use of the rhythmic pattern ♫♩ ♫♩ .

Dŏi kong and dŏi pamah are also played in lai yai but follow a more rigid melody although with embellishment permitted. The following version was played by a young student named Ahtit:

Example 94. Dŏi kong played by student Ahtit.

Dŏi pamah similarly follows a set pattern but uses the pitch b rarely found in other dŏi:

Example 95. Dŏi pamah played by student Ahtit.

The following example of Tawng-koon called ruam dŏi ("mixed dŏi") represents a more skillful performacne in which the playing more closely approximates the accompaniment. The tempo, 146, also typifies the usual solo tempos, which range from 132 to 146 in recordings. (Example 96)

Example 97 is a transcription of another performance by Tawng-koon of dŏi kong and represents the work of a highly skilled player who has transcended accompaniment for a more original display of technique and manipulation of sound combinations.

In nung daloong (shadow theatre) dŏi tamadah differs from the ordinary version in its crisp rhythm and tendency to more sixteenth notes. Solo kaen players imitate this style calling it dŏi nung daloong, which is played similarly to dŏi tamadah in lai yai. Since nung daloong is especially

Example 96. Ruam döi (mixed döi), mm. 1-47, played by Tawng-koon.

Example 97. Dŏi kong, complete, played by Tawng-koon.

"isanized" only in Roi-et province, players from other areas unfamiliar
with this style nung daloong would not know who such a piece for kaen.

Example 98. Dŏi nung daloong, excerpt, played by Tawng-koon.

Dŏi hua non dan, also called lum ngio dawng dawn ("swinging pods of
kapok"), is quite unlike all previous dŏi in that it is played in sootsanaen
or less commonly in bo sai and soi, at a slow tempo, and may be written
in 12/16 or 6/8 meter. Tawng-koon also plays this dŏi in bo sai, and while
the characteristic melodic patterns permit recognition, the sonorities are
of course different. Dŏi hua non dan, as played by Tawng-koon in sootsanaen (Example 99), is especially sonorous due to complete triads played
with the c pair, the third added manually, the fifth from the drone.
There is in sootsanaen a general lack of dissonance stemming from its
single drone. Older players, such as Soot-tee do not close the high g' with
kisoot but hold only the lower g.

<h3 style="text-align:center">Lum plün</h3>

In attempting to play lum plün, the more lively of the two theatrical
styles, players consciously imitate the singers in the parlando-rubato slow
introduction but combined both singing and accompaniment styles in the
fast section in tempo giusto. If the player wishes to extend his performance, he may return to the slow part as if a new character is about to
enter the stage. Tawng-koon, the only player to record lum plün solos,
normally played a sequence of slow-fast-slow-fast giving the performance
an ABAB form. (Example 100)
While many players can accompany lum dŏi and lum plün, not every
player will play this material solo. They are not basic kaen repertory but
part of the group imitating various Northeastern vocal styles which players
perform for fun. Older men, who perfected their styles before the advent
of lum dŏi and lum plün cannot or will not play these solos, leaving them

Example 99. D̈ŏi huan ᶇon ḏan played by Tawng-koon.

(Example 100 continued on following page)

(Example 100 continued on following page)

Example 100. Lum plün, complete, played by Tawng-koon.

to the more eclectic younger generation of players.

Tawng-koon also plays a piece shown in Example 101 that is called gok kah kao ("the white thigh"). After an opening imitating lum tang yao in lai noi, he begins a tempo giusto section which he says imitates a fawn (dance) piece he heard years ago during a mawlum plün performance of SungSin-sai in Ban-pai in which a female wearing shorts impersonated a male. Probably no other player in Northeast Thailand plays a piece by this title, however. The title alludes to the sensual and hidden parts of the female anatomy, adding a spicy element to the kaen improvisation.

Example 101. Gok kah kao, mm. 1-17, played by Tawng-koon.

Miscellaneous Pieces

Although the convivial song maeng dup dao is well-known throughout Northeast Thailand, very few kaen players perform it as a solo. Tawng-Koon's solo maeng dup dao played in lai soi, however, is not the melody of the song but rather the faster tune played by the ensemble of the old mawlum moo maeng dup dao troupe which had its origin in the villages near Tawng-koon's home. Other players asked to perform a piece by this title would more likely play the song. Another piece peculiar to Tawng-koon is pleng look toong samai an wong, an imitation of the popularized kaen play-ing of the Central Thai actor Samai An-wong who plays this instrument in the movies. Tawng-koon plays his pleng look toong in lai noi.

Kaen players easily imitate the chant of the revellers who go about during boon bung fai (the rocket festival) singing ribald songs and begging for whiskey money. Two kaen players, Tawng-koon and Soobin, volunteered solo performances of sung bung fai. Tawng-koon played in lai noi with only the high a' sounding as a drone and the chant played in octave pairs (See Example 102).

Example 102. Sung bung fai, complete, played by Tawng-koon.

Similarly, Tawng-koon's imitation of suat sarapun, a kind of laymen's chant once common in villages of the Northeast, is in lai noi (Example 103).

In summary, the player's basic repertory consists of the five lai--soot-sanaen, bo sai, soi, yai, and noi--in addition to maeng poo dawm dawk and a second called lom put pai, lom put prao, lom put chai kao, or pootai. Any competent player also will have accompanied mawlum and can there-fore play solo versions of certain vocal styles such as lum doi. The re-maining examples discussed included little known pieces such as goolah hab noon, pieces characteristic of younger players such as lai rot fai, and novelty pieces associated with one or two players such as gok kah kao.

Example 103. Suat sarapun, complete, played by Tawng-koon.

Many more examples falling into the last category, such as Tawng-koon's playing of Siamese classical songs, may be discovered when a more extensive survey is made, but few of these would have musical significance. Players will continue to invent new songs and imitate new styles; perhaps some of these less traditional pieces will eventually take their places along with maeng poo dawm dawk and lum put pai.

Khmer kaen playing

Little information regarding the possible use of the kaen in Kampuchea is available, but the Khmer living in Northeast Thailand, particularly around Soo-rin, have borrowed this instrument which they call ken from the Northeastern Thai. The Khmer do not make their kaen but buy them from Oobon and Roi-et provinces. I have recorded and interviewed but one Khmer kaen player, Mr. Mui, from a village near Jom-pra district town in Soo-rin province. Mui, who was about sixty, knew only one mode, lai yai. He did not know the term lai yai, however, nor did he know the other lai, a limitation perhaps attributable to the Khmer's recent adoption of the kaen. Mui's primary function was to accompany Khmer narrative singing called jariang which resembles mawlum.

Mŭi performed three solos, all entitled according to function. The first was in the style of mamuat (from maemot meaning "witch"), the Khmer spirit ceremony related to mawlum pee fah among the Lao. The second, called buat nak, was a march played during the ordination procession around the village. This piece is also known by a Khmer title which means "the dog jumps over the paddy wall," referring to the crossing of dikes in the fields when the procession moves to a distant temple. Lastly, Mŭi performed a piece which boys played while returning home at night after talking to their girlfriends, a function also common in Lao villages. This piece he also called dum rai yule dai ("the elephant shakes its trunk") or gun jine jay tome ("the big toad").

Northeastern kaen players are fond of imitating Khmer kaen playing under two titles, jariang kamen[10] and sui kayom hua chang. Tawng-koon's jariang kamen played in lai yai resembles most closely Mŭi's solo interludes during the jariang performance recorded the same night. Both rely heavily on the rhythmic pattern ♪♪♪♪ and remain within a narrow melodic range. Although he could not understand the words, Tawng-koon had often listened to jariang when visiting two of his several "wives" in Boori-rum province. By comparing the following excerpts, it will be seen that Tawng-koon successfully imitated the style and sound of Khmer playing (See Examples 104 and 105).

Example 104. Interludes from jariang accompaniment, mm. 1-26, played by Mŭi.

Example 105. <u>Jariang kamen</u>, mm. 1-16, played by Tawng-koon.

The second piece played by Northeasterners is called <u>sui kayom hua</u> <u>chang</u> ("a Sui on the head of an elephant"). The Sui or Soai live among the Khmer in the Soo-rin area, but there is some confusion as to which group the title may refer. According to Seidenfaden[11] the Soai are a mixture of Pootai and So peoples, the latter Mon-Khmer, who live in Muk-dahan district, Nakawn-panom province. The Thai, however, also refer to the Mon-Khmer Kui people living in the provinces of Soo-rin, Sisaget, Oobon, and Roi-et with the term Soai. It is no doubt the Kui rather than the distant Soai to whom the title refers. While elephants are common in the Soo-rin area, there is no known tradition for playing the <u>kaen</u> seated upon the animal's head, which is implied by the title. The title probably originated when an isolated player was seen in this position or simply through the imagination of Lao players.

<u>Sui kayom hua chang</u>, also played in <u>lai yai</u>, displays two prominent characteristics. The first is the constant sixteenth-note movement within a small range which may be seen in the following example played by Soottee. The second is the pattern of alternating <u>a</u>'s and <u>c</u>'s as seen in mm. 10-13. Müi's <u>mamuat</u> for the Khmer spirit ceremony closely resembles <u>sui kayom hua chang</u> both in the sixteenth-note movement and the <u>c/a</u> motive shown in mm. 9-10 and m. 22 of Example 107. One major difference is that the rhythmic drive generated by Soot-tee's playing of this pattern was less energetic in that of Müi.

Example 106. <u>Sui kayom hua chang</u>, mm. 1-26, played by Soot-tee.

Example 107. <u>Mamuat</u>, mm. 1-25, played by Mŭi.

NOTES

1.   Morton, The Traditional Music of Thailand, p. 12.

2.   Kerr, Lao-English Dictionary, 2: 987.

3.   Gerald P. Dyck, "They Also Serve," in Selected Reports in Ethnomusicology, vol. 2, no. 2 ed. Davis Morton (Los Angeles: University of California, 1975), p. 207.

4.   All the men listed are farmers except Tawng-koon, Joi, and Wichian who were blind. All had four years of education except Soot-tee who had seven.

Name	1974 Age	Address	Province
Boonlü Yochana	48	Kosum district	Mahasarakam
Brasüt Mapon	28	Wung-pai, city district	Mahasarakam
Joi	28	Ban Lao-gawng, Barabü district	Mahasarakam
Koon Saeng-sawat	36	Ban Nawng-waeng-kuang, city district	Roi-et
Kumbun Tumin-tarat	40	Ban Nawng-waeng, Barabu district	Mahasarakam
Loon Silatoolee	60	Ban Nawng-waeng-kuang, city district	Roi-et
Pun Chonpairot	50	Ban Nawng-waeng-kuang, city district	Roi-et
Sawut Dalao	28	Kosum district	Mahasarakam
Sian Jun-wiset	28	City district	Mahasarakam
Somjit Chok-bandit	35	City district	Kawn-gaen
Soobin Promrut	48	City district	Mahasarakam
Soot-tah Sawutpon	57	Ban Nawng-waeng-kuang, City district	Roi-et

Soot-tee Chai-dilüt	67	Ban Kawn-gaen, city district	Roi-et
Sui Sitawng	69	Ban Tawng-lang, city district	Kawn-gaen
Tawng-koon Siaroon (deceased)	35	Ban Nawng-koo-kok, city district	Roi-et
Wichian (deceased)	ca.35	from Oobon, living in Chiangmai	Chiangmai

5.   Morton, The Traditional Music of Thailand, p. 15.

6.   Somdet Pra Maha Wirawong, Northeast Thai-Central Thai Dictionary, p. 27.

7.   Kerr, Lao-English Dictionary, 1: 23.

8.   Lebar, Hickey, and Musgrave, Ethnic Groups, p. 94.

9.   Letter from Dr. Charles F. Keyes dated January 30, 1975.

10. Jariang refers to Khmer singing, and kamen is the Thai pronunciation of Khmer.

11. Seidenfaden, The Thai Peoples, p. 111.

Conclusions

An old proverb says, "He who inhabits a pile house, eats sticky rice, and plays the <u>kaen</u>, he is a true Laotian."[1] The musical culture of Northeast Thailand expresses the true Lao culture though politically part of modern Thailand and separated from Laos across the Maekong river. While <u>lum</u> singing and <u>kaen</u> playing are not the only musical expressions in this region, they are the most significant. They preserve and convey to the next generation the essentials of the Lao view of life. <u>Lum</u> in Laos is closely related though more conservative since Thailand's small neighbor has been plagued by colonialization, war, and unstable government holding back the modernization which has given music in Northeast Thailand a new lease on life though also accelerated the rate of change.

At least five fundamental forces and forms of expression may be identified as the "origins" of the various types of <u>mawlum</u>: animism, Buddhism, story telling, ritual courtship, and male-female competitive folksongs. Animism has many forms of expression and ritualists, and not all of them sing, but the <u>mawlum pee fah</u> are among the best known, and their singing represents untrained, even illiterate, folk expression although founded in written literature. Buddhism represents both learning which leads to the contests of wit found in <u>lum jot gae</u>, a type of <u>mawlum glawn</u>, and story telling since <u>tet</u>, sermons retelling both the previous lives of the Buddha and epic-length local tales, leads to <u>mawlum pün</u> and <u>mawlum moo</u>. Similarly, secular story telling, <u>an nungsü pook</u>, can be viewed as a proto-melodic form of <u>lum pün</u> singing. <u>Panyah</u>, formalized courtship and testing of wits, together with the <u>pleng pün müang</u> in which young people contest each other in singing, lead directly to <u>glawn gio</u>, the courting songs that dominate <u>mawlum glawn</u>.

Theorizing about music has never interested traditional players and singers to any degree, but there is a rudimentary music theory nonetheless. The terms <u>lum tang sun</u> and <u>lum tang yao</u>, though of fairly recent origin, differentiate two basic approaches to text setting and scale. <u>Lum tang sun</u> indicates syllabic text setting and implies the use of the pentatonic G A C D E scale (which I have called the <u>sun</u> scale) in contradistinction to <u>lum tang yao</u> which indicates melismatic text setting and implies the use of the pentatonic A C D E G scale (which I called the yao scale). Kaen players use the term lai to describe improvisations involving numerous elements--melody, rhythm, "harmony," and form among others; they further differentiate five lai with the terms sootsanaen, bo sai, and soi for those following the sun scale and yai and noi for those following the yao scale. The sixth and seventh pitches in the tuning system may be added in performance but are called siang som or sour pitches. A change of mode within a mawlum performance, from the sun scale to the yao scale, is called seetundawn.

The future of mawlum singing in Northeast Thailand can only be constant change, possibly at a more rapid pace than observed during recent memory. The key factor is popular demand and its help-mate, money. Performers will do whatever the public requires because they cannot earn any money without audiences. The concept of the private artist going against the tide is unknown. If a man's musical genre loses its popularity, he simply ceases singing or changes to another genre. The Thai as a whole are much taken with Western things even as they berate the West for "ruining" their culture. And yet as they continue to demand popular forms of music in Western fashion, they have changed mawlum from an intimate gathering into a crowd situation where overloaded speakers spew forth both music and feedback, and they continue to demand that their entertainments be "modern," "progressive," and "youthful." Eventually there may be a reaction, a turning back to Thai ways when the superficiality and alienness of these things, often the worst of the West, threaten completely to overwhelm Thai culture.

Under these pressures of modernization the traditional genres will continue to change. Mawlum moo may become a medley of popular songs and mawlum plün may fall deeper into stereotyped situations and mindless, throbbing rhythms meant to please the increasingly affluent and youthful audiences. Mawlum glawn may all but disappear from the stage and become a genre heard mainly on the radio in thirty-minute programs. Mawlum pün may disappear before the end of this century, and the old men who formerly read (an nungsü pook) the epic stories at funeral wakes may die without being able to pass on their art. And yet Northeast Thai music is not dying, and to the Northeasterner it is not being corrupted either. It is merely responding to the dynamics which are affecting culture and life in general. What has made musical art expressive of Lao culture for centuries will continue to do so.

NOTE

1. Mme Anne Marie Gagneaux, "Le khene et la musique Lao." <u>Bulletin des amis du Royaume Lao</u> 6 (Deuxieme semestre, 1971), p. 175.

Appendix A
Translations of Texts
in Examples

Example 2. An nungsü from Sio Sawat read by Soot-tee.

1. Now I shall talk of Sio Sawat's teaching which the old Lao scholar wrote. I do this to follow the old tradition which all find good.
2. This story for teaching was first written in manuscript and was very long. I have sought to rewrite it and modernize it, isolating the main ideas and then embellish them.
3. To make it easier to listen to, it is written as a glawn poem. If there are faults, please forgive them.
4. In the city of Paranasee there is an elderly couple which has two boys.
5. The older boy is named See Salio, the younger boy Sio Sawat. The old couple raised their children carefully.
6. When the older child was sixteen, the father, wishing to plot out their futures, called his two children to him in order to teach them.
7. First he asked them a question. He said he had two houses, one finished, the other one not.
8. I love both of you, he said, and I want each of you to take the house that suits you best. I will give you whichever house you desire.
9. Then suddenly Sio Sawat told his father that he did not want the finished house. See Salio was very happy and asked for the finished house.
10. Thus the father knew how his child thought, that they were different, that one was clever and one was not.

Example 3. An nungsü from Jumba-seedon read by Loon

1. Then two handsome boys,
2. One the elder, the other the younger, asked their grandmother about themselves.
3. Then she told them the story.
4. When Queen Akee tried to kill you
5. Your grandfather, you, and I had to leave your mother.

6. Soon after you were born, you were put into jars,
7. And the jars were put into the river and let float away.
8. Your merit protected you from evil.
9. Two of your grandparents
10. Raised you as their own children.
11. Then Queen Akee, a very sinful person, tried another evil deed.
12. She put poison in something which you ate, and you both died.
13. You were reborn as Jumba trees.
14. Queen Akee had told her servants to put the poison in wheat,
15. And now she had her servants cut down the trees and throw them into the river.
16. The trees floated upstream instead of down.

Example 5. Lum glawn (tang sun) "lum plün" sung by Boonpeng

1. Greeting to all.
2. This is enough for now. [changing phrase]
3. Let us change to a new glawn poem.
4. Please come with me.
5. It is now a good time to enter the forest,
6. To see many kinds of trees in the forest.
7. Walking across the plain,
8. You can see many kinds of trees.
9. There are jundai, jundaeng, and puang pee trees;
10. The rah daree flower displays a beautiful color.
11. This flower is found in the forest.
12. But the gah-long and gah-lao flowers are found near the hills.
13. I enjoy seeing these,
14. To smell the flowers and sing.
15. I meet you when I am far away.
16. I am very sad and melancholy in my heart.
17. I hear the sound of the wind blowing against the dried leaves.
18. The animals are frightened and chase after each other.
19. This forest has both plains and hills,
20. With clumps of various kinds of trees.
21. I see them and walk past them.
22. There are also banana trees, sugar cane, and orange trees.
23. Leaving the village, I pass the forest.
24. The next day I got to the top of the hill
25. Where I saw many deer and monkeys playing happily.
26. All of these things are seen in the forest.

Example 6. Lum glawn (tang sun), "glawn gio" sung by Boonpeng

1. Oh la naw.
2. You are a handsome one.
3. Please divorce your wife and then marry me.
4. I will also divorce my husband and we will marry each other; can you?
5. Oh la naw, you are a handsome man.
6. One day I looked at the stars in the clear night,
7. And found the moon and many stars.
8. But for myself, I could find no one.
9. There were no clouds to be seen.
10. I tried to call you, but you did not come.

11. I peered into the eternity,
12. The sunshine is interrupted by clouds for a few moments.
13. But Boonpeng has waited for you many times.
14. The thread on the spool is tangled and should be rewound with patience,
15. But to know your heart is impossible.

Example 7. Lum glawn (tang sun), "glawn gio" sung by Ken

1. Oh la naw.
2-4. You are a beautiful girl and look like the leaf on the lotus when the wind blows and it sways in the pond.
5. Oh la naw, you are the prettiest one.
6. Oh my dear,
7. Listen to me, you pretty girl,
8. Let me court you.
9. I am like an elephant needing help from the tiger.
10. I am like a boat needing help from the ocean.
11. I am like a beggar, like Choochok in Wetsundawn, and need help.
12. I am an old man; my eggs [testicles] have turned yellow with age.
13. Please keep the old buffalo until it dies.
14. Please take care of the malodorous thing, for it may do you good later.
15. Please touch my dung, for this may be better than smelling my gas.
16. If you take care of the old elephant, you can keep its tusks.
17. Nowadays I dare not look at girls.
18. My heart nearly breaks when a pretty girl approaches.
19. But regardless, my heart still tries to get close to girls.

69. Even though I am very old, I like to see my image in the mirror.
70. The Buddha said that the body will change.
71. My feet and hands are wrinkling with age.
72. Yet if anyone calls me father [old man], I feel angry like a tiger.
73. Hellow, friend, don't complain too much.

Example 8. Lum glawn (tang sun), "glawn gio" sung by Choompon

1. Oh la naw.
2. [In Pali] Greed, anger, and foolishness,
3. Patience, patience,
4. [In Lao] Patience, patience,
5. Don't be greedy, angry, or foolish
6. The Buddha said,
7. If you meet a bad person, he will lead you to the wrong things.
8. If you meet a good person, he will lead to right things.
9. If you meet a bad person, he will make you poor.
10. If you want to be in trouble, get divorced.
11. If you want a lot of trouble, get two wives.
12. If you want to be aggressive, study the law.
13. If you want to lose everything you have, play cards and gamble.
14. If you drink a lot of alcohol,
15. After a year
16. Even though you were very rich,
17. Finally you will have nothing left.

18.   Oh la naw.
19.   One performance is past.
20.   Is this not true, audience?
21.   Now is the second time.
22.   Whom do I meet today? Oh, the same one, Miss Plünpit
23.   Yesterday we did some courting.
24.   And we almost fell in love.
25.   She and I have felt a little bit in love.
26.   Today I would like to sing something that is worthy.
27.   Listen to me, all in the audience, you must be careful of your
28.   Hand, your mouth, and other parts.
29.   If you say a bad word, it will damage you.
30.   Your mind should not be angry; be patient.
31.   We are not supposed to touch or take things that belong to others.
32.   When you do this, you will run away.
33.   That means you did a bad thing.
34.   Speaking evil may cost you your head.
35.   Please be careful and keep in mind younger people.
36.   Speaking bad words is not good for society.
37.   Your mouth can land you in jail.
38.   Please be careful everytime you speak.
39.   An evil mouth will keep you in trouble until you die.
40.   You will find out about evil mouths in the dharma.
41.   This small hole called the mouth can make you poor.
42.   Bad words are not supposed to be heard by others.
43.   The mouth is for right and good words.
44.   If you speak bad words or tricky words,
45.   You will die because of your mouth.
46.   Please don't speak in anger.

Example 9.   Lum glawn (tang sun), Kawn-gaen style by Plünpit

1.   Now listen to me, all in the audience, and the host.
2.   It has been said that if we are talkative, we cannot keep the dharma.
3.   One who loves climbing up trees will someday fall down.
4.   If you enjoy climbing trees, be careful.
5.   Listen to me, Northeasterners, Central Thai, and Southern Thai,
6.   And people of the North, please listen to my poem.
7.   If I sometimes make mistakes, forgive me.
8.   Please hurry, kaen player.
9.   Did you hear something?
10-
12.   Did you hear something from the top of the bush; something is
        jumping on that bush.
13.   You can see the birds, but also a monkey.
14.   You can hear a cat's meow.
15.   You can see they are jumping over the green bush.
16.   Along the woods there are also deer to be seen.
17-
18.   You can see a small tiger following its prey.
19.   Because tigers eat too much, there are now few deer left.
20.   The tiger keeps chasing and the wind is gusty.
21.   Finally, because the wind is so strong, the tiger must stop.
22.   Now let me go near the place where the dove is singing.

23. Many kinds of birds are singing, and also a cock is crowing.
24. From there I go close to the big forest.
25. I smell many kinds of wood in the forest.
26. Along the trail I saw many open flowers,
27. And some kinds of trees have open flowers too.
28. Some look like the dao ruang at home.
29. I also smell the ga yawn flower.
30. There is also a clump of sa mung.
31. Now we are come to the end of the singing.
32. Please take care of me.

Example 17. Lum tang yao sung by Boondah

1-2. Oh thunder, thunder near the lake close to Hat-yai.
3. Why does the thunder not sound here where I await it.
4. Waiting for . . . .
5. Oh, that's it, my dear.
6. Well, Bra-muan-see,
7. Now we have finished tang sun and come to tang yao.
8. Let both of us turn to lum gio [courting poetry].
9. What are your ideas, my golden carillon.
10. Do you care about me, even a little bit?
11. I have already prepared a crossbow to shoot a bird;
12. But the bird jumps out of its hiding place and I cannot follow.
13. As it used to be said, first the pipe is hollow, but then it closes.
14. The canal will leave the stream, the buffalo will say goodbye to the cows,
15. The salt will leave the som dum salad and tuna will leave the chilly sauce;
16. Wild cats will be bored with dried eel and dried fish.
17. It is not turning out well for me, though I have strong feelings for you.
18. I am surprised how a snake will leave another snake.
19. A travelling tiger will go far away from the place where flying squirrels and mice live.
20. I feel sorry that the petals of the flowers whither and fall.
21. All of these seem to be like you and me as we must depart.
22. The silk doesn't feel sorry about the carpet; much will go far from the writer.
23. I feel sorry for losing a beautiful ring.
24. Who shall be able to wear that ring? My fortune is not good enough.
25. My dear.

Example 18. Lum doi (tamadah, pamah, kong) sung by Boonpeng and Wichian

doi tamadah

1. Oh my dear.
2. Oh my dear singer,
3. As handsome as you are, do you want to sleep in bed with me?
4. Please divorce your current wife and come to me.
5. If your wife divorces you, please send back the gifts she gave you earlier.

6. I need you to go with me to my home village.
7. Please come near me if you are a divorcee.
8. Please come nearer if you are a divorcee.
9. I am also willing to divorce my husband to be your wife.
10. But I fear you may not be interested in me.
11. Oh my dear handsome man, do you want to go to bed with me?
12. If you do, I will protect you from the mosquitos.
13. My dear handsome one,
14. My dear handsome one,
15. You good looking one,
16. You tall and smart one.

döi pamah

17. Love is not as sweet as sugar.
18. I have little fortune and I must follow you.
19. I have come to dance on the Burmese tune.
20. My uncle and aunt, please listen to me carefully.
21. Please come to me dear,
22. Please come to me dear.
23. I will take you to Piboon district,
24. Where we can see the Moon River flowing over the rapids.
25. The stream is high at the gaeng sa pü [rapids].
26. If you don't believe me, please go with me tomorrow.

döi kong

51. It has been a long time since I met you.
52. My heart is beating; you are as beautiful as the full moon.
53. Could you smile a little bit, then let me talk to you.
54. Could you smile a little bit, then let me talk to you.
55. When I meet you, I lose control of my heart.
56. As long as I gaze on you, I am never bored.
57. How beautiful you are, you Thai star.

Example 19. Lum döi (pamah, kong, tamadah) sung by Kumboon

döi pamah

1. I have been deeply in love with you, but I don't want the kind of
    love that is sweet on the outside and bitter on the inside.
2. I have been deeply in love with you, but I don't want the kind of
    love that is sweet on the outside and bitter on the inside.
3. The merit which I have accumulated has helped me meet you.
4. Please feel sympathy for me,
5. For even though I die, I will leave my heart to you;
6. I will leave my heart to you.

döi kong

1. How handsome you are as long as I look at you.
2. How handsome you are as long as I look at you.
3. If I get you, I will keep you in my arms and give you a light kiss
    like the spirit that overtakes you when asleep.

4. Then my dear handsome one will die for me.

dŏi tamadah

1. You have fooled me into waiting for you for many days, and I grow thin.
2. Every day I wait for you but I get nothing; I just sit lonely.
3. I am very tired of feeling hopeless.
4. I don't know what to do and I fear the foolish words of men.
5. You told me to wait for your dung, eh; why don't I eat your gall too
6. Why aren't you ashamed of fooling me since I am a beautiful girl.
7. If you desire to eat much, you will have little;
    If you don't want to eat, then you will become thin.
8. You fooled me each day a little bit more, but you had better be careful or I won't need you anymore.
9. You see, my dear?
10. You see, my dear?
11. Who has a pretty eye.
12. You don't want to have a singer-friend,
13. You don't want to have a singer-lover,
14. You don't want to have a singer-wife;
15. Please go away quickly.
16. Maybe you think you are handsome;
17. That's why you don't need me,
18. Don't need me.

Example 34. **Dŏi hua non dan** sung by Kumboon

1-3. Oh my dear, oh my dear, as I meet you, handsome man,
4-5. My good man, I want you to marry me.
6-7   Where are you from? Where do you live?
8.   Are you Thai, Miao, Vietnamese, or Indian?
9.   You look strange like foreigners; do you live near or far away?
10.   Please tell me where your home village is.
11.   Do you live at Ban Dae or Ban Doom?
12.   Do you live in Selapoom district?
13.   Would you tell me if you love me? When I meet you I feel very sad,
14.   You, the handsome man from a faraway place,
15.   You, the handsome man that I dream of when I sleep alone, sleep alone.
16-
17.   Oh my dear, nothing can make me forget you though we will be separated for a long time.
18-
19.   My good man, as long as the tiger has stripes on its body,
20.   As long as the sand does not turn into mud,
21.   As long as my breasts do not shrivel up,
22.   As long as the red ants do not loose their narrow waists,
23.   As long as the gold foil doesn't turn black like a pot, I shall wait for you.
24.   You, the handsome man, do you know if my lover is coming?
25.   You who has a very beautiful neck,
26.   You who has a very beautiful neck.

Example 36. Lum pün (Orapim) sung by Tawng-yoon

1. I'll tell you an old story.
2. All of you, please listen to me.
3. I will tell you the story of Orapim
4. And of the city of Pimai and Pai-sing who came to construct the city.
5. At that time it was in Lao territory.
6. The king who ruled the city was called Payah Pomma-tut,
7. And his younger sister was called Orapim,
8. And she carried a child in her womb to be named Dah-ban,
9. And there was a parasol for the child.
10. It was ordained that the city would be defeated because of Orapim.
11. Pimai was ruined before Wiangjun.
12. Let us talk about the Cambodian nation.
13. They wish to make Pimai part of their territory.
14. First they sent a spy into the city
15. Whose name was Bah-jit.
16. He was accompanied by two soldiers, and the trio pretended to sell fish.
17. Bah-jit lead the group in order to get information.
18. The soldiers were named Tao Gaeo and Tao Kwun.
19. A few other soldiers accompanied them.
20. After they got to Pimai, they stayed there
21. And sold fish.

Example 37. Lum pün (Jumba-seedon) sung by Tawin

9-
10. The Buddha has been gone for many years.
11. I wish to pay respect to the Buddha by placing his image above my head.
12. And I a student pay respect to the Three Gems: Buddha, dharma, and sangha.
13. Please forgive me if I do not remember all of you.
14. Who have come to hear the doctrine,
15. As it was the same in the past,
16. To tell the old people.
17. Now I'll begin the story.
18. I will explain this well-known story.
19. Each student has his own teacher and learns something a little different.
20. Please listen to me whether it is good or bad.
21. Let's stop here.
22. Just for a minute.

Example 39. Mawlum moo (Nyah gin bling) sung by the Pet-boorapah
            troupe

1-2. Now, tonight the moon is shining brightly over the mango trees.
3. As I turn towards the field I see many clouds.
4. There are also bats flying overhead.
5. My companion knows that I am planning to go see my girlfriend.

15. I love her very much, but I can't tell her.
16. Tonight I made up my mind to go and talk to a friend
17. And then try to remember his words to use in <u>pa-nyah</u>.
18. After he has decided what the words will be.
19. I shall go talk to my girlfriend this evening.
20. I will get my fiddle and try slowly to produce quality sounds.
21. I am leaving the house to see my friend.
22. First.

Example 40. <u>Mawlum plün</u> (<u>Saen Kawn Long</u>) sung by the Kwunjai-
          Müang-lat troupe.

1. After I open the curtain, I shall be looking for the worker.
2. It is the third month; I must look for the worker.
3. Oh my dear girl.
4. It is the time for singing a Lao song.
5. And then I will sing in the Thai style.
6. You in the audience, you need not be frightened.
7. No one can sing as well as I do.
8. My voice and melody never falter.
9. It only gets better and better, like thunder in the sky.
10. Grandmother, please watch me and listen to me.
11. I never dress myself up.
12. I am afraid I will make you forget your place and forget sleeping.
13. I am afraid tomorrow morning you won't have any soaked rice to
    steam.

Appendix B

Dimensions of a *Kaen Baet* (Sixteen Tubes)

Pipe	Pitch	Pipe Length	Speaking Length	Diameter	Reed length
R-1	A	96.1 cm.	74.5	1.3	1.1
L-2	B	96.1	67.2	1.2	1.1
R-2	c	96.1	65.1	1.2	1.1
L-3	d	80.2	57.7	1.3	1.1
L-4	e	80.2	51.4	1.2	1.1
L-5	f	76.2	49.4	1.1	1.1
L-6	g (left)	76.2	42.9	1.1	1.1
R-3	g (right)	80.2	42.3	1.2	1.1
R-4	a	80.2	37.9	1.2	1.1
R-5	b	76.2	33.8	1.1	1.1
L-1	c'	96.1	31.5	1.3	1.1
R-6	d'	76.2	28.7	1.1	1.1
R-7	e'	72.8	25.0	1.1	1.1
L-7	f'	72.8	24.3	1.1	1.1
L-8	g'	72.8	20.6	1.0	.9
R-8	a'	72.8	18.2	1.2	1.1

Glossary

The following glossary has been alphabetized according to the system of romanization followed in the text. Following each term in parentheses is the term written in Siamese (Central Thai) letters. Following this is a transcription of the term in the Haas romanization system. Completing the line is a brief definition of the term.

A number of problems had to be solved with compromises. As noted earlier, in Northeastern Thailand the local Lao language is written in Central Thai spellings where there are equivalent terms and in a phonetic system where there are not but pronounced in Lao regardless of spelling. Pronunciation varies from province to province and even within a province. We have chosen the pronunciation of the Roi-et/Mahasarakam area since that was the locale of the research and most of the musicians.

The Lao language in the Roi-et/Mahasarakam area has seven tones. In the Haas romanization they are indicated with symbols:

1.	Low	màa
2.	Mid	ma
3.	Mid-high	máa
4.	Mid-rising	m̃a
5.	Rising	mǎa
6.	High-falling	mâa
7.	Low-falling	mā̄a

The Haas romanization has one unusual feature: it transcribes the <u>actual</u> pronunciation of the word and not the literal sound of the spelling. In some cases the changes are minor such as changing <u>ch</u> to <u>s</u>. In other cases the changes are much greater. Alternate but standard pronunciations (especially in terms of tone) are given in brackets. In cases where the Lao might write one term, such as one which is normally a Siamese term, but read another, that word is given inside the symbols < >.

The author wishes to express his deep appreciation to Mr. Jarunchai Chonpairot for pronouncing each term clearly and discussing various matters dealing with them and to Ms. Yoko Tanese for romanizing the terms.

(NOTE: Terms are alphabetized according to the spellings used in the text. Following that is the original spelling in Siamese letters, then the romanization following the system of Mary Haas.)

aeo lao (แอ่วลาว   ɛ́ɛw lâaw): a Siamese term referring to Northeast Thai traditional singing.

ajan (อาจารย์, ʔaacaan): teacher.

an nungsU (อ่านหนังสือ   ʔaán nǎŋsɏ̌ɏ): literally "to read a book" or letter, but it also refers to epic-length stories read from palm-leaf manuscripts at funeral wakes in chanted style.

awk kaek (ออกแขก   ʔɔ̀ɔŋ khɛ̀ɛŋ): a muslim or Malay-style melody used to open a performance of Siamese ligeh theatre.

baht (บาท   bàad): the basic unit of Thai currency, currently worth U.S. $.05.

bai dan (ใบทาง   bajtaan): a kind of palm leaf used for the sounding material in the sanoo (musical bow).

boon (บุญ   bun): the Buddhist concept of merit; also a festival.

boon prawetsundawn (บุญพระเวสสันดร   bun phà wèedsandɔɔn): a boon (festival) during which the story of Prince Wetsundawn, the penultimate life of the Buddha before enlightenment, is chanted.

boon bung-fai (บุญบั้งไฟ   bun bâŋ fâj): the rocket festival held at the end of the dry season.

bot (บท   bòd): a stanza of a poem.

bee bai dawng glui (ปี่ใบทองกล้วย   píi bajtɔɔŋ kûaj): kazoo instrument made from banana leaf, in cone shape.

bee goo fUang (ปี่กูเฟือง   píi gúu fɁaŋ [ffiaŋ]): aerophone made of a rice stalk.

bee chawah (ปี่ชวา   píi sà[sa]wâa): double-reed aerophone made of wood with flared bell, literally, Javanese oboe.

bee sanai (ปี่สะไน   píi sà nâj) : free-reed aerophone made of a buffalo horn.

bee saw (ปี่ซอ   píi sɔ́ɔ): free-reed pipe of Northern Thailand (see look bee kaen for Northeastern Thai version).

bee tae (ปี่แตร   píi thɛ́ɛ): trumpet-type instrument to signal time.

bo-kwah (โป้ขวา   poo khǔa): on the kaen hok, pipe R-1.

bo-sai (โป้ซ้าย   poo sâaj): on all kaen, pipe L-1; the name of a kaen mode.

bong-lang (โปงลาง   pooŋ lâaŋ): wooden cow bell imitated in Northeastern music.

boon (ปูน   puun): a powder, either red or white, made from shells.

bra-tet-tai (ประเทศไทย   pà thêedthâj): the Siamese name for Thailand, the "Land of the Free."

bUt-pah-gung (เปิดผ้ากั้ง   pèəd phàa kâŋ): literally, "open the curtain," the phrase sung in mawlum plUn before an actor enters the stage.

chadok (ชาตก   sâa dòg): the Siamese word for jataka, a story of an incarnation of the Buddha before enlightenment.

chap-yai (ฉาบใหญ่   sàabnjâj‹sèɛ›): large-sized cymbals, a Siamese instrument.

ching (ฉิ่ง   síŋ): small cymbals used to keep the audible beat of Siamese court music, sometimes used in Northeast Thailand also.
chun (ชั้น   sǎn): a level of tempo in Siamese court music, chan in Morton.

duang (ดวง   duaŋ): classifier word for kaen.
dün dong (เดินดง   dəəndoŋ): literally, "to walk in the forest," a type of
poem describing nature used in various types of mawlum singing.
dün glawn (เดินกลอน   dəənkɔɔn): the same as dün dong.
dabaeng (กะแบง   sàdtàabeeŋ): a kind of tree used to make the kaen
windchest.
dakian { กะเทียน   tàkhîan <khêen>): same as above, but another variety.
dao (เดา   tāw): the windchest of the kaen. The term means "gourd"
or "breast."
dapon (กะโพน   tàphôon): Siamese court drum in barrel shape with two
laced heads.
dŏi (เดย   tɔ̄əj): the third type of singing in a lum glawn performance,
probably derived from dai meaning south (southern Laos). Types:

dŏi duan hah (เดยเดือนห้า   tɔ̄əjdyan [dian] hâa   ): a slow version of
lai bo-sai.
dŏi hua non dan (เดยหัวโนนทาน   tɔ̄əjhǔa nɔ̌ɔntaan): sung or played
in 6/8 meter following the sun scale, derived from lum kawn-
sawun in southern Laos.
dŏi kong (เดยโขง   tɔ̄əjkhǒoŋ): fixed melody sung in lum glawn, literally dŏi of the Maekong river.
dŏi mak-ngiu-dawng-dawn (เดยหมากงิ้วดองดอน   tɔ̄əjmàag ŋíw tɔ̄ɔŋ tɔ̄ɔn   ):
another name for dŏi hua non dan, meaning "swinging pods of
kapok."
dŏi nung daloong (เดยหนังตะลุง   tɔ̄əjnǎŋ tàlúŋ): a version of dŏi
tamadah used in Northeastern shadow theatre.
dŏi pamah (เดยหมา   tɔ̄əj phà[pha]māa): fixed melody sung in lum
glawn, literally of Burma.
dŏi see poom düm (เดยศรีภูมิเดิม   tɔ̄əj sǐi phûumdəəm): an old name
for dŏi tamadah.
dŏi tamadah (เดยธรรมดา tɔ̄əjthâmmàdaa): regular type of dŏi
following the yao scale and improvised according to lum principles.
dua (ตัว too): a letter of the alphabet. Dua müang is Northern Thai
script while dua tai noi is old Lao script.
dua bra-gawp (ตัวประกอบ   toopàkɔ̀ɔb): in theatre, soldiers.
dua dalok (ตัวตลก   tootàltà]lǒg): the comedian in mawlum moo and
mawlum plün.
dua gong (ตัวโกง too kooŋ): the enemy of the leading male in mawlum
moo.

fawn (ฟ้อน   fɔ́ɔn): traditional dancing in Northeast Thailand.

gabawng (กะบอง   kà bɔɔŋ): an old-fashioned type of light in rural Northeast Thailand powered by a kind of tree sap.
gaem (แก้ม   kɛ̂ɛm): cheek, a term commonly used in singing texts.
gae noi (แกนอย   cɛ́ɛ nɔ́ɔj): On the kaen baet, R-6.

gajum (กะจ้ำ   kàcăm): a village ritualist, usually male, who intercedes with the village spirits.

galüng (กะเลิง   kàlə̀əŋ): the name of a kaen piece in the E mode.

gap (กาพย์   kàab): a form of poetry in which the last word of a line rhymes with the third word (and another accented word) of the following line.

gatin (กฐิน   kàthǐn): a Buddhist festival in October during which laymen present the monks with new robes and other gifts.

gawn dut (กลอนกัด   kɔɔntǎd): the Lao term for glawn gap poetry.

gawn see (กลอนสี่   kɔɔnsíi): the Lao term for glawn see poetry.

gawn yun (กลอนเญิ้น   kɔɔn njə̀ən): the Lao term for ordinary glawn poetry.

glawn (กลอน kɔɔn): generic term for poetry as well as a specific form written in four-line stanzas and having a tonal pattern.

glawn betdalet (กลอนเบ็ดเกล็ก   kɔɔnbĕdtàlĕd): miscellaneous poems in a singer's repertory.

glawn dün dong (กลอนเทินดง   kɔɔndəəndoŋ): poems describing a walk through the forest and the natural scenes there.

glawn gap (กลอนกาพย์   kɔɔnkàab): a form of poetry; see gap.

glawn jot (กลอนโจทย์   kɔɔncòod): poems for a contest of knowledge, also called glawn dowatee (กลอนโทวาที   kɔɔntòowàathíi).

glawn lawng kong (กลอนลองโขง   kɔɔnlɔŋkhǒoŋ): poems describing a trip down a river, especially the Maekong river.

glawn lum lah (กลอนลำลา   kɔɔnlâmlâa): poems for saying good-bye to the audience.

glawn nitan (กลอนนิทาน   kɔɔnnithâan): poems that tell stories.

glawn pitigam (กลอนพิธีกรรม   kɔɔnphithíikam): poems for ceremonies.

glawn sasanah (กลอนศาสนา   kɔɔnsàadsànǎa): poems about religion and the Buddha.

glawn sat (กลอนสาท   kɔɔnsàad): poems for bragging and showing off the voice.

glawn see (กลอนสี่   kɔɔnsíi): a form of poetry having four syllables per line, the last syllable often rhyming with the first of the following line.

glawng (กลอง   kɔɔŋ): generic term for drum. Types include the following.

glawng düng (กลองทึ่ง   kɔɔŋtʉ̄ŋ): a shallow, one-headed frame drum called rumana in Central Thailand.

glawng hang (กลองหาง   kɔɔŋhǎaŋ): a long, single-headed waisted drum also called glawng yao (กลองยาว   kɔɔn njâaw).

glawng jing (กลองจิง   kɔɔŋ cíŋ): pairs of two-headed, laced drums in barrel shape beaten in contests to attain the highest pitch; also called glawng sang (กลองเสิง   kɔɔŋ sĕŋ).

goi kwah (ก้อยขวา   kɔ̌j khǔa): on the kaen baet, R-7.

goi sai (ก้อยซ้าย   kɔ̌j sâaj): on the kaen baet, L-7.

gok kah kao (กกขาขาว   kŏgkhǎa khǎaw): a kaen piece by Tawng-koon meaning the white thigh or other sensual part of the female body.

goolah hawng hai (กุลาฮ้องไห้   kúlâahɔ́ŋhàj): literally, the Goolah people cry, and referring to a broad expanse of fields south of Roi-et city.

goolah hab noon (กุลาหาบนุน   kúlâahàabnun): literally, the Goolah carry bales of kapok, and referring to a kaen piece imitating the gait.

grabrong (กระโปรง   kàpooŋ): a kind of wrap-around skirt.

gratom (กระทม thom   ): a kind of wood used in making the kaen windchest.

graw (เกราะ   kɔ̌ɔ‹khɔ̌ɔ›): a village signal box made of wood.

grup sepah (กรับเสภา   kǎbsěe phâa   ): a pair of wood castanets used to accompany chanted recitations called sepah in Central Thailand.

gun (กัณฑ์ kan): a chapter or section of a Lao story, especially Wet-sundawn

gup gaep (กับแกบ kabkêeb): the Northeastern term for grup sepah, castanets.

hang (หาง hǎaŋ): meaning tail and referring to the decorative finial on the kaen windchest.

hoon (หุน hǔn): the jaw harp in Northeast Thailand, also called hǔn (หืน hy̌n,).

hup toong (อับทุ่ง hab thoŋ): on the kaen jet, pipe R-3 and on the kaen baet, R-4.

isan (อีสาน íliɜsaan): a Sanskrit term meaning northeast and referring to Northeastern Thailand; see also pak isan.

jariang (เจรียง cà lîaŋ): in the Khmer area of Northeast Thailand, a kind of singing accompanied by kaen that resembles mawlum; also called jarin (จะริน cà lîn): by the Khmer speakers.

jong graben (โจงกระเบน cooŋ kà been   ): a kind of wrap-around traditional trousers often worn in traditional theatre.

jum (จ้ำ cȃm   ): a village ritualist who intercedes with the village spirits.

jungwa (จังหวะ caŋwá?   ): a musical term meaning rhythm.

kaen (แคน khɛ̂ɛn): the free-reed bamboo mouth organ of the Lao people.

> kaen baet (แคนแปด   khɛ̂ɛnpɛ̀ɛd): the standard instrumental today, sixteen tubes.
> kaen go (แคนโก khɛ̂ɛnkôo): the smallest kaen, six tubes.
> kaen gao (แคนเก้า khɛ̂ɛnkȃw   ): the largest kaen, eighteen tubes.
> kaen hok (แคนหก khɛ̂ɛnhȏg): same as kaen go, six tubes.
> kaen jet (แคนเจ็ด khɛ̂ɛncȇd   ): the standard instrument in Laos, fourteen tubes.

kaen wong (แคนวง   khɛ̂ɛn wôŋ): an ensemble of kaen, usually of differ-ent sizes at different octaves.

kai (ไก khāj): an old literary term for kaen found in Lao literature.

kai (คาย khâaj): the articles of worship used in the mawlum pee-fah ceremony.

kamin (ขมิ้นkhàw[khà]mȉn): a yellow ginger-like root also called tumeric used with boon powder to seal the reeds of the kaen.

kao pansah (เข้าพรรษา   khȃwphȃnsǎa   ): during the rainy season, the Buddhist lenten period.

kata aw (คาถาอ้อ   khâathǎa ʔɔ̌ɔ): magic words, usually in Pali, to protect a singer.

kawlaw (ขอลอ khɔ̌ɔ lɔɔ): the vertical xylophone found principally in Galasin province.

kawng-wong (ฆองวง   khɔ̌ɔŋ wóŋ): a Central Thai court instrument having tuned knobbed gongs mounted on a circular frame.

kawn-lek (ฆอนเหล็ก   khɔ̌ɔn lèg): the hammer used by the kaen maker.

kayoong (กะยูง   khà njûŋ): a wood used in making kaen windchests.

kisoot (ขี้สูด   khîi sùud): a black wax product of the maeng kisoot insect, used to seal the kaen pipes into the windchest.

klui (ขลุย khǔj): a vertical bamboo fipple flute typical of Central Thai music.

kon (โขน khǒon): the masked dance drama of the Central Thai court.

kon-chai (คนใช้ khôn sǎj): servant characters in theatre.

kroo (ครู khûu): from the Sanskrit guru meaning teacher.

krua mai (เครือไม้   khŷa mǎj): a kind of tough grass used to bind kaen tubes.

kruang boochah (เครื่องบูชา   khyaŋ buu sǎa   ): articles of worship in ceremonies.

kum aw (คำอ้อ khâm ʔɔ̌ɔ   ): magic words, mostly in Pali, used by performers.

kum boopabot (คำบุพบท   khâm bùbphà bɔ̌d): a prefix to a regular line of glawn poetry.

kumpee (คัมภีร์ khâmphîi   ): palm-leaf books.

kum soi (คำสร้อย   khâm sɔ̌ɔj): a suffix to a regular line of glawn poetry.

kup (คับ   khǎb): a term which means to sing and implies a relationship with the word tones. See also lum.

kwai (ควาย khûej   ): buffalo, especially the water buffalo.

kwun (ขวัญ khwǎn): a spiritual essence which flees at times of stress and must be called back by a pram in the sookwun ceremony.

lai (ลาย   lâaj): mode, especially in kaen music.

    lai bo sai (ลายโป้ซ้าย   lâaj pôo sáaj   ): mode on the sun scale, C D F G A.

    lai bong lang (ลายโปงลาง   lâaj pooŋ lâaŋ): kaen piece imitating cow bell in E mode.

    lai bit/but satanee (ลายปิดเปิดสถานี   lâaj pǐd/pɔ̀ɔd sà thǎanîi   ): performance of lai yai used to begin and end mawlum program on the radio.

    lai noi (ลายน้อย   lâaj nɔ́ɔj): mode on the yao scale, D F G A C.

    lai rot fai (ลายรถไฟ   lâaj rod fâj): kaen piece imitating a steam engine.

    lai saw (ลายซอ   lâaj sɔɔ): kaen piece imitating a northeastern fiddle.

    lai se (ลายเซ   lâaj sêe): a title for lai yai.

    lai soi (ลายสร้อย   lâaj sɔ́ɔj): mode on the sun scale, D E G A B.

    lai sootsanaen (ลายสุดสะแนน   lâaj sǔd sà nɛɛn   ): mode on the sun scale, G A C D E.

    lai yai (ลายใหญ่   lâaj njǎj): mode on the yao scale, A C D E G.

    lai yai hua dok mawn (ลายใหญ่หัวดอกหมอน   lâaj njǎj hǔa tɔ̌ɔg mɔ̌ɔn   ): a title for lai yai.

lai yai poo kio poo wiang (　　　ลายใหญ่ปู่เขียวปู่เวียง　lâaj njáj phûu khǐaw phûu wîaŋ　　　): a title for lai yai.

lai yai poo tao ngoi kaw (　　　ลายใหญ่ปู่เฒ่าเงยคอ　lâaj njáj phûu tâw ŋôaj khɔɔ　　　): a title for lai yai.

lai yai sao yik mae (ลายใหญ่สาวหยิกแม่　lâaj njáj sǎaw jîg mɛɛ　　): a title for lai yai.

lakon (ละคร　lákhɔɔn): Central Thai classical dance drama.

lap (หลาบ　làab): a measurement unit for kaen reed metal.

lek-see (เหล็กซี　lég sîi): a metal stick used to burn holes through kaen tube nodes and to burn finger holes into pipes.

len sao (เล่นสาว　lên sǎaw): formalized courting, also called panyah.

ligeh (ลิเก　í kee): Central Thai folk theatre, known in the Northeast in Siamese, Khmer, and Lao permutations.

loha (โลหะ　lóo hǎʔ): the metal used to make kaen reeds.

lom pu chai kao (　　　ลมพัดชายเขา　lôm phad sâaj khǎw) : kaen piece in lai yai or lai noi imitating the wind blowing through the hills. Also called lom put pai (ลมพัดไป　lôm phad pháj) and lom put prao (ลมพัดพร้าว lôm phad phâaw), the wind blowing the bamboo and the wind blowing the coconuts, respectively.

look bee kaen (ลูกปี่แคน　lûuŋ pîi khêen): a single bamboo tube with free reed in the Northeast, called bee saw in North Thailand.

look kaen (ลูกแคน　lûuŋ khêen): an individual kaen tube.

look wiang (ลูกเวียง　lûuŋ wîaŋ): on the kaen baet, pipe R-5.

lü (ลื้อ　lýy): a Northern Thai script.

lum (ลำ　lâm): (1) a long story, usually about a person, told in verse, such as lum prawet, the story of Prince Wetsundawn; and (2) "to sing" according to word tones, or generically, Northeast Thai singing.

lum ban sawk (ลำบานซอก　lâm bâan sɔɔg): a regional style of singing from Southern Laos.

lum ching choo (ลำชิงชู้　lâm sîŋ súu): a type of lum glawn in which three singers, usually two male and one female, act out the competition of a love triangle.

lum dŏi (ลำเตย　lâm tǝ̌j): the third section of singing in a lum glawn performance; see dŏi.

lum dut (ลำตัด　lâm tàd): a type of Central Thai folksong accompanied by drum in which there is a strong element of male-female competition.

lum glawn (ลำกลอน　lâm kɔɔn): a Northeast Thai singing genre in which male and female singers alternate, often feigning a developing love affair.

lum gup gaep (ลำกับแก้บ　lâm kab kɛɛb): a form of lum in which a single singer accompanies himself with two pairs of wooden castanets called gup gaep.

lum jot-gae (ลำโจทย์แก้　lâm còod kɛɛ): a form of lum glawn formerly common in Kawn-gaen province in which two singers competed in matters of knowledge.

lum kawn-sawun (ลำคอนสวัน　lâm khɔɔn sà wǎn): a style from Southern Lao.

lum mahasai (ลำมหาชัย　lâm mǎhǎa sǎj): a style from Southern Laos.

lum moo (ลำหมู่　lâm múu): a theatrical genre, mostly serious, which grew out of lum pün.

lum moo maeng dup dao (ลำหมู่แมงทับเท่า   ลâmmúumêɛŋ tǎbtáw   ): an
early form of <u>lum moo</u> that originated in Roi-et province. The title
comes from the convivial song, "Maeng dup dao" (an insect) that is
sung.

lum num (ลำนำ   lâm nว̀m   ): melody derived from a poem.

lum pee fah (ลำผีฟ้า   lว̂mphǐifáa   ): a sung ceremony in which someone
made ill by spirits is cured; see also <u>lum tai tŭng</u>, <u>lum pee taen</u>, <u>lum
song</u>.

lum pee taen (ลำผีแถน   lว̂mphǐithɛ̌ɛn   ): see <u>lum pee fah</u>.

lum plŭn (ลำเพลิน   lว̂m phə̀ən   ): a theatrical genre, often light, which
originated in Oobon province and later came to resemble <u>lum moo</u>.

lum pŭn (ลำพื้น   lว̂m phýyn   ): an older genre of <u>lum</u> in which a solo
singer performs an epic-length story.

lum rŭang (ลำเรื่อง   lว̂mlyaŋ[liaŋ]): another term for <u>lum pŭn</u>.

lum sam glŭ (ลำสามเกลอ   lว̂msǎamkəə): a genre of <u>lum glawn</u> in
which three males, one an official, one a farmer, and one a
shopkeeper, argue the virtues of their professions and sometimes
comment on politics.

lum sam sing ching nang (ลำสามสิงห์ชิงนาง   lว̂msǎamsǐŋsǐŋnว̂aŋ   ):
a permutation of <u>lum sam glŭ</u> in which the three males, by point-
ing out their profession's virtues, compete for a fourth singer, a
female.

lum song (ลำทรง   lว̂m sôŋ): see <u>lum pee fah</u>.

lum tai tŭng (ลำไทเทิง   lว̂mthâjthə̀əŋ): see <u>lum pee fah</u>.

lum tang sun (ลำทางสั้น   lว̂mthâaŋsว̂n): the first portion of <u>lum
glawn</u> sung to the <u>sun</u> scale in tempo giusto.

lum tang yao (ลำทางยาว   lว̂mthâaŋ njว̂aw): the second portion of <u>lum
glawn</u> sung to the <u>yao</u> scale in parlando-rubato.

mae gae (แม่แก๋   mɛɛ kɛ̌ɛ): on the <u>kaen baet</u>, pipes L-2 and L-3.

mae goi kwah (แม่กอยขวา   mɛɛ kɔ̌ɔj khǔa): on the <u>kaen baet</u>, pipe L-4.

mae goi sai (แม่กอยซ้าย   mɛɛkɔ̌ɔjsว̂aj): on the <u>kaen baet</u>, pipe L-5 and
L-3 on <u>kaen hok</u>.

mae mai glawn look (แม่หม้ายกลอนลูก   mɛɛmว̂aj kว̀ɔm lûuŋ): literally,
the widow sings to her child, the title for <u>kaen</u> pieces usually in <u>lai
noi</u>.

mae panyah (แม่พญา   mɛɛphว̀ njว̂a): the mother character in theatre,
sometimes a queen.

mae se (แม่เซ   mɛɛ sêe): on the <u>kaen hok</u>, pipe R-1 and on <u>kaen baet</u>,
R-2.

mae wiang (แม่เวียง   mɛɛ wîaŋ): on the <u>kaen baet</u>, pipe L-2.

maeng dup dao (แมงทับเท่า   mêɛŋtǎbtáw): a convivial song with bawdy
text that was incorporated into an early form of <u>lum moo</u>; the title
refers to an insect.

maeng kisoot (แมงขี้สูด   mêɛŋkhîisùud): the insect that makes the black
wax used to seal kaen tubes into the windchest.

maeng poo dawn dawk (แมงภู่ดอมดอก   mêɛŋ phuutɔɔm tɔ̀ɔg): the title of
a <u>kaen</u> piece in <u>lai bo-sai</u> meaning "bees around the flowers."

mahoree (มโหรี   mǎhǒolǐi): originally "music," and later a Central Thai
court ensemble mixing strings and tuned percussion; also a <u>kaen</u> piece
by Tawng-koon.

mai bawk baek (ไม้ป่อนแบก   māj pɔ̄g pɛ̀g): a combination shaken and scraped idiophone used to accompany certain regional styles of lum in Southern Laos.

mai bradoo (ไม้ประดู่   māj pà dúu): a kind of wood used for the kaen windchest.

mai-ek (ไม้เอก   māj ʔèeg): a tone mark which resembles an apostrophe (').

mai goo kaen (ไม้กูแคน   māj kúu khɛ̄ɛn): the bamboo tubes of the kaen.

mai hia (ไม้เฮี้ย māj hīa): a type of bamboo used for kaen tubes; also called mai sang (ไม้ซาง māj sâaŋ).

mai mü ling (ไม้มือลิง   māj mŷy lîŋ): a wooden tool used by kaen makers to straighten tubes.

mai saen (ไม้แซน   māj sɛ̄ɛn): a metal tool used by kaen makers push the reed into the pipe and to manipulate the reed tongue.

mai sah (ไม้ซา   māj sâa): a piece of rough bamboo used to file reed tongues.

mai-to (ไม้โท   māj thôo): a tone mark which looks like a check mark (✓).

maka boochah (มาฆะบูชา   mâakha buu sâa): the day in the Buddhist calendar in February which is similar to the Western All Saints' Day.

mamuat (มะมวด ma mūad): a Khmer-Thai spirit ceremony similar to lum pee fah.

maw doo (หมอดู   mɔ̌ɔ duu): a seer or fortune teller.

maw kaen (หมอแคน   mɔ̌ɔ khɛ̄ɛn): a skilled kaen player.

maw kwun (หมอขวัญ   mɔ̌ɔ khwǎn): a ritualist, often called pram, who calls back the kwun in the sookwun ceremony.

maw lek (หมอเลข   mɔ̌ɔ lêeg): a fortune teller who works with numbers.

mawlum (หมอลำ   mɔ̌ɔ lâm): a traditional Northeast Thai singer; see lum.

mawlum pcc fah (หมอลำผีฟ้า   mɔ̌ɔ lâm phǐi fâa): female ritualist/singers who intercede for someone made ill by spirits.

maw maw (หมอมอ   mɔ̌ɔ mɔ̂ɔ): another type of fortune teller.

maw sawng (หมอส่อง   mɔ̌ɔ sɔ̀ɔŋ): a little known ritualist who meditates for understanding.

maw song (หมอทรง   mɔ̌ɔ sôŋ): a diviner and diagnostician.

maw tam (หมอธรรม   mɔ̌ɔ thâm): an exorcist of spirits.

maw wichah (หมอวิชา   mɔ̌ɔ wisâa): experts in love magic, protection, and other matters.

maw yah (หมอยา   mɔ̌ɔ jaa): traditional herbal doctor.

ma yio sai dawng (หมาเยี่ยวใส่กอง   mɔ̌ɔ njiaw sàj tɔɔŋ): an imaginary kaen piece the title being a parody of more conventional descriptive titles; meaning: "the dog pees on dry leaves."

meet dawk (มีดกอก   mīid tɔ̀ɔg): a long handled knife used in kaen making.

mong (โหม่ง   mòoŋ): a knobbed gong usually hung by a string in a frame.

mut (มัด mad): a packet of palm-leaves, i.e., part of a traditional book.

nam taeng (หนามแท่ง   nǎam thɛ̀ɛŋ): a kind of wood used for kaen wind-chest.

nang-ek (นางเอก   nâaŋ ʔèeg): the leading female actress in theatre.

nang-rawng (นางรอง   nâaŋlɔɔŋ): the second leading female in theatre.

nen (เณร   nêen): a Buddhist novice, under the age of twenty-one.

ngun hŭan dee (งันเฮือนดี   ŋân hŷandii): a house-warming party and wake held on the three days after a person has died, the occasion for an nungsŭ reading.

nitan (นิทาน   nithâan): a story.

nitan pŭn mŭang (นิทานพื้นเมือง   nithâan phŷyn mŷaŋ): a long story of local origin as opposed to a jataka story.

nung bra mo tai (หนังประโมไทย   nǎŋ pà môothâj): Northeastern Thai shadow puppet theatre.

nung daloong (หนังตะลุง   nǎŋ tàlûŋ): shadow puppet theatre in South and Central Thailand, sometimes used for Northeastern theatre as well.

nungsŭ bai lan (หนังสือใบลาน   nǎŋ sǯybajlâan): a traditional palm-leaf book.

nungsŭ pook (หนังสือผูก   nǎŋ sǯy phùuɡ): same as nungsŭ bai lan.

padalong (ผ้าทะโหล่ง   phàatà lòoŋ): a kind of trousers worn in theatre.

pak dai (ภาคใต้   phāaɡ tāj): South Thailand.

pak glang (ภาคกลาง   phāaɡ kaaŋ): Central Thailand.

pak isan (ภาคอีสาน   phāaɡ ísǎan): Northeast Thailand.

pak nŭa (ภาคเหนือ   phāaɡnɣa): North Thailand.

Pah kuap (ผ้าควบ   phàakhûab): a kind of trousers worn in ceremonies; see pah salong.

pa-nyah (ผญา   phà njǎa): formalized courting and reciting of passages from old literature.

pah sarong (ผ้าโสร่ง   phàasàlòoŋ): same as pah kuap.

payah taen (พญาแถน   phà njâathěɛn): a kind of god or chief of the spirits.

paw panyah (พอผญา   phɔɔ phà njâa): the father or king figure in theatre.

pee (ปี   phǐi): a spirit or ghost.

pin (พิน   phîin): the traditional Northeastern Thai plucked lute, also called sŭng).

pinpat (พิณพาทย์   phîn phāad): an older term for ensembles, especially those of the Siamese court.

pleng (เพลง   phêŋ): a song with a fixed melody.

pleng look groong (เพลงลูกกรุง   phêŋ lūuɡ kuŋ): an urban popular song.

pleng look toong (เพลงลูกทุ่ง   phêŋ lūuɡ thuŋ): a rural popular song based on a regional style.

poo chui (ผู้ซวย   phúu sɔj): the second leading male in theatre.

pook (ผูก   phùuɡ): a pile of twenty palm-leaves in a manuscript.

poo rai (ผู้ร้าย   phúu lāaj): the enemy of the leading male.

poot (พูด   phūud): a verb meaning to speak.

poo tai (ผู้ไท   phúu thâj): upland Lao living in South Laos and Northeast Thailand.

pra (พระ   phaʔ): a Buddhist monk.

pra-ek (พระเอก   pha ʔèeɡ): the leading male in theatre.

pram (พราหมณ์   phâam): the ritualist in sookwun, derived from Brahman.

pra-rawng (พระรอง   pha lɔɔŋ): the second leading male in theatre.

ramana lum dut (ระมะนาลำตัด   làmmanāalâmtắd   ): a large single-
headed frame drum used in Central Thai lum dut.

ranat (ระนาด   lànāad): the Siamese xylophone used in the court
ensembles.

rawng (ร้อง   lɔɔŋ): to sing a fixed melody, a Central Thai term.

roo bao (รูเป่า   hûu pàw): on the kaen, the windchest hole into which
you blow.

roo lin (รูลิ้น   hûu līn): the holes in the kaen pipes for the reeds.

roo nup (รูนับ   hûu nab): the finger holes of the kaen.

roo pae (รูแพ   hûu phɛ̂ɛ): the pitch holes in the kaen pipes, hidden
from view.

ruam dŏi (รวมเกย hûamtɜ̄j   ): a performance on the kaen in which the
various dŏi (kong, pamah, and tamadah) are mixed into a medley.

rumwong (รำวง   lâm wóŋ): formerly a kind of popularized and simplified classical dancing, now an entertainment found at fairs in which
males pay a small fee to dance with a girl for a fixed period of time.

rūsee (ฤาษี   lɯ̂y sǐi): a hermit monk, a practitioner of magic.

sadang (สตางค์ sàtaaŋ): the smallest unit of Thai currency, 1/100 of
a baht.

samakom mawlum (สมาคมหมอลำ   sàmâakhômmɔ̌ɔlâm): a mawlum
association, booking agent.

sanaen (สะแนน   sànɛ̀ɛn): on the kaen hok, pipe -2, on the kaen baet,
R-3 and L-6.

sangha (สังฆะ   sǎŋkha?): the community of monks.

sanoo (สนู   sànūu): a musical bow attached to large kites and played
by the wind.

saw bip (ซอปิ๊บ   sɔɔpíd): a two-stringed fiddle with a metal box for a
body.

saw duang (ซอด้วง   sɔɔ dûaŋ): the Siamese two-stringed fiddle with
cylindrical body.

sawk (ศอก   sɔ̀ɔg): a unit of measurement for length, about an arm's
length.

saw mai pai (ซอไม้ไผ่   sɔɔ mâj phǎj): a Northeastern Thai village fiddle
made of a section of heavy bamboo with two strings raised above
the tube.

saw oo (ซออู้   sɔɔ ʔūu): the Siamese two-stringed fiddle with coconut
body.

see tun dawn (สีทันดอน   sǐithân dɔɔn   ): the phenomenon in lum of
changing from the sun to the yao scale in the midst of lum tang sun
while maintaining tempo giusto; also called see pun dawn (สีพันดอน
sǐiphândɔɔn   ).

senah (เสนา   sěenâa): in theatre, a servant character.

sep kwah (เสพขวา   sèebkhǔa): on the kaen baet, pipe R-8.

sep sai (เสพซ้าย   sèebsāaj): on the kaen baet, pipe L-8.

siang som (เสียงส้ม   sǐaŋ sôm): literally, the "sour notes," i.e., the two
remaining pitches in the tuning system beyond the pentatonic scale
tones.

sin (ซิ่น   sìn): a wrap-around skirt.

sio (สิ่ว   sǐw): a chisel used in kaen making, found in two sizes, large
and small.

sok (โชก/โสก   sòog): a custom of placing the hands on a stick to determine good luck.

songkran (สงกรานต์   sǒŋkaan): the Buddhist New Year, held in April.

soo-kwun (สู่ขวัญ   sùu khwǎn): a ceremony in which a ritualist calls back the kwun.

sootsanaen (สุดสะแนน   sǔdsànɛ̂ɛn   ): a kaen mode following the sun scale, G A C D E.

suan-lai (สวนใล   sǔanlâj): a type of oboe no longer known, probably related to Cambodian sralai and Siamese bee.

suat sarapun (สวดสาระภัญ   sùadsǎalàphân   ): a kind of laymen chant or singing in the temple.

sui kayom hua chang (สวยขยมหัวช้าง   sǔajŋǒmhǔasáaŋ): a kaen piece in lai yai imitating a Sui (ethnic group) playing the kaen on the head of an elephant.

sumput ukson/sara (สัมผัสอักษร/สระ   sǎmphǎd ʔàŋsɔ̌ɔn/sàlàʔ): rhyme, the former being alliterative, the latter being vowel rhyme.

sun (สั้น   sàn): one of the two scale systems, pitches G A C D E.

sung (สังข์   sǎŋ): a conch shell trumpet.

sung (ซึง   sŷŋ): the plucked lute of Northeast and North Thailand.

sung (เซิ้ง   sýyŋ): responsorial singing, used at festivals.

suppa-gawt (สัพพะกอด   sàbphàkɔ̀ɔd): a kind of rhyme where two words sound the same except in tonal inflection.

sutra-soomeroo (สุตรสุเมรุ   sǔdsàmêen): "mountain sutra," possibly the origin of the term sootsanaen.

tai noi (ไทยน้อย   thâjnɔ́ɔj): old Lao script.

tai wiang (ไทเวียง   thâjwîaŋ): old Lao script, another term for tai noi.

tam (ธรรม   thâm): Buddhist script used in North Thailand, from dhamma.

tang (ทาง   thâaŋ): a regional style of singing or playing, less commonly mode.

tao (ท้าว thâaw): the leading male of lum plǔn.

tet (เทศน์   thêed): Buddhist sermons.

tet lae (เทศน์แหล่   thêedlɛ̀ɛ): Buddhist sermons that are written in glawn poetry and sung for entertainment as well as edification.

tiam (เทียม thîam): a medium, usually female.

ton (โทน   thôon): a goblet-shaped wood or ceramic drum with one hand.

toong (ทุง   thuŋ): on the kaen baet, pipe R-1.

tumboon (ทำบุญ   thâmbun): a festival or party associated with creating Buddhist merit.

tung (ทั่ง thâŋ   ): an "anvil" used in kaen making consisting of a block of wood with a flat-headed spike driven into it.

ukson (อักษร   ʔàŋsɔ̌ɔn): a consonant; consonant classes including ukson dum (อักษรต่ำ   ʔàŋsɔ̌ɔntâm   ), ukson glang (อักษรกลาง ʔàŋsɔ̌ɔnkaaŋ), and ukson soong (อักษรสูง   ʔàŋsɔ̌ɔnsǔuŋ).

wah (ว่า waa   ): a verb meaning to sing Siamese folksongs.

wai kroo (ไหว้ครู wàajkhûu): a ceremony to honor a teacher.

wak (วรรค waŋ): line of a glawn poem.

  wak hawng (วรรคทอง   waŋhɔ̌ɔŋ): the third line.

  wak hup (วรรคฮับ   waŋhab): the second line.

wak sa-dup (วรรคดับ   wagsàdãb): the first line.

wak song (วรรคส่ง wag sôŋ): the fourth line.

wat (วาท wāad): another term for tang.

wisaka boochah (วิสาขะบูชา wisǎakhã̌buu sǎa): a Buddhist festival combining into one day the birth, enlightenment, and death of the Buddha.

wong dondree (วงดนตรี wôŋ dontii): literally, a music ensemble, but referring specifically to Western popular ensembles.

wot (โหวท wòod): a circular bundle of bamboo tubes in panpipe form thrown by children in the fields to produce the sound.

wua kün poo (วัวขึ้นภู ŋûa khỳn phûu): a title of a kaen piece also called bong lang or lai bong lang played in the E mode imitating a cow ascending a hill.

wut (วัด wad): a Buddhist temple.

yah nang (ยานาง/หญ้านาง   jaa nâaŋ/njàa nâaŋ): a tough grass used to bind the kaen tubes.

yam tae (ยามแต njâamthἔ): an old term that referred to the period before noon.

yao (ยาว njâaw): one of the two scale systems, A C D E G.

yuan (ยวน njûan): a Northern Thai script.

yutdipung (ยัติภังค์   njadtìphâŋ): enjambment, i.e., bridging the caesura in a line of glawn poetry with a multi-syllable word.

Select Bibliography

General Works Pertaining to Thai and Lao Culture

Archaimbault, Charles. "Le cycle de Nang Oua-Nang Malong." France-Asia n.s. 17 (November-December 1961): 2581-2604.

Bang-kum. Sung Sin-sai. Edited by Sila Viravong. Vientiane, Laos, 1972.

Benedict, Paul K. "Thai, Kadai, and Indonesian: A New Alignment in Southeast Asia." American Anthropologist n.s. 44 (1942): 576-601.

Bitard, Pierre. "La légende de Nang Têng On." Bulletin de la Société des Etudes Indochinoises 31 (1956): 113-33.

Bree-chah Brinyanoh, Pra-maha. Brapenee boran pak isan [Old Customs of Northeast Thailand]. Oobon, Thailand, 1967.

Brown, J. Marvin. From Ancient Thai to Modern Dialects. Bangkok: Social Science Association Press, 1965.

Chula Chakrabongse, H.R.H. Prince. Lords of Life. London: Alvin Redman, Ltd., 1960.

Clarac, Achille and Smithies, Michael. Discovering Thailand, 2nd ed. Bangkok: Siam Publications, 1972.

Coedès, George. "La littérature laotienne en Indochine." In L'Indochine. Edited by S. Levi. Paris: 1931.

Dhani Nivat, Prince. "The Rama Jataka, a Lao Version of the Story of Rama." Journal of the Siam Society 36 (1946): 1-22.

Encyclopédie de la Pléide. S.v. "Littérature Laotienne," by Solange Bernard-Thierry.

Finot, Louis. "Recherches sur la littérature Laotienne." Bulletin de l'Ecole Française d'Extrême-Orient 17 (1917): 1-221.

Graham, Walter A. Siam. 2 vols. London: Alexander Moring, Ltd., 1924.

Griswold, A. B. Thoughts on the Romanization of Siamese. Bangkok, 1969.

Haas, Mary R. Thai-English Student's Dictionary. Kuala Lumpur: Oxford University Press, 1964.

Hall, D. G. E. A History of South-East Asia. 3rd ed. New York: St. Martin's Press, 1970.

Hang Minh Kim. "Rimes Lao et rimes Vietnamiennes." Bulletin des Amis du Royaume Lao 2 (July-September 1970): 114-23.

Kerr, Allen D. Lao-English Dictionary. 2 vols. Washington, D.C.:
    Catholic University of America Press (Consortium Press), 1972.
Keyes, Charles F. Isan: Regionalism in North Eastern Thailand. Cornell
    Thailand Project Interim Reports Series, no. 10, Data Paper no. 65.
    Ithaca, New York, 1967.
Klausner, William J. "Popular Buddhism in Northeast Thailand." In Cross-
    Cultural Understanding. Edited by F. S. C. Northrop and Helen H.
    Livingston. New York, 1964.
Lafont, Pierre Bernard. Bibliographie du Laos. Paris: École Française
    d'Extrême-Orient, 1964.
Lebar, Frank M.; Hickey, Gerald C.; Musgrave, John K. Ethnic Groups of
    Mainland Southeast Asia. New Haven: H.R.A.F. Press, 1964.
_____, and Suddard, Adrienne. Laos. New Haven: H.R.A.F. Press, 1960.
Le May, Reginald. An Asian Arcady: The Land and Peoples of North
    Siam. Cambridge: W. Heffer and Sons, 1926.
Maha Sila Viravong. History of Laos. Translated from Lao by the United
    States Joint Publications Research Service. New York: Paragon Book
    Reprint Corporation, 1964.
_____. Sunta-luksana [Lao Versification]. Vientiane, Laos, 1961.
Manich Jumsai, M. L. History of Thai Literature. Bangkok: Chalermnit
    Press, 1973.
_____. Understanding Thai Buddhism. Bangkok: Chalermnit Press,
    1973.
Mosel, James N. "Sound and Rhythm in Thai and English Verse." In
    Pasah lae nungsü [Languages and Books], pp. 28-34. Bangkok, 1959.
_____. A Survey of Classical Thai Poetry. Bangkok: Bangkok World
    Press, 1959.
_____. Trends and Structures in Contemporary Thai Poetry. Data
    Paper no. 43, South East Asia. Ithaca, New York, 1961.
Pavie, Auguste. Mission Pavie Indo-Chine 1879-95. 11 vols. Paris:
    Ernest Leroux, 1898-1904.
Phouvong Phimmasone. "Cours de littérature Lao." Bulletin des Amis du
    royaume Lao 4-5 (January-June 1971): 5-70.
Phya Anuman Rajadhon. Essays on Thai Folklore. Bangkok: The Social
    Science Association Press of Thailand, 1968.
Phya Anuman Rajadhon. Five Papers on Thai Custom. Data Paper no.
    28, South East Asia. Ithaca, New York, 1958.
_____. Life and Ritual in Old Siam. Edited and translated by William
    J. Gedney. New Haven: H.R.A.F. Press, 1961.
Prem Chaya. The Story of Khun Chang Khun Phan. Bangkok: Chatra
    Press, 1955.
Seidenfaden, Erik. "The So and the Puthai." Journal of the Siam Society
    34 (1943): 145-82.
_____. The Thai Peoples. 2nd ed. Bangkok: The Siam Society, 1967.
Siam and Laos as Seen by our American Missionaries. Philadelphia:
    Presbyterian Board of Missions, 1884.
Simmonds, E. H. S. "Tai Literatures." Bulletin of the Association of
    British Orientalists n.s. 3 (December 1965): 40-53.
Solheim, Wilhelm G. III. "The 'New Look' of Southeast Asian Prehistory."
    Journal of the Siam Society 60 (1972): 1-20.
_____. "Reworking Southeast Asian Prehistory." Paideuma 15 (1969):
    125-39.
Songwon Chotsookrut. Brapenee tai pak nüa [The Customs of Northern
    Thailand]. Bangkok: Odeon Book Store, 1969.

Thao Nhouy Abhay. "Folklore Laotiane--Xin Xay." Bulletin de la Société
  des Etudes Indochinoises 4 (1934): 75-91.
Wirawong, Somdet Pra-maha. Potjanah-noogarom pak isan pak glang
  [Northeast Thai-Central Thai Dictionary]. Bangkok, 1972.

Works Pertaining to Thai and Lao Music

Ajalbert, J. Les chansons de Sao Van Di. Paris: Michaud, n.d.
Berval, Rene de. Kingdom of Laos. Translated by Mrs. Teissier du Cros,
  et al. Saigon, South Vietnam: France-Asie, 1959.

The following articles in the Kingdom of Laos pertain:

Souvanna Phouma, Prince. "Music," pp. 87-96.
Archaimbault, Charles. "The Sacrifice of the Buffalo at Vat
  Ph'u," pp. 156-61.
Thao Nhouy Abhay. "Courts of Love and Poetry," pp. 206-09.
Thao Khene. "The Khene-Maker," pp. 217-20.
Faure, Marie-Daniel. "The boun Bang-fay (Rockets Festival,
  6th Month)," pp. 272-82.
_____. "The Boun Pha-Vet (4th Month)," pp. 294-300.
Finot, Louis. "Laotian Writings," pp. 307-27.
Phouvong Phimmasone. "Literature," pp. 336-44.
Thao Nhouy Abhay. "Versification," pp. 345-58.
_____. "Sin Xay," pp. 359-78.

Bidyalankarana, H.H. Prince. "The Pastime of Rhyme-Making and Singing
  in Rural Siam." Journal of the Siam Society 20 (1926): 101-27.
_____. "Sebha Recitation and the Story of Khun Chang Khun Phan."
  Journal of the Thailand Research Society 33 (1941): 1-22.
Bowring, Sir John. The Kingdom and People of Siam. 2 vols. London:
  1857; reprinted ed., London: Oxford University Press, 1969.
Brandon, James R. Theatre in Southeast Asia. Cambridge, Mass.: Harvard
  University Press, 1967.
Brengues, Jean. "Les Mo Lâm: la chanson au Laos." Revue Indo-chinoise
  n.s. 2 (1904): 588-92.
Coedès, George. "Origine et evolution des diverses formes du théatre
  traditionnel en Thailande." Bulletin de la Société des Études Indochin-
  oises 38 (1963): 489-506.
Compton, Carol J. Courting Poetry in Laos: A Textual and Linguistic
  Analysis. Center for Southeast Asian Studies Special Report No. 18,
  DeKalb, Illinois: Northern Illinois University, 1979.
Cort, Mary Lovina. Siam: or, The Heart of Farther India. New York: A.
  D. Randolph and Company, 1886.
Cripps, Francis. The Far Province. London: Hutchinson and Company,
  1965.
Daniélou, Alain. La musique du Cambodge et du Laos. Pondichéry [India]:
  Publications de l'Institut Français d'Indo-logie, 1957.
Dhanit Yupho. Thai Musical Instruments. Translated by David Morton.
  Bangkok: Department of Fine Arts, 1960.
Dyck, Gerald P. "They also serve." In Selected Reports in Ethnomusi-
  cology, Vol. II, no. 2, pp. 205-16. Ed. by David Morton. Los Angeles:
  University of California, 1975.

Encyclopédie de la musique (Albert Lavignac). S.v. "Histoire de la musi-
que dans l'Indo-chine," by Gaston Knosp.
Escoffier, André. Dan le Laos au chants des khènes, poèmes. Hanoi:
Imprimerie d'Extrême-Orient, 1942.
Gagneaux, Mme. Anne Marie. "Le khene et la musique Lao." Bulletin des
Amis du royaume Lao 6 (1971): 175-81.
Gironcourt, Georges de. "Recherches de géographie musicale en Indochine."
Bulletin de la Société des études indochinoises 17 (1943): 3-174.
Graham, A. W. Siam: A Handbook of Practical, Commercial, and Political
Information. London: Alexander Moring, Ltd., 1912.
Gréhan, M. A. Le Royaume de Siam. 3rd ed. Paris: Challamel Aime,
Libraire-Editeur, 1869.
Guillemet, Mme. Eugene. Les chants du khène Laotien. Hanoi: Imprimerie
d'Extrême-Orient, 1923.
Helmholtz, Hermann L. F. On the Sensations of Tone. 2nd English ed.,
revised, based on 4th German ed. of 1877 by Alexander Ellis. London:
1885; reprint ed., New York: Dover, 1954.
Henri d'Orleans, Prince. Around Tonkin and Siam. London: Chapman and
Hall, Ltd., 1894.
Hipkins, A. J. Musical Instruments Historic, Rare, and Unique. London:
A. and C. Black, 1921.
Hornbostel, Erich M. von. "Formanalysen an siamesischen Orchester-
stücken." Archiv fur Musikwissenschaft 2 (1919/1920): 306-33.
Humbert-Lavergne, Madeleine. "La musique à travers la vie Laotienne."
Zeitschrift für Vergleichende Musickwissenschaft 2 (1934): 14-19.
Jarunchai Chonpairot. Kaen wong [Kaen Ensembles]. Mahasarakam,
Thailand: Mahasarakam Teachers College, 1972.
Jao-pra-yah Ti-pah-gor-ra-wong. The Dynastic Chronicles, Bangkok Era,
the Fourth Reign (B.E. 2394-2411) (A.D. 1851-1868). 2 vols. Trans-
lated by Chadin Flood. Tokyo: The Centre for East Asian Cultural
Studies, 1966.
Kaufmann, Walter. Musical Notations of the Orient. Bloomington,
Indiana: Indiana University Press, 1967.
Kham-Ouane Ratanavong. Learn to Play the Khene/Apprenez le Khène.
Vientiane, Laos: Bulletin des Amis du Royaume Lao, 1973.
Khanthong Thammavong. Kaen. Vientiane, Laos, 1968.
Kloss, M. "Notice de M. Kloss sur un instrument à vent provenant du
Laos." Bulletin de la Société des Études Indo-chinoises (1897): 86-88.
Knosp, Gaston. Laotian Songs. Bangkok, 1922.
_____. "Rapport sur une mission officielle d'etude musicale en Indo-
chine." International Archiv für Ethnographie 20 (1911): 121-51, 165-
88, 217-48; 21 (1912): 1-25, 49-77.
Lefèvre-Pontalis, Pierre. Chansons et fêtes du Laos. Paris: Ernest Leroux,
1896.
Leonowens, Anna Harriette. The English Governess at the Siamese Court.
Boston: Fields, Osgood, and Co., 1870.
Liang Tsai-ping. Chinese Musical Instruments and Pictures. Taipei:
Chinese Classical Music Association, 1970.
List, George. "Speech Melody and Song Melody in Central Thailand."
Ethnomusicology 5 (1961): 16-32.
Ly-Hang. "Musique et danse Laotiennes." Musica 99 (1962): 13-17.
Malm, William P. Japanese Music and Musical Instruments. Rutland,
Vermont: Charles E. Tuttle, 1959.

Mattani Rutnin, ed. The Siamese Theatre: A Collection of Reprints from the Journals of the Siam Society. Bangkok: The Siam Society, 1975.

Mersenne, Marin. Harmonie universelle, 3 vols. Paris, 1636; reprint ed. Paris: Éditions du Centre National de la Recherche Scientifique, 1965. English ed. trans. Roger E. Chapman in 1 vol. The Hague: M. Nijhoff, 1957.

Miller, Terry E. "Free-Reed Instruments in Asia: A Preliminary Classification." In Music East and West: Essays in Honor of Walter Kaufmann, pp. 63-100. Ed. by Thomas Noblitt. New York: Pendragon Press, 1981.

_____. An Introduction to Playing the Kaen. Kent, Ohio: By the author, 1980.

_____. "The Musical Culture of Northeast Thailand." In Program of the 4th Festival of Asian Arts, pp. 56-7. Hong Kong: The Urban Council, 1979.

_____, and Jarunchai Chonpairot. "The Musical Traditions of Northeast Thailand." Journal of the Siam Society 67-1 (1979): 1-16.

_____, and _____. "The Ranat and Bong-lang: The Question of Origin of the Thai Xylophones." Journal of the Siam Society 69(1981): 145-63.

_____, and _____. "Review-Essay: The Problems of Lao Discography." Journal of Asian Music 11-1 (1979): 124-39.

_____, and _____. "Shadow Puppet Theatre in Northeast Thailand." Theatre Journal 31-3 (1979): 293-311.

Mom Dusdi Paribatra Na Ayuthya. The Regional Dances of Thailand. Bangkok: Foundation for Advancement of Educational Materials, 1962.

Montri Tramote. Ganlalen kawng tai [Thai Entertainments]. Bangkok: Prachan Press, 1954.

Moonee, Tanjaokoon-tamtirarat-maha. "Ruang lum kaen" ["The Story of the kaen"]. In Maradok chao isan [The Heritage of Northeast Thailand], pp. 393-420. Bangkok: Prayoot Press, 1962.

Morton, David. The Traditional Music of Thailand. Los Angeles: Regents of the University of California, 1968.

Murchie, Gordon W. "Mohlam." In Sawaddi-15 Years (1956-1971), pp. 81-85. Bangkok: American Women's Club, 1971.

Neale, Frederick Arthur. Narrative of a Residence in Siam. London: Offices of the National Illustrated Library, 1852.

The New Grove Dictionary of Music and Musicians. S.v. "Laos," by Terry E. Miller.

Oobalee-koonoo-bamajan, Pra. Ruang kaen [The Story of the kaen]. Bangkok, 1964.

Program of the Northeast Music Festival. Mahasarakam, Thailand, 1972.

The following articles pertain:

Jarunchai Chonpairot. "Mawlum," pp. 1 18.
Pawnsee Chaisara. "Pa-nyah," pp. 19-25.
Jarunchai Chonpairot. "Maw kaen," pp. 32-39.

Program of the Northeast Music Festival. Mahasarakam, Thailand, 1973.

The following articles pertain:

Jarunchai Chonpairot. "Mut pit lum lawng laeo lum doi kao sai gun" ["When lum tang yao is finished, we sing lum doi

together"], pp. 1-8.
Pan Wong-uan. "Nae num hai roo juk lae isan" ["An Intro-
duction to Northeastern Thai lae"], pp. 9-12.
Miller, Terry E. "An American Musical Scholar in
Mahasarakam--Why?" pp. 16-20.
_____. "Maw kaen American" ["An American kaen player"]
pp. 21-27.
Dasee. "Plik bra wut sat jak kruang don dree" ["Reworking
the history of musical isntruments"], pp. 40-43.
Sachs, Curt. The History of Musical Instruments. New York: W. W.
Norton, 1940.
Scott, A. C. Traditional Chinese Plays. 2 vols. Madison, Wisconsin:
University of Wisconsin Press, 1967.
Smith, Hermann. The World's Earliest Music. London: William Reeves,
1904.
Smithies, Michael. "Likay: A Note on the Origin, Form, and Future of
Siamese Folk Opera." Journal of the Siam Society 59 (1971): 33-64.
_____, and Euayporn Kerdchouay. "Nang Talung: The Shadow Theatre
of Siam." Journal of the Siam Society 60 (1972): 377-87.
Smyth, Herbert Warington. Five Years in Siam, from 1891-1896. 2 vols.
London: John Murray, 1898.
_____. Notes of a Journey on the Upper Mekong, Siam. London: John
Murray for the Royal Geographical Society, 1895.
Som Patrsandorn. "The Story of the kaen, klui, saw, and bia." Written
down by A. Bushpages. Wittaya-sarn, January 8, 1958, pp. 13-14.
Stern, Theodore, and Stern, Theodore A. "'I pluck my Harp': Musical
Acculturation Among the Karen of Western Thailand." Ethnomusicology
15 (1971): 186-219.
Tambiah, S. J. Buddhism and the Spirit Cults in North-East Thailand.
Cambridge: Cambridge Unviersity Press, 1970.
_____. "Literacy in a Buddhist Village in North-East Thailand." In
Literacy in Traditional Societies, pp. 86-131. Edited by J. Goody.
Cambridge: Cambridge University Press, 1968.
Thao Rangsy Souttathamma. Dooriya-lekah [Music Notes]. Vientiane,
Laos, n.d.
Thompson, Peter Anthony. Siam: An Account of the Country and the
People. Oriental Series, vol. XVI. Boston: J. B. Millet Co., 1910.
Tiao Sisavane Tchittarath. "The Khene Player." Friendship (Lao-Ameri-
can Association) 6 (1969): 12-16.
Trân vǎn Khê. La musique Vietnamienne traditionnelle. Paris: Presses
Universitaires de France, 1962.
_____. Viêt-Nam. Paris: Buchet-Chastel, 1967.
"A Traveller." "Siamese Amusements." Southern Literary Messenger 23
(May, 1857): 362-72.
Yung, Bell. "Creative Process in Cantonese Opera I: The Role of
Linguistic Tones." Ethnomusicology 27-1 (January, 1983): 29-47.

Discography

The following recordings are either devoted to Lao music or include selections. Most of them were reviewed by the author and Jarunchai Chonpairot in "Review-Essay: The Problems of Lao Discography" in Asian Music 11-1 (1980): 124-39. One other was reviewed by the author as indicated in parentheses.

Loas. Recorded by Alain Danielou. (UNESCO Collection. A Musical Anthology of the Orient) One 12 inch, 33 r.p.m. mono disc. Barenreiter Musicaphon BM 30 L 2001. Descriptive notes in English, French, and German by Alain Danielou.

Laos. Recorded by Jacques Brunet. (Musiques de l'Asie traditionnelle, vol. 2) One 12 inch, 33 r.p.m. mono disc. Playa Sound PS 33502. Jacket notes in English and French by Jacques Brunet.

Laos: Musique pour le khene/Lam Saravane. Recorded by Jacques Brunet. Two 12 inch, 33 r.p.m. stereo discs. Ocora 55837/8. Jacket notes by J. Brunet. (Reviewed by the author in Ethnomusicology 25-3 [September, 1983]: 561-3.)

Laos: l'art du khene. Recorded by Jacques Brunet. (Collection musique du monde, no. 26.) One 12 inch, 33 r.p.m. stereo disc. Galloway Records GB 600 545 B. Jacket notes by J. Brunet.

Music of Thailand. Recorded by Howard K. Kaufman. One 12 inch, 33 r.p.m. mono disc. Ethnic Folkways Library, FE 4463 (1960, 1962). Pamphlet, 5 pages by Howard K. Kaufman.

Thailand: Lao Music of the Northeast. Recorded by Terry E. Miller. One 12 inch, 33 r.p.m. simulated stereo disc. Lyrichord LLST 7357. Jacket notes by T. Miller. (This album includes examples of kaw law, pin, hoon, and kaen, the latter playing all five modes [lai] and two programmatic pieces. The other side includes a complete lum glawn cycle.)

Traditional Music of Southern Laos. Recorded by Jacques Brunet. (UNESCO Collection. Musical Sources. Art Music of South-East Asia, IX-4, Alain Danielou, general editor) One 12 inch, 33 r.p.m. stereo disc. Philips 6586 012. Jacket notes by J. Brunet.

Visages du . . . Laos. Recorded by Marc Reinhorn. One 12 inch, 33 r.p.m. mono disc. Le Chant du Monde LDX-A-4331. Booklet notes by Marc Reinhorn.

Index

Palm-leaf manuscripts, 10ff, 25
     an nungsü (reading a manuscript), 25ff, 40, 88

Poetry, 47-8, 101ff, 135, 175
     glawn, 11-13, 101ff
     glawn gap, 13, 106, 131, 133, 139
     glawn see, 106-7, 131

Ritualists (village), 64-6

Scale, see Mode

Scripts (writing systems), 9ff

Spirits, 63-4

Theatre
     mawlum moo, 37, 51, 54, 61, 62, Chapter 3 (73ff), 176ff
     mawlum plün, 37, 51, 62, Chapter 3 (73ff), 184ff, 284ff
     shadow puppet, 105

U.S.I.S., 56

Wai kroo (ceremony to honor teacher), 46, 86, 232

About the Author

TERRY E. MILLER is Associate Professor of Ethnomusicology and Associate Director of the Center for the Study of World Musics at Kent State University. He has published privately *An Introduction to Playing the Kaen* and *The Covered Bridges of Tuscarawas Country, Ohio*. His articles have appeared in *Asian Music, Journal of the Siam Society, Theatre Journal*, and *Music East and West*. He has also edited two phonograph records—*The Song of the Phoenix* and *Thailand: Lao Music of the Northeast*.